Before the Movies

Before the Movies

American Magic-Lantern Entertainment and the Nation's First Great Screen Artist, Joseph Boggs Beale

by Terry and Deborah Borton

Foreword by Charles Musser

British Library Cataloguing in Publication Data

Before the Movies: American Magic-Lantern Entertainment and the Nation's First Great Screen Artist, Joseph Boggs Beale

A catalogue entry for this book is available from the British Library

ISBN: 9780 86196 711 7 (Hardback)

Published by
John Libbey Publishing Ltd, 3 Leicester Road, New Barnet, Herts EN5 5EW,
United Kingdom
e-mail: john.libbey@orange.fr; web site: www.johnlibbey.com
Direct orders (UK and Europe): direct.orders@marston.co.uk
Distributed in Asia and North America by **Indiana University Press**, Office of Scholarly Publishing,
Herman B Wells Library—350, 1320 E. 10th St., Bloomington, IN 47405, USA. www.iupress.indiana.edu

Printed and bound in China by 1010 Printing International Ltd.

Table of Contents

Cover Picture: *This dramatic scene is the climax of the 10-slide magic-lantern set of* Curfew Shall Not Ring Tonight. *Joseph Boggs Beale created the set's illustrations in 1894, just before the first movies were seen in America. The poem itself was written in 1866, by American author Rose Hartwick Thorpe. It tells the story of a young woman at the time of Cromwell's England who saves her condemned lover by silencing the curfew bell that is to signal his death.* Curfew Shall Not Ring Tonight *was a favorite in the vast repertoire of magic-lantern screen entertainment during the Victorian era.*

Fig. 1. Joseph Boggs Beale (1841–1926) created over 250 sets of magic-lantern images, about half of which were stories, songs, and hymns. [Beale Collection.]

Foreword

An effective stereopticon lecture is a message to both the eye and the ear, enforced by the lecturer's own burning conviction.
Anonymous[1]

Driving up the Connecticut River Valley, one passes through an endless expanse of green. The sensation of having been sent back in time soon becomes palpable. There are no malls and no houses. Eventually one approaches a Victorian-era summer retreat that tries to remain true to its past. Here, just before reaching an old-time Seventh Day Adventist campground, one reaches the residence of Terry and Deborah Borton. Their garden, which overlooks the river, sustains the sensation of meeting another time halfway. Then, one enters the Bortons' home and encounters the fitting culmination to such a journey: a veritable shrine to Joseph Boggs Beale (1841–1926). Several of Beale's paintings grace the living room wall, while display cases feature Beale lantern slides. The bookshelves are filled with volumes that he illustrated. Notebooks hold facsimiles of old photographs, correspondence, and one of Beale's report cards for his students. The corner cabinet contains a china tea set that uses Beale's images as decoration. Moreover, this is only the visible part of a more massive collection: the "good stuff" is housed elsewhere – in some archive, secured storage vault or museum.

The Bortons have focused their investigations on Beale in an immersive undertaking that may seem quaint or antiquarian to some members of the academe. Through amazing detective work, they have located records and artworks that were dispersed around the country and documented others that were destroyed by fire. They have also tracked down old garbage bags stuffed with materials that were fortuitously saved by one of Beale's neighbors as his house was being emptied for the real estate market. The Bortons have let this material speak to them in ways that I recognize from my years working on the life and career of Edwin S. Porter. This process becomes so consuming that both Terry and I have found ourselves dating our checks for another century (e.g. the year 1889 rather than 1989). If I sometimes found myself talking to Porter (Mr. E.S.P.) in my waking dreams, Terry sports mutton-chop sideburns that resemble Beale's to the extent that his wife will allow. The Bortons have stalked their subject: if Beale was alive

---

1 Anonymous, *India* (type script manuscript in the Borton Collection).

today, he might easily have them arrested for their excessive zeal. Either that or Beale would allow them to write his "authorized" biography.

Ultimately the Bortons offer us an historical narrative that foregrounds and contextualizes a *catalog raisonné* of Beale's artworks produced for the C.W. Briggs Company, one of the leading American producers of lantern slides between 1880 and 1920. In the world of Film Studies, the *catalog raisonné* takes the form of filmographies. All too often a filmmaker's biography is written first, and his filmography becomes an afterthought at the back of the book. This is unfortunate, for these seemingly innocuous inventories reveal patterns and provide roadmaps that are never obvious. Crucial gaps and mysteries emerge that must be explored lest what is hidden stays hidden. Paolo Cherchi Usai has remarked that filmographies are the necessary starting point for any historical undertaking in film studies.[2] As *Before the Movies* makes clear, this is equally true for studying the magic lantern. However, if filmographies are as common in Film Studies as *catalog raisonnés* in the field of art history, this is the first such sustained effort in magic lantern scholarship.

Although the Bortons have focused their attention on Beale for *Before the Movies*, their interests are much broader – as one might expect from the president of the Magic Lantern Society of the United States and Canada, and her travelling lantern-showman spouse (director of the American Magic Lantern Theater). This becomes clear when one leaves the Borton House and crosses the dirt road to a bungalow with ceiling-to-floor displays of ephemera promoting a vast array of lantern shows. Suddenly I felt like a young boy let loose in a candy shop. A broadside for *The Stereopticon or Mirror of Rebellion*, dated Saturday, October 29, [1864], lists the numerous Civil War photographic slides that were projected, with particular emphasis on the battles of Vicksburg and Petersburg. Another programme features Harry Ellsworth Feicht's 1903 illustrated lecture on *Oberammergau: Its People and Its Play* at Cincinnati's Pike Opera House. Now, in *The Emergence of Cinema*, I wrote about John Stoddard's stereopticon lectures on *The Passion Play of Oberammergau* of 1880 and 1890, and E. Burton Holmes's illustrated lectures on *Oberammergau* in 1900, which combined slides and films: so I naturally found Freicht's efforts to be intriguing.[3] Feicht (1862–1918), who had been a successful manager of the Grand Opera House and Park Theater in Dayton, Ohio, showed "230 colored views" (no films) under the auspices of the Interstate Lecture Bureau based in Cincinnati. His presentation had its own special claim: fluent in German, Feicht was "the only American who ever lectured to the performers of Oberammergau on the subject of their play".[4] This resulted in a series of endorsements in July 1901, which he used in promoting his American exhibitions.[5] And then there is a 1929 flyer for a series of stereopticon lectures at the Colored Seventh Day Adventist Church in Birmingham, Alabama, during February 1929. In short, here is

2   Paolo Cherchi Usai, *Silent Cinema: An Introduction* (London: British Film Institute, 2000), 90–103.

3   Charles Musser, *The Emergence of Cinema: The American Screen to 1907* (New York: Scribners, 1990), 39, 208–209.

4   "Pictorial Reproduction – Oberammergau: Its People and Its Play" (Cincinnati, Ohio The Interstate Lecture Bureau Co., [1903].

5   Ibid, 2–4.

a room full of both context for and distractions from the subject of this book, the man in the other house: Joseph Boggs Beale.[6]

Beale has not had a Wikipedia entry (though the Bortons are about to post one as this book goes to press). There have been a few scattered exhibitions of his work, but nothing has cohered in a way that has made him a recognizable figure in American cultural life during the forty-year period of his greatest productivity: between roughly 1880 and 1920, (which is not to dismiss his pre-1880 work as an illustrator or the continued circulation of his images post-1920). Why has Beale failed to gain traction in the scholarly community? Perhaps because he was virtually unique in what he did and so has escaped familiar categories. And yet for this very reason he forces us to confront unfamiliar aspects of creative production in an era when technological reproducibility was increasingly pervasive, often in transitory ways that flourished before the arrival of the movies but were then buried by them. Here the traditional artist met new industrial methods in ways that we have still not adequately understood – and it is Beale who gives us a unique opportunity to do so. In seeking to understand and appreciate Beale's artistry, we not only encounter Walter Benjamin's iconic essay "The Work of Art in the Age of Technological Reproducibility", we must give it new substance.[7]

Beale was the central creative force in the production of lantern slides for Caspar W. Briggs, who owned and operated one of the largest lantern-slide businesses in the United States. Briggs commissioned Beale to draw and paint images (usually sets of images) in black and white, which his company would then photograph and turn into lantern slides – a process that was greatly simplified by the successful, widespread introduction of dry plate photography ca 1879.[8] Workers, operating in an industrial process that bore some resemblance to the assembly line, tinted the slides but the quality of the final images – specifically the number of colors being used – varied in relation to the final selling price. (Of course, some slides were never tinted at all.) Beale's remarkable monochromatic paintings, most of which survive, are intermediate art works. Although he occupied the central creative role in the process, he was nonetheless caught between the initial conception (Briggs) and the final finishing by anonymous employees. Although Beale was careful to acquire a deluxe version of his slides as the full realization of his efforts, he rarely selected the colors nor approved the final results. In this sense we can truly recognize that the work of art had lost its unique aura – its detachment from traditional artistic practices. These slides are not even comparable to a photographer's prints that are made under his/her supervision and with his/her approval. Moreover, and this is critically important: it was not – and is not – the slides themselves that were meant to be seen. It was their projections on a screen. These slides were themselves

6   The results of such distractions can be found in Terry Borton, "238 Eminent American 'Magic-Lantern' Showmen: The Chautauqua Lecturers", *The Magic Lantern Gazette* 15:1 (Spring 2013), 3–34.

7   Walter Benjamin, "The Work of Art in the Age of Technological Reproducibility", in *Walter Benjamin: Selected Works, Volume 4, 1938–1940* (Cambridge, MA: Belknap Press, 2003) edited by Howard Eiland and Michael W. Jennings, 251–283.

8   Although Briggs apparently continued to use the older collodion process, which offered a finer grained image than dry plate emulsions – important for projection, the introduction of dry plate photography was an overall boon to the lantern world and generated new opportunities and pressures on Briggs that must have encouraged his hiring of Beale and other artists.

only intermediate elements for a larger cultural performance – an illustrated lecture that was produced by someone else altogether. Beale, so far as we know, never gave illustrated lectures himself.

The Bortons open up another, albeit related path for looking at Beale's work in relationship to his contemporaries working in the same milieu – and the same city of Philadelphia. Certainly the city was the center of the magic lantern world in the United States during the late nineteenth century, but it was much more than that. It was a milieu that generated and attracted artists, photographers and entrepreneurs who were fascinated with issues of technological reproducibility. It was a world of new media – the Silicon Valley of its day. This includes figures such Thomas Eakins (1844–1916), who was three years Beale's junior. As the Bortons point out, Beale and Eakins attended the same high school and briefly competed for the same job teaching art. Both worked as painters and both worked with and in relation to photography, but in very different ways. Henry R. Heyl (1842–1917) was another Philadelphia inventor who developed a modified magic lantern or "phasmatrope" in 1870. This wheel-like attachment held 16 photographic slides mounted radially along its outer edge. The pictures were successively passed along in front of the light source (using an intermittent mechanism and a shutter) with the views repeated as many times as the exhibitor desired. Heyl, who also invented the stapler in 1877, undoubtedly took some of his inspiration from Coleman Sellers (1827–1907), who patented "the kinematoscope", an improvement on the stereoscope that showed movement through a succession of images, in 1861. Then there is the painter Thomas Pollock Anshutz (1851–1912), who moved to Philadelphia in 1875 and worked with Thomas Eakins. Both collaborated with Eadweard Muybridge, who was based in Philadelphia in the 1880s, making his serial photography and stop motion studies – the very decade that Beale was beginning his relationship with Briggs. In 1886 Robert Henri (1865–1929) moved to Philadelphia and enrolled in classes at the Pennsylvania Academy of Fine Arts under Anshutz and by the 1890s was beginning to gather around him key painters of the Ash Can School – just as Beale began working full-time for Briggs. The Bortons characterize Beale's work as extending a realist tradition. If so, his realism was quite different from that of Eakins, Anshutz and Henri – more romantic, more patriotic and more ideologically normative. His illustrations were generally designed to bring a visual intensity to the lives of presidents and the canonical stories that constructed a shared Anglo-American culture. Unlike the other three, Beale never studied in Europe and was relatively untouched by the dynamism of the French art scene. He helps to define what we think of as the Victorian era.

Despite this book's title, *Before the Movies*, the Bortons are strikingly ambivalent about the relationship of Beale & Briggs' lantern programs to subsequent cinema. If Beale's slides were energetic and "cinematic" in their construction of space and composition, their depiction of action, and their use of eye-line matches; the Bortons indicate that these methods would have to be rediscovered by later filmmakers. There is only one figure who appears at the very periphery of this book – Sigmund Lubin – who would lead Philadelphia's transition from the magic lantern or stereopticon to the cinema.

Clearly the lantern show and cinema share complex histories. Practically every moving picture program until 1903 combined slides (if only title slides) with film. Illustrated songs flourished in the early storefront movie houses or nickelodeons from 1905–1908. Timing is worth noting. The arrival of projected motion pictures in 1896 did not seem to adversely affect Briggs' business. It was only when cinema became a form of mass culture and mass communication in 1908 (with the standardized release system, as well as new modes of production and representation) that Briggs' business faced rapid decline, with Beale losing his full-time job in 1909. Beale stopped making illustrations for Briggs' business altogether ca. 1917–1920, the very moment that the Classical Hollywood Cinema/the vertically integrated studio system fell into place.

A foreword cannot begin to exhaust this book's many merits nor the areas of analysis and further research that it invites. One final observation I cannot resist involves the tension between an international or cosmopolitan outlook and a nationalistic alternative. As the Bortons show, Briggs and other business leaders active in the American lantern industry sold numerous lantern-slide programs made in Great Britain and France. Briggs and Beale were committed to Americanizing the stories being offered in the catalogs of T.H. McAllister, George Kleine and other retailers. Their main competition came from England and the process of building up domestic production involved a sustained, decades-long effort. This may help to explain, I suspect, why the first nationalistic reaction by the American film industry to the "invasion" of European machines was directed towards the British with films such as *The Monroe Doctrine* (Edison, 1896) rather than – given the Lumières' prominence – the French. The effort to Americanize the screen would have a long, cyclical history. Edwin Porter tried to make films with specifically American subjects in 1902–03 (such as *Uncle Tom's Cabin* and *The Great Train Robbery*) as well as American productions of international subjects (*Jack and the Beanstalk*). A few years later, as Richard Abel has pointed out, the Motion Picture Patents Company was used to contain and marginalize Pathé and Gaumont.[9] It was not until the Great War, which disrupted European production while leaving US filmmaking untouched, that the screen became predominantly American on a global scale. Beale clearly had an important place in this history of cultural nationalism.

If the Bortons seemingly invite us to consider new areas of future scholarship (many more bungalows of riches), we must appreciate and celebrate what they have achieved in this monograph – a task with a remarkably high degree of difficulty. To evoke the anonymous epigraph that begins this foreword, *Before the Movies* is itself like an effective stereopticon lecture in that its striking images and eloquent text (if read aloud – and why not?) offer a message (and perhaps transcendent pleasures) for both the eye and the ear, powerfully enforced by the Bortons' own burning convictions.

Charles Musser, *Yale University*

---

9   Richard Abel, *The Red Rooster Scare* (Berkeley: University of California Press, 1999), 151–175.

Chapter 1

The Magic Lantern

Introduction

This reference book documents a largely unexplored chapter in American pre-cinema and art history, the magic-lantern entertainment that was widespread in the nation's culture before the movies arrived in 1896.[1] From 1859 through the 1920s, millions of people a year enjoyed a rich variety of projected entertainment – magic-lantern stories, songs, and hymns that were specifically mass-produced for the screen. This study is a comprehensive survey of the American artists who produced that entertainment in its early period. The book's purpose is one of media archeology – to determine which artists created the different lantern sets, and when. It concentrates particularly on the nation's most prolific lantern artist, Joseph Boggs Beale (Fig. 1). Beale's extensive body of lantern art is documented in detail so that it can be assessed in the larger contexts of screen practice and Victorian culture.

Chapter 1 provides a brief history of the magic lantern (or "stereopticon", as it was often called),[2] concentrating especially on the company Beale worked for, that of C.W. Briggs, and on Beale himself. *Chapter 2* delves deeply into Beale's work, describing the provenance, attribution, and dating of the images he produced for lantern-slide manufacturers, and the production processes involved. *Chapter 3* examines all non-Beale lantern entertainment, both foreign and domestic, which was widely available in America from 1859 to 1896. *Chapter 4* discusses each of the American artists who were producing this work and compares their production to that of Beale, demonstrating that Beale created the vast majority of American-made mass entertainment for the screen in the generation before the movies, and that it was seen by millions. *Chapter 5* explores the cinematic quality of Beale's projected art, and concludes that both in terms of quantity, quality, and

---

1   Picking a date for the "birth of the movies" is perforce somewhat arbitrary. Charles Musser in *The Emergence of Cinema: The American Screen to 1907, Volume 1* (Berkeley: University of California Press, 1990), 109 cites the showing of Edison's vitascope at Koster & Bial's Music Hall in New York on April 23, 1896 as the event that "effectively launched projected motion pictures as a screen novelty in the United States". Since we are interested in movies as an effective competitor for magic-lantern entertainment, we have selected that date for the purposes of this discussion. (Musser also discusses a number of other early examples of projected moving images: 43–89, 91–116.) For an extensive discussion of moving picture projection before 1896, including a number of major European producers, see Deac Rossell, "The Public Exhibition of Moving Pictures Before 1896" *KINtop* 14/15 (2006): 169–205.

2   The "magic lantern" was the first slide-projector. In America it was often called a "stereopticon". The term usually denoted a large lantern (rather than the smaller children's lanterns) and was meant to suggest a more sophisticated and adult form of entertainment and education than that of the "magic" lantern. "Sciopticon" was sometimes used in a similar manner. The British used the term "optical lantern" for the same purposes.

cultural impact, he can be considered America's first great screen artist. *The Catalogue Raisonné (Appendix 1)* is the data core of the book. It provides detailed information about each of Beale's 2,073 images, presented in 2,618 differently-named lantern slides, and a sample picture from each of the sets the slides are divided into.

Since much of the magic-lantern material in *Before the Movies* may be new to many readers, *Before the Movies* is heavily annotated, both with source information and additional explanation.[3] Underlined terms in the text and in the figure captions are techniques that are usually thought of today as part of the "art of the movies", but which Beale and others employed regularly in producing lantern-slide entertainment. A discussion of Beale's use of these cinematic techniques appears as part of the exploration of Beale's work in Chapter 5.

A companion volume to this book, called *Cinema Before Film,* is in preparation.[4] It builds upon the data and research here, but is written in a more popular style and is intended for a general audience. It covers Beale's biography, puts him in the social and economic context of his time (especially the introduction of the movies), and provides a much more extensive examination of his cinematic art.

Context

In *The Emergence of Cinema,* Charles Musser begins his history of the early days of film not with the first movies, but with several prior forms of screen media. In particular he concentrates on the magic lantern, since, like the movies, the lantern projected images on screen and did so over the course of a quarter of a millennium before the birth of the movies (Fig. 2). While discussing the magic lantern, Musser makes the point that when we examine cinema history we should look carefully at "screen practice", that is, what is happening on screen, rather than simply at the devices that produce the screen images. It is primarily in this realm of screen practice that he finds connections between the first magic-lantern screen art and that of the movies.[5]

We have chosen to focus our discussion of magic-lantern screen practice on the genre of entertainment such as stories and songs, rather than lectures on travel and science or (with one "story" exception) the secret society rituals of the Masons and similar groups. These latter genres, while the dominant forms of magic-lantern presentation in the Victorian period, had much less connection with what we think of today as the movies than did magic-lantern stories and songs. In travel and science lectures, the individual slides were selected for their didactic effect, and the continuity between them was established by the logic of the subject matter. But in the case of magic-lantern stories, songs, and hymns, the individual slides were selected

3   The best single source for additional information on all aspects of the magic lantern, including the companies and techniques discussed here, is David Robinson, Stephen Herbert, Richard Crangle, eds., *Encyclopaedia of the Magic Lantern* (London, England: The Magic Lantern Society, 2001).

4   Terry Borton, *Cinema Before Film: America's First Great Screen Artist, Joseph Boggs Beale* (in preparation).

5   Musser, note 1, 15–48.

for artistic purposes in order to create a narrative whole – to establish a scene, to portray a highpoint of drama, to create a denouement. Dramatic stories and songs also suggested dramatic artistic techniques for changing perspective, lighting, angle of presentation, costuming, and blocking. Shaping complex stories into coherent form with a limited sequence of lantern scenes required special attention to issues of editing and continuity. Thus, it is in the magic-lantern presentation of entertainment that the cinematic qualities of magic-lantern art can most easily be seen.

"Ideal" Triple Lantern.

While Musser and others have discussed magic-lantern entertainment and its relation to the movies, they have not examined in detail the earliest years of magic-lantern entertainment in America.[6] Without greater specificity, it is difficult to take the discussion much further. As Richard Crangle points out in his article, "What Do Those Old Slides Mean? Or Why the Magic Lantern Is Not an Important Part of Cinema History", discussions of the magic lantern culture itself and of its relation to the broader area of cinema studies have been severely hampered by the lack of detailed information on provenance, attribution and dating – the contextual details necessary to understand lantern screen art in its own terms, and to put it in a broader historical framework.[7] That has certainly been true of the American slide industry, where there has been no detailed and systematic published study of "who did what when". In this book, we take the first steps in that direction by concentrating on Beale's lantern illustrations.

Fig. 2. A combination magic-lantern and movie projector, produced by the Stereopticon and Film Exchange about 1899, soon after the advent of film in America. The two lanterns on top make up a traditional "bi-unial" magic lantern for superimposing one picture over another, creating slow dissolves, or "flashing" from one slide picture to another (jump cutting). The lantern on the bottom could be used for lantern shows (making a "tri-unial" magic lantern for additional special effects), or it could be used to supplement a lantern show with the newest form of screen entertainment – the movies. [Beale Collection.]

6   In addition to Musser's work (ibid), David Robinson, *From Peep Show to Palace: The Birth of American Film* (New York: Columbia University Press, 1996) and Deac Rossell, *Living Pictures: The Origins of the Movies* (Albany: State University of New York Press, 1998) treat the American magic-lantern era, but only briefly. Richard Abel, ed., *Encyclopaedia of Early Cinema* (London and New York: Routledge, 2005) contains an informative article on the magic lantern, but it barely mentions the American lantern industry. The opening volume of the *Screen Decades* series by André Gaudreault, ed., *American Cinema: 1890–1909* (New Brunswick, New Jersey: Rutgers University Press, 2009) contains only a few paragraphs about the lantern. The most thorough study of the American magic lantern is Xenophon Theodore Barber's unpublished "Evenings of Wonder: A History of the Magic Lantern Show in America" (Ph.D. diss., New York University, 1993). Barber gives an excellent and detailed overview of the field, but does not assay the kind of year-by-year slide chronology or comparative assessment of American lantern entertainment provided here.
For other information on the magic lantern see the many excellent publications of the Magic Lantern Society at www.magiclantern.org.uk/. Past issues of the research journal of The Magic Lantern Society of the United States and Canada, *The Magic Lantern Gazette*, are available at http://library.sdsu.edu/scua/online-materials/magic-lantern-pubs/gazette. Another good source is *Lucerna – the Magic Lantern Web Resource*, at http://www.slides.uni-trier.de/.
The best collection of American magic-lanterns, lantern slides, catalogs, and related materials – one that gives a sense of how extensive the industry was – is that amassed by curator Jack Judson at the Magic Lantern Castle Museum in San Antonio, Texas. The museum is not open to the public, but it welcomes researchers to its collection and library.

7   Richard Crangle, "What Do Those Old Slides Mean? Or Why the Magic Lantern Is Not an Important Part of Cinema History" in Simon Popple and Vanessa Toulmin, eds., *Visual Delights: Essays on the Popular and Projected Image in the 19th Century* (Trowbridge, England: Flicks Books, 2000), 17–24.

Fig. 3. Christiaan Huygens, a well-known Dutch scientist, probably invented the magic lantern but thought of it as a toy, and did nothing to promote its use. [Beale Collection.]

A Short History of the Magic Lantern

The magic lantern was the first projector. It operated by focusing the light from a lamp though a system of lenses so that it could project an image painted on glass that had been inserted amid the lenses. The lantern was probably invented in 1659 by Christiaan Huygens, an eminent Dutch scientist who, among many accomplishments, was the first to discover that the "rings of Saturn" were actually disks of debris surrounding the planet (Fig. 3). Though the lantern began in a scientific context, and continued to be used for science and educational purposes for the next 250 years, it almost immediately became an entertainment medium as well. At first only a few knew how the magic lantern made images appear out of nothing – hence the "magic" in its name. Shows were small because of the limited illumination, and tended to be for the wealthy, but even in this early period the performances might include images that moved on screen, created with slipping slides and other ways of moving pieces of glass.

By the 18th century the lantern had become a common form of entertainment for the general public, presented by wandering showmen who carried the lantern and a few slides on their backs. Often called Savoyards because many came from the Savoy region between Italy and France, they spread out across Europe, projecting ghosts and angels, simple stories, and dramatizations of recent battles. Knowledge of the lantern spread across the world too, carried by diplomats, missionaries, colonists, and adventurers. The first documented American screen entertainment was more than 250 years ago, in Salem, Massachusetts on December 3, 1743. This "Magick Lanthorn" show, promoted in the *Boston Evening Post*, was produced by John Dabney, a mathematical instrument maker, "for the Entertainment of the Curious".[8] The early lantern period belonged to such individual showmen, some of whom appear to have created their own hand-painted slides. As early as 1804, "Phantasmagoria Shows", which featured skeletons that became larger and larger on screen, were touring the East Coast of America.

---

8   Lanthorn Show: *Supplement to The Boston Evening Post* 436 (December 3, 1743). Judson Collection, The Magic Lantern Castle Museum, San Antonio.

By the mid-19th century, the lantern was well established throughout Europe (most especially in England) and in America. The development of limelight, a brilliant illuminant also used for lighthouses, meant that shows could be projected to audiences of thousands, though managing the technology was difficult and dangerous. Slides became more elaborate, and methods were devised for producing high-quality color images in large quantities. At the same time, inexpensive toy lanterns were manufactured, especially in Germany, and became commonplace in middle-class households, both in Europe and in America.

Also by mid-century, new forms of lantern shows were becoming popular. Dissolving Views (in which one image changed into another) were a common feature, as were lectures that demonstrated various scientific phenomena. Some shows were strictly entertainment. Such performances were like stage productions, largely dependent on the artistic and presentational skills of a single showman/artist/promoter creating one performance at a time. No matter how successful the run, shows such as these could not hope to reach a national audience.[9]

What transformed the American magic-lantern into the first projected mass medium was the development of photographic lantern slides by the Langenheim Brothers in 1849. Suddenly it was possible to rapidly reproduce not only images of nature such as travel scenes and portraits, but also copies of engravings or paintings. At about the same time, the development of kerosene (paraffin) and other illuminants led to small, easily managed lanterns. That meant that the potential market for lanterns and slides exploded from relatively few showmen, to thousands who gave shows in theaters, churches, lodges, club meetings, and their own homes.[10]

American Screen Entertainment in 1895

By 1895 American magic-lantern shows had become a mass-entertainment medium, though most of the shows were in fact illustrated lectures (Fig. 4). A study by the authors using newspaper references in Middletown, Connecticut and surrounding Middlesex County for the first three months of 1895 found about three shows and lantern lectures a week in the county.[11] (A similar study, based on the *Brooklyn Daily Eagle* in New York, found about four and a half performances a week reported there during the same period, and many more in later years.)[12] From the Middlesex sample, using census data, we estimated (very roughly) the number of shows nationally at between 75,000–150,000 a year, given by 30,000–60,000 lanternists. As is suggested by the relationship between these two numbers, most of these lanternists would have been small-time local performers.

9   Musser, note 1, 26–33; Barber, note 6, 24–79.

10   A more extended history of the magic lantern can be found in the books and web site mentioned in note 6.

11   Terry and Debbie Borton, "How Many American Lantern Shows in a Year?" in *Realms of Light: Uses and Perceptions of the Magic Lantern from the 17th to the 21st Century, eds.,* Richard Crangle, Mervyn Heard, Ine van Dooren (London: The Magic Lantern Society, 2005), 105–115.

12   Authors' email correspondence with Kent Wells, May 18, 2008. Wells did not find the same proportion of "magic-lantern" entertainment performances as in Middlesex County; almost all were "lectures".

Fig. 4. Magic-lantern shows were a widespread form of public education in the 1890s. Travel lectures, such as this one, were one of the most common kinds of performance, but entertainment variety shows that mixed lectures with stories, songs and comedy were also popular. The image above promotes the slides of the largest distributor of Beale slides, T.H. McAllister.
[Beale Collection.]

Rising above the local showmen were the superstars such as John L. Stoddard, America's most famous lantern lecturer. While he did not happen to appear in our Middlesex County sample, he was active in the big cities at this time, as were several others of national stature, including Alexander Black, discussed later. The thousands of little-known lantern showmen supported a sizeable magic-lantern industry – some three hundred American manufacturers and distributors of magic-lanterns and slides, the largest of which offered 150,000 slides for sale – and the actual lantern-image creators, such as Beale himself.[13]

The lantern performances in Middlesex County were not at the local opera house, which booked lavish shows from New York and Boston. Instead, lantern shows were held in churches and meetings halls, though these were not small venues. Some held 1,000 people, and often they were full. The lantern shows operated as a second-tier of entertainment, much as the local multi-plex cinema does today. The lantern slides themselves were usually photographic. Most of the showmen probably used slides bought or rented from distributors; some clearly took their own pictures. The most popular subjects were lectures on travel, science, or religion, to which the lantern effects added an entertainment quality, so that the shows filled much the same niche as today's Discovery Channel, History Channel, or *Nova*.

About 15 percent of the shows were not stand-alone lectures, but contained illustrated entertainment, often in a variety format that mixed travel or other didactic subjects with stories, songs, and the animated comedy created by slipping slides or other lantern special effects. Though such shows made up a small percentage of the general lantern field, the overall amount of activity was so large that if our estimate of the total is correct, 15 percent of it would amount to 11,000 to 22,000 entertainment shows a year. Assuming the lower end of this range, and assuming an average audience of 100 per show, about a million Americans a year would have been enjoying these kinds of

13   150,000 slides: "Superb New Lantern Slides", T.H. McAllister Co. advertisement in *National Geographic*, 1911. Number of distributors: Nancy A. Berg, "List of Magic Lantern and Slide Manufacturers", compiled 1987, updated 1989. Unpublished manuscript. Many of these were small distributors. If the lower end of the number of lanternists (30,000) is divided by these 300 manufacturers and distributors, each would have only 100 customers, another indication that our estimate is indeed reasonable.

public presentations of story and song entertainment on screen in 1895, before the movies, and indeed, well into the 20th century.[14]

An even larger audience probably saw stories and songs presented on screen by children in their homes, and by adults in churches and secret societies. These venues were not open to the general public, and hence did not have their activities reported in the press. Children's lantern shows were a favorite Victorian pastime, and many slides were produced for them. Churches presented Bible stories and hymns on screen and it is likely that millions saw them in church groups and Sunday Schools each year. Likewise, Secret Societies such as the Masons used lantern slides regularly in their meetings. As we will see, an enormous number of lantern slides, including stories and songs, were created for these three groups, most especially by Joseph Boggs Beale.

Fig. 5. Casper. W. Briggs (left), the leading producer of illustrated lantern slides, stands beside William Henry Jackson (right), the famous photographer, at a 1939 celebration of their accomplishments at the American Museum of Photography. They are standing before the Museum's display of Briggs lantern slides, including those of Joseph Boggs Beale.
[Beale Collection.]

C.W. Briggs, and His Vision of Magic-Lantern Entertainment

Providing the slides for magic-lantern entertainment was primarily the business of one lantern-slide firm, the C.W. Briggs Company of Philadelphia.

Casper Briggs was the son of Daniel Briggs, an early lantern dealer and one of the pioneers of photographic lantern slides (Fig. 5). In 1868 Casper Briggs took over his father's business and in 1872 moved it from Massachusetts to Philadelphia, which was rapidly becoming the center of the lantern industry. In 1874, Briggs bought out the business of the Langenheim Brothers, making Briggs one of the largest American companies in the field.

Given the photographic lineage of the combined Briggs/Langenheim company, and the existing market for photographic travel slides, it would seem natural that Briggs might concentrate in this area, but he did not do so. Perhaps he thought the field was too crowded. Or perhaps, as Charles Musser suggests in the Foreword, he thought it would become even more so with the introduction of dry plate photography which opened the production of travel slides to anyone with minimal skill and effort. (Dry plate, a much simpler process than the wet collodion photography that preceded it and that Briggs continued to use, was developed in 1871; the first factory opened in 1879.) Or perhaps Briggs wanted to pursue his own interests in art and drama. Whatever the reason, he shifted from being a retail distributor of photographic slides to being a wholesaler, "selling to the trade". He began to specialize in coloring slides for the entire lantern

14 For a discussion of a major lantern use in the first quarter of the 20th century – primarily illustrated lectures, but also including Beale stories and songs, see Terry Borton, "238 Eminent Magic-Lantern Showmen: The Chautauqua Lecturers", *The Magic Lantern Gazette* 5, (Spring 2013): 3–34.

industry, and – of special interest to this study – he began to concentrate on creating illustrated (rather than photographic) images by using photography to reproduce etchings and paintings.

Shortly after buying Langenheim, Briggs developed a vision of building an American screen repertoire of illustrated story, song, history and religion, rather than relying on imports from England, which in the 1870s had a more established lantern industry. At that time there was very little in the way of American story and song slide sets.[15] Briggs imagined a future when American-made magic-lantern entertainment would be readily available on the screens of the nation's homes, theaters, church halls, and fraternal organizations. Though he made some accommodations to economic realities over the next 30 years, Briggs stuck with that vision, gradually building up an impressive body of work.[16]

At first Briggs created story sets by simply photographing existing etchings, as the Langenheims had done before him. The results were often disappointing. The hatch marks of the etchings were distracting when blown up on screen; often the dark areas were muddy. Rarely were there enough sequential images to illustrate a complete story. Even if there were, the images might not be of the same aspect ratio – the same size and shape – or in an aspect ratio that fit the needs of the lantern. In 1877, Briggs hired a free-lance artist named Herman Faber to try to improve the images. The procedure was to photograph the engravings and etchings, make very light prints of them, and then "over-paint" the images to make them more suitable for projection. The edges might also be "pieced-out" or "matched-out" by extending the illustration to create a standard aspect ratio so that the picture would fill the area illuminated by the lantern, and the images would not change shape on screen when projected sequentially. In 1880–81, Briggs hired two other free-lance artists, Augustus Tholey and Joseph Boggs Beale. Both did some over-painting and matching-out, but Beale in particular began to create original work, and in 1892 started working full-time for Briggs, creating mostly original magic-lantern art for the screen.

The process of developing an original set of slides began when Briggs selected a subject. Beale then created a storyboard of the set to illustrate a story or song. After approval, he drew a sequence of master drawings – usually four to twenty-four – about 13" square in a monochrome wash of watercolor and gouache (opaque watercolor), pen, and sometimes highlights of white oil paint. Briggs often called these wash drawings "designs"; the terms "designs", "wash drawings", and "drawings", are used interchangeably in the following text.

The Briggs factory photographed the designs and then, to make the slides, printed the resulting collodion negative images as black and white positives on collodion emulsion-covered glass plates.[17] Some were sold as inexpensive black-and-white slides; others were hand-colored in the factory

15   See *Tables 1* and 2, Chapter 3.

16   Louis Sipley (?), "The Pictures of Casper W. Briggs", *Pennsylvania Arts and Sciences 1* (1936): 228–231.

17   Most lantern manufacturers switched to dry plate photography about 1880, but Briggs apparently continued to use collodion. See Louis Walton Sipley, "Civil War Pictures", "The Magic Lantern", "Photographs on Glass", *Pennsylvania Arts and Sciences*, 4 (July, 1937): 28, 43, 93.

(Fig. 6). Finally, the 3" circular glass images were covered with a protective glass, and set in 4" x 7" wooden frames. (Alternatively, cheaper 3-1/4" x 4" all-glass versions – called "Economy" slides – were bound around the edges with tape.) Briggs might make hundreds or even thousands of copies of a single image, and in total sold millions of slides. As a wholesaler, he did not market to individual buyers. Instead, he sold slides to 112 different distributors, including almost every major lantern company in the country, and was thus able to blanket the nation with Beale's images.

Since Beale was the major creator of Briggs illustrated slides, his career will be examined first.

Fig. 6. A slide from Beale's 1890 set for William Gilbert's play of *Pygmalion and Galatea* is a good example of Beale's intricate magic-lantern "designs", and of the meticulous coloring for which the Briggs factory was known. Rich and realistic details are portrayed in a painterly fashion. The series of slides for the set was made with cutouts of the figures, using a matte technique against a standard background, so that one image dissolved into the next, creating the illusion that the marble statue of Galatea had been brought to life. [Beale Collection.]

Joseph Boggs Beale

Beale was born in 1841 in Philadelphia, to a large and well-connected clan. His father was a prominent dentist. His great aunt on his mother's side was Betsy Ross, who probably inspired the many American flags to be seen in Beale's drawings (Fig. 7). The family was religious; attending many church services a week, often at different churches and denominations. His many brothers and sisters also provided a ready audience for the family's amateur theatrics and musicals, in which Beale was often the lead player. In particular, as a 14 year-old boy he created a toy panorama, a painting about two feet high and 126 feet long, containing a series of story illustrations which scrolled across a small proscenium stage. Beale's Uncle Edmund probably inspired this project. Uncle Edmund was a professional panorama showman, performing all over the world, including before Queen Victoria. He also performed often in Philadelphia before the admiring eyes of young Joseph, who would then go back to work on his own panorama, which he eventually presented – with great fanfare – before Uncle Edmund himself. At an early age then, Joseph was learning how to make a series of pictures tell a story on screen.[18]

18 Beale's life as a young man is documented with excerpts from Beale's diary in Nicholas B. Wainwright, "Education of an Artist: The Diary of Joseph Boggs Beale, 1856–1862", *Pennsylvania Magazine of History and Biography* 97 (October 1973): 485–510. The full text of Beale's boyhood diary is at The Historical Society of Pennsylvania in Philadelphia. The description here of Beale's life in Philadelphia relies on both.

Fig. 7. Beale's magic-lantern slide of his famous ancestor, Betsy Ross (Set 166, 1899?). Beale became involved in the effort to have Ross recognized as the creator of the first American flag. [Beale Collection.]

The family also attended a wide variety of other entertainments – minstrel shows, presentations of dwarfs, theatricals, and, of course, magic lantern shows. Most of these were small affairs in churches, but Beale also attended one of the first performances of the larger and more powerful "stereopticon", presented in a major theater. The show was a travelogue, presenting photographic images. Beale was suitably impressed, and commented in his diary that the audience seemed "very much pleased". Even as a boy he could appreciate the power of this visual medium.

Beale received an excellent liberal arts education at Central High School, the academic high school of Philadelphia and so prestigious an academy that it was allowed to award a BA. Beale was, not surprisingly, especially gifted in art, which was a very demanding course at Central. The curriculum had been designed by Rembrant Peale of the famous Peale family of artists, and focused on realistic drawing, stressing especially the mastery of perspective. Both Beale and his schoolmate, Thomas Eakins, learned these lessons well.

Immediately after graduating in 1862, Beale won a competitive examination to become Professor of Art at Central, out-scoring Eakins, who would later become the 19th Century's foremost American naturalist painter. Beale taught at Central for several years, attended classes at the Pennsylvania Academy of the Fine Arts, and was an early member of the Philadelphia Sketch Club.[19] He was active in politics, a member of the Undine Rowing Club (the same club to which Eakins belonged), and enjoyed being a young man about town. The Civil War, a trauma that was tearing the country apart, did not seem to loom large in his consciousness.

Then in June of 1863, the Rebel armies advanced up the valley of central Pennsylvania, and came within striking distance of Philadelphia. The city was in a panic. Beale and his brother Steve enlisted in the 33rd Pennsylvania Volunteers, Blue Reserves. He became regimental artist, but also saw fighting near Chambersburg, Pennsylvania, an experience that informed his many lantern slides of the Civil War (Fig. 8). After two months at the front he returned to Philadelphia, where he took a short vacation hunting and fishing, and then returned to teach at Central.

19   David Sellin, "Thomas Eakins and the Philadelphia Sketch Club" in *Thomas Eakins and His Fellow Artists at the Philadelphia Sketch Club* (Philadelphia: The Philadelphia Sketch Club, 2001) 1–3.

Fig. 8. Beale's images of the Civil War, such as this slide from *Marching Thro' Georgia* (Set 51, 1891), reveal his intimate knowledge of camp life, and often make use of dramatic <u>key lights</u>. [Beale Collection.]

Fig. 9. Beale's lantern slide of the "Hanging Gardens of Babylon" from *Seven Ancient Wonders of the World* (Set 179, 1894). The image demonstrates his mastery of perspective techniques like <u>size diminution</u> – learned in high school, and perfected while creating his many Chicago architectural drawings. [Beale Collection.]

One day in the fall of 1865, Beale attended a baseball game between the Philadelphia Athletics and the Brooklyn Atlantics, sketchpad in hand. Baseball was becoming a consuming American interest, so Beale submitted his drawing to *Harper's Weekly,* where it was published on November 18, 1865, his first work to be published for a national audience. A year later, on Sept. 22, 1866, he published "Burning of the Union League" in the same publication. His career as a professional artist was launched, as he was now appearing in the same pages as artistic giants like Thomas Nast and Winslow Homer. Soon after he moved to New York, where he became a staff

artist for another major illustrated newspaper, *Frank Leslie's Weekly*. As an "artist reporter", Beale was in an environment that required artists to work swiftly, meeting the weekly deadlines, but also to present accurate renditions of the swirling life of the 19th Century. It was excellent training for an artist who would later be asked to create thousands of "realistic" magic-lantern scenes from his imagination alone.[20]

In 1868, Beale married Marie Louise Taffard (also spelled Taffart). The young couple lived in New York while Beale worked at *Leslie's* and free-lanced for other publications. In 1870 they moved to Chicago, where Beale worked for Baker and Company, a firm that provided wood engravings for a wide variety of clients. Unfortunately, the Chicago fire of 1871 destroyed Beale's early Chicago work, but the fire's devastation, and the fierce determination of the city to rebound, led to a frenzy of new construction, including many lavish office buildings. Many of the owners of these buildings wanted engravings of them, and Baker and Company was kept busy creating them. Beale, with his excellent training in perspective, seems to have been especially busy, often correcting the work of others at the firm. Again, he was receiving excellent training for his future career as a magic-lantern artist, where one of the hallmarks of his work would be his fluid depiction of architecture, with the "camera angle" changing with every slide (Fig. 9).[21]

In 1881, Beale returned to Philadelphia, probably because his wife, who was also a Philadelphia native, was dying. There, as we shall see during the following chapters, he began what was to be a 39-year career as the foremost magic-lantern artist in the Briggs Company, and indeed, in the nation.[22] When the nickelodeon movie craze exploded in 1909, he was laid off[23] but continued to create lantern designs on a free-lance basis until 1917–20.[24]

20 Letter of Joseph Boggs Beale to Harper and Brothers, Sept. 15, 1909 in the BC. This letter summarizes Beale's artistic career.

21 Beale kept a portfolio of his work during the Chicago period. This scrapbook, together with a number of preparatory sketches (BC), demonstrate the wide range of activities Beale was called upon to illustrate, and his role as the one who fixed up the work of others at Baker and Company.

22 Louis Sipley, who purchased the Briggs Company, gives the date that Beale started with Briggs as 1880, but Beale, in a letter to his nephew, says he arrived back in Philadelphia in 1881. Beale's date is used here. His earliest signed and dated work in is 1881, *The Two Paths of Virtue and Vice*. For the Sipley Date: Louis W. Sipley, "In Celebration of the One Hundredth Year of the C.W. Briggs Company", ... invitation to a "Private Exhibition of Works", 29–30 June, 1939. For the Beale date: Joseph Boggs Beale to William Louis Taffard, September 27, 1914. Both are in the BC.

23 Letters of C.W. Briggs to Joseph Boggs Beale, Aug. 20, 1909, and Joseph Boggs Beale to Harper and Brothers, Sept. 15, 1909 in the BC.

24 We believe that the end of Beale's career should be given as the date-range, 1917–20. Explaining the reasons for that designation takes some discussion:
Casper W. Briggs sold his company to his son and nephew in 1917–18, so the business relationship between him and Beale was terminated at that point, and with it perhaps any relationship between the company and Beale, although that is by no means certain. (See note 43 for sale information.) Beale's last copyright-dated lantern-slide set was *The Man Without a Country* in 1917, but we do not believe that this date should be used to designate the end of Beale's magic-lantern career, as other slides may have been done later, and the final catalog that contains them has a number of special characteristics which suggest that a later date is appropriate. Determining the date of the end of Beale's career requires understanding the date of this final catalog.
The catalog is called the *Catalogue of Economic Series Lantern Slides*, (the following is handwritten) "Beseler Lantern Slide Co". The catalog is located at GEH and, despite the Beseler label, is attributed by them to "C.W. Briggs Company of Philadelphia, 1918–30". Briggs often provided un-branded *Economic* catalogs to dealers for their use, allowing these firms to brand them with their own company's name as Beseler did here, so the GEH attribution to Briggs is probably correct.
Since the catalog contains the 1917 *Man Without a Country*, the 1918 date chosen by GEH as the earliest date of publication for this Briggs catalog is reasonable. However, since we have no 1918 catalog in our catalog matrix, we use 1917 as the lower end of the date range for our *Catalogue Raisonné*.
GEH gives 1930 as the later end of the catalog's date range. But the catalog features a Set called *The Passion Play of Ober-Ammergau 1910*. The *Passion Play* was given every decade, and photographs of it were readily available, as it was a staple of the lantern trade. The Briggs catalog would certainly not have promoted the "old" 1910 version of the Play past 1920, and since it does not contain the "new" 1920 version, the catalog is even more unlikely to have been produced after that year. Hence, we believe that the later end of the catalog's date range should be 1920.
This Briggs 1917–20 *Catalogue of Economic Series Lantern Slides* contains the last published evidence of new Beale work – five new Sets and 35 miscellaneous new images. Since throughout this book we use catalogs to date Beale's slides, we have also chosen to use the Briggs catalog's end date, 1917–1920, as the end of Beale's magic-lantern career.
There are later undated Briggs religious and history catalogs. They are published by "Briggsco", the name that Louis Sipley sometimes

Today Joseph Boggs Beale is an obscure figure, little known, even by cinema scholars. To correctly evaluate the importance of his work, we need to answer a number of questions: What is the provenance of Beale's lantern-slide materials – how did they come to be where they are? To what degree can we trust the various custodians of this material? What lantern-slide images did Beale create? Can we indeed be sure that that Beale created them? What is the basis for that attribution and how certain is it? How many lantern images or sets did he create? To what degree are the images original to Beale? When were they created, and for what purposes? In what formats and for what multiple uses did they appear? How large an audience did Beale reach? How does his work compare to that of others who were creating lantern entertainment at the same time?

used between the time he bought the Briggs company in 1929, and closed it in 1939. However, the Briggsco catalogs contain no new Beale images. See C.W. Briggs Company, *Catalogue of Briggsco Religious Lantern Slides*, and *Catalogue of Briggsco History Lantern Slides* (Philadelphia, 1929–1939?)
Beale's life will be covered in detail by Terry Borton's forthcoming book, *Cinema Before Film*.

Chapter 2

Provenance, Attribution, Dating – An Introduction to Beale's *Catalogue Raisonné*

Overview

This chapter provides general answers to questions about the provenance, attribution, dating and multiple formats of Beale's work, and also serves as an introduction to the *Catalogue Raisonné* of *Appendix 1*, which contains specific details on these subjects for each of Beale's images. For each set that Beale created or contributed to, the *Catalogue* provides the title and its *Catalogue* ID number, an indication of its popularity, the author of the text illustrated by the slides, the number of Beale images in the set compared with the total available, and, in most cases, a picture from the set. For each of Beale's individual magic-lantern slides the *Catalogue* gives the sources of attribution, and, if needed, date, and location of wash drawings.[25]

The *Catalogue* is organized by set within subjects (Fig. 10).[26] This subject organization emphasizes the types of story and song material that Beale created, and keeps similar images together on the same page rather than (for instance) juxtaposing a Religious and Comic Story just because both begin with an "A". This subject-oriented approach also makes the Catalogue much easier to search by slide and by image. (A chronological organization was not used because it lacks these advantages, because there are some sets that cannot be dated precisely, and because there is little chronological change in Beale's style after his initial experimental period.) *Appendix 2* gives a chronological listing of sets. An alphabetical listing can be found in the Index.

The subject organization of the *Catalogue* also suggests the different markets for Beale's slides.

A primary market for the large concentration of Literature and History slides was schools, as suggested by the fact that the marketing for these slides

25 Since the format of Beale's magic-lantern drawings is almost always 13" square, and slide sizes were standardized, the size and formats for individual wash drawings and slides are not included in the *Catalogue* information.
Six drawings are of a dramatically different size-range, from about 19.5" square to 21.7" square: "Field of Cloth of Gold"; "Execution of Robt. Emmett"; "Siege of Limerick, 1691"; "Trial of Daniel O'Connell"; "Christian Martyrs in Coliseum"; and "The Resurrection". All are in the BC. There is no indication of why these images are larger than normal. For slide sizes, see notes 37 and 38.

26 In Fig. 10, the "Number of New Images" indicates the number of images first used in these subjects. The "Number of Repeated (Images)" indicates the number that were first used in sets for other subjects, and then *reused* in these subjects. The "Total Number of Images" is the sum of the two. For a full explanation of multiple use see the "Multiple Use" section under "Individual Slide Information" in the *Introduction to the Catalogue Raisonné*.

Literature	Religion	History	Secret Society	Other
# New Images: 770	651	312	170	170
# Repeated 24	246	37	216	22
Total # Images: 794	897	349	386	192
Long Poems	Hymns	American History	Masons	Temperance
Novels and	Biographies	Biographies	Oddfellows	Comic Singles
Long Stories	Bible Texts	General History	Knights of Pythias	and Dissolves
Plays and Operas	Old Testament	Current Events	Patriotic Order	Miscellaneous
Parlor Poetry	New Testament		of America	
Popular Songs	Miscellaneous		American	
Religious Literature			Mechanics	
Short Stories			Moose Lodge	
Comic Sketches			Etc.	

Fig. 10. Subject Organization of the *Catalogue Raisonné*

was concentrated there at the end of the Briggs Company.[27] Slide collections and posters also suggest that both families and traveling show-men used the Literature sets for entertainment shows.[28] The market must have been substantial, because Briggs continued to produce a large number of slides for it over a long period. It was most likely the collapse of the market for entertainment slides, caused by competition from the movies, which led to the end of Beale's full-time employment in 1909, and the eventual slow demise of the Briggs Company.[29]

The subject organization of the *Catalogue* also emphasizes the large number of Religion slides, which suggests that churches (particularly Protestant churches) were a major market. In 1890, one third of all adult Americans were church members.[30] Bible stories and hymns illustrated with lantern slides were a standard part of Sunday School. Indeed, in 1894 Beale produced 36 slides for the International Sunday School Lessons that were specifically designed to be used, one slide a week, in a coordinated national Sunday School program.[31] Adult evening functions were another use of slides in churches.

Secret Societies – the Masons, the Knights of Pythias, The Patriotic Order of America – were another major market that is suggested by the subject organization of the *Catalogue*. A large number of slides were created for these Societies because screen presentations of their rituals were common in all these groups. For instance, according to the current national secretary of The Knights of Pythias, every Knights' lodge at the turn of the last century had a lantern and most members – our estimate is 250,000 – saw Beale slides at least monthly (Fig. 11).[32] One can assume that other Societies used Beale

27 For instance, Louis Sipley?, *Brigsco Filmslides: A Catalog of Educational Filmslides for use with Standard 35 MM Still Projection Apparatus* (Philadelphia, Briggsco, 1940?).

28 For instance, Beale lantern-slide sets for children, and several showmen's posters in the Beale Collection.

29 See Briggs/Beale letters, notes 20, and 43–44.
    The other two large markets for slides would have continued. History materials would still appeal to schools, since they did not have movies. The Secret Societies also did not use movies, and the market was in fact growing as the Society membership expanded up the mid 1920s. (See note 32.) Hence it must have been the market for lantern entertainment – stories and songs – that collapsed in 1909, though neither Briggs nor Beale say this explicitly.

30 U.S. Department of Interior, *Abstract of the Eleventh Census: 1890, Second Edition* (Washington, D.C.: Government Printing Office, 1896) 259.

31 See Sets # 124 and 142, and accompanying notes.

32 Author's phone interview with Don Grant, Supreme Secretary, Supreme Lodge of The Knights of Pythias, Morton, PA, Oct, 28, 2010. According to Grant, the Knights had about 500,000 members in 1900, and about 900,000 in 1924. Beale did not begin producing slides for the Knights until 1891, and so in 1900 a certain percentage of the members would have been watching pre-Beale sets of slides. We assume half, or 250,000 and use that figure in the text and Fig. 11.

slides in a similar manner as did the Knights, since Beale produced most of the images used by most of the Societies, and, as can be seen by looking through their sets in the *Catalogue*, there was a large overlap in the way the Societies handled their rituals. In 1920, at about the peak of the Societies' popularity, 30 percent of American men were members of one of these groups. Making some assumptions, it is possible to get a rough estimate of the total number of men watching Beale's images in fraternal organizations in various years. We estimate that in 1900, one and a half million men were watching Beale slides every month in their Secret Society lodges, and by 1920, six million.[33]

Fig. 11. Damon rushes to save his friend Pythias in Beale's dramatic 1896–97 addition of a triple <u>dissolve</u> to an 1891–94 story set (# 216) used by the Knights of Pythias fraternal organization. About a quarter-million members of the Knights in 1900 would have seen such Beale scenes projected monthly in their lodges. [Beale Collection.]

The *Catalogue's* overall organization by subject, then, shows where Beale was putting his creative effort, and, by implication, who was watching those screen presentations, and where. The thousands of individual entries in the *Catalogue* provide much more specific data about particular sets or slides. Because the *Catalogue* presents this information in a limited space, it requires precise definitions and uses abbreviations to summarize the provenance attribution, dating, and multiple format use for each set and slide. Those definitions and abbreviations will only be mentioned briefly in this chapter. They are summarized in a Quick Key before the *Catalogue* and discussed in detail in the *Introduction* to the *Catalogue (Appendix 1)* and its accompanying notes.

Issues in the Provenance, Attribution, and Dating of Beale's Images

Determining the provenance, attribution, and dating of Beale's individual images – the foundation of a *catalogue raisonné* – is essential for assessing his work, as it is for that of any artist. These issues are especially important in Beale's case because his opus is unique. Nowhere else in the world is there

33 For the estimate of Secret Society membership in 1920 see David T. Beito, *From Mutual Aid to the Welfare State: Fraternal Societies and Social Services, 1890–1967* (Chapel Hill, North Carolina: University of North Carolina Press, 2000) 2. The Census reported about 39,000,000 men in the country in 1900, and 54,000,000 in 1920. See Rogers C.B. Morton, *Historical Statistics of the United Sates, Colonial Times to 1970, Part 1.* (Washington, D.C., Bureau of Census, 1975) 9. If 30 percent of the male population in 1920 were Secret Society members, that would be about 12 million. By that time most Secret Societies were using Beale slides, but since they had been using other slides before Beale and some might still be, to be conservative we cut that number in half, suggesting that about 6 million were watching Beale slides every month in 1920.
Calculating a similar number for 1890 is more difficult, because various Secret Societies began using Beale slides at different times. The Knights of Pythias had about half the membership in 1900 that it had in the 1920s. (See note 32.) If we assume that the same was true of other Societies, that would mean six million members in 1900, and if we reduce that number by three quarters, to be conservative about those watching Beale slides, then one and a half million seems like a reasonable estimate.

such a large body of documented imagery by a single magic-lantern artist who was explicitly creating for screen projection. Beale's wash drawings, slides, sketches, letters, scrapbooks, portfolios, and related materials are a treasure trove for the study of his style, his techniques of on-screen story-telling, and – more broadly – for examining American cinematic art before the movies.

However, there are a number of difficulties affecting the documentation of the three areas of provenance, attribution and dating. First among them is the sheer quantity of non-Beale slides sold by American magic-lantern catalogs – roughly 40,000 in the catalog of T.H. McAllister alone – and there were at least a dozen lantern catalogs of this size by the mid-1890s, plus scores of smaller ones.[34] While the vast majority of the slides in these catalogs were photographic, many were not. In the McAllister catalogs, for instance, five to six thousand were hand-drawn images, most of which were not specifically created for the screen but were made by photographing existing etchings or drawings to make slides. There were many foreign sets, and a few sets by American magic-lantern artists other than Beale. Amid this mass of material, it is easy to think that a slide, or slide set, is by Beale when it is not.

The second difficulty affecting the documentation of Beale's work is the quantity of his own material. Beale created (or contributed to) over 250 sets or groups of slides, covering literature such as *Evangeline* and *The Merchant of Venice*; songs such as *Dixie's Land, The Star Spangled Banner,* and *Auld Lang Syne*; history and current events; Bible stories and hymns; temperance stories and songs; fraternal and Secret Society stories, songs and rituals; and comic stories and sketches. Altogether, this work amounts to more than 2,000 images. Each image usually exists in four primary formats – wash drawings; negatives (including original negatives, negative storage sleeves with notes, and occasionally pirated negatives);[35] plus slides of two formats (4" x 7" wood-framed slides, and 3-1/4" x 4", all-glass Economy slides).[36] Many images exist in five other formats (song slides with words beside the images, Gem slides for children, Victor Animatograph "Lightweight" slides, and filmslides (filmstrips) and 35mm slides.[37] A few are found in 12 other rare formats.[38] In total then there are twenty-three different image formats,

34   T.H. McAllister, *Catalogue of Stereopticons, Dissolving View Apparatus and Magic Lanterns, with Extensive Lists of Views for the Illustration of All Subjects of Popular Interest* (New York, 1893). See note 100 for documentation on some of the other major catalogs, and *Appendix 4* for a list of all the catalogs that carried Beale images.

35   The Sipley Collection in the George Eastman House International Museum of Photography and Film (GEH) has many Briggs negatives, including most of Beale's negatives along with their original protective sleeves and their accompanying notes. Examples of pirated negatives are in the BC.

36   Slides were first produced as a "light", or four positive slide images printed together on a single pane of glass. Examples are at GEH and in the BC. The Economy slides were generally later than the wood-framed, were much cheaper, and after 1900 were promoted in a Briggs-produced *Catalogue of Economic Lantern Slides* that was carried by many American lantern companies, either as a separate unit, or worked into their usual catalogs. Though prices varied, in general wood-framed colored slides were $1.50, and colored Economy slides were $.50.

37   Some Beale song images come in two forms of Economy slides – with and without words. "Gem" slides were a children's format, usually 8-1/2" x 2-1/2", taped around the edges, and usually containing three black and white images. (See discussion of children's slides, pp. 43–44.) The Victor Animatograph Company's "Lightweight" slides were a late format, 3-1/4" x 4", made with celluloid framed in light cardboard. About 135 different filmslides (filmstrips) were produced using Beale slides, and many were produced in the 35mm format. (See discussion pp. 44–46.)

38   In addition to the relatively common formats, there were twelve others in which Beale images are rarely seen: (1) Children's slides of 7" x 1-3/4", taped, black and white, with four images. (2) The Victor Animatograph Company's "Viopticon" format, a 2-3/4" x

totaling about 13,000 artifacts, which might provide clues to Beale's provenance, attribution, or dating.

The third difficulty in documenting Beale's work is the fact that it was done in the Briggs Company's production environment. Occasionally Beale re-did the work of other Briggs artists, or Beale over-painted or adapted the work of well-known artists such as Gustave Doré or F.O.C. Darley. It is difficult to be sure of a Beale attribution in these adaptations, as the original artist made the basic choices of *mise-en-scène*, etc. rather than Beale. Occasionally (though not often) several artists worked on a story set, making it hard to tell who was doing what. In fact, Briggs once commented about the problem of identifying artists to Louis Sipley, who purchased his business and went on to establish the American Museum of Photography. Briggs claimed that, "nobody but myself can tell which [artist] is which".[39] That was a bit of an overstatement, as Beale's original work is usually identifiable, provided enough sources are used, but the other artists are indeed very difficult to distinguish.

Adding to the confusion about attribution are the obfuscations of Arthur Colen, a Philadelphia art dealer who was owner of The Modern Galleries. Colen purchased many lantern wash drawings from Briggs in 1935, and began an aggressive public relations and marketing campaign with the intent of selling or merchandizing the images. Colen claimed that almost all the drawings he purchased were "Beale" to make them easier to market, though he probably knew from Briggs that in several sets Beale did not do all of the images. Colen at first also intentionally misled the local and national press into thinking that Beale's work was for possible book illustration, rather than magic-lantern shows, and claimed that they had never before "seen the light of print or public exhibition".[40] No doubt he thought this would make the drawings more marketable, and, as we shall see, the response to his claims certainly proved him right. Even years later he did not mention the existence of the slides themselves in his promotional materials, though he did sell some slides with the drawings.[41] Unfortunately, Colen's tendency to be slippery with the truth casts doubt on all his statements about

2-1/4" slide made with celluloid in a heavy cardboard frame – the precursor of 35 mm. (3) Color slides, 2" x 2" frame on 35 mm film from the Society for Visual Education's "SVE Library of Kodachromes", advertised, for instance, in *Grade Teacher 40* (February, 1943):77, also called "miniature slides". (4) Color slides, 2" x 2", all glass with taped edges, possibly home-made. (5) Tiny slides about 2" x 1" containing ten images, used for Edison's Home Kinetoscope. (6) Briggs "Safety Slides", a 1" square image bound in 3-1/4" x 4" metal and cardboard frames, meant to be used without cracking in the extreme heat of movie projectors. (7) "British" format, 3-1/4" x 3-1/4", (probably pirated). (8) Masonic images in 3-1/4" x 4" metal frames, sometimes called "Metal-Mat Slides". (9) Images on celluloid, surrounded by 3-1/4" x 4" fiberboard, manufactured by Buffalo Stereopticon Entertainers. (10) Six 3" images fixed in a large circular metal wheel published by the Pettibone Company. (11) Three or six 3" images in a two-foot long wooden frame, also published by Pettibone. (12) The DeMoulin Bros. 3-1/4" x 4" slides in 4" x 7" cardboard frames. The later three formats were only used by fraternal societies. Copies of all but the Kinetoscope and Pettibone slides are in the BC; the Kinetoscope slide is at GEH, the circular Pettibone at the MLCM.

39 C.W. Briggs to Louis W. Sipley, Dec. 17 (1940?). Sipley Collection, GEH.

40 "The Professor", *Time 26* (August 19, 1935): 44–45. Technically, Colen's claim that Beale's *drawings* had never "seen the light of print or public exhibition" was true since the drawings were Briggs "in-house art". However, Colen conveniently neglected to mention that these same *images* had been publicly exhibited before millions in slide format.
Almost all the drawings Colen purchased from Briggs were by Beale. The fact that Colen did <u>not</u> buy a large number of drawings by other Briggs artists that would seem to have been saleable is an indication that he was looking for "Beale" drawings, or at least drawings that he could pass off as Beale. Hence, a Colen provenance for a drawing is one indication that Beale did at least some work on the set it is in.

41 In addition to the Beale drawings he purchased, Colen created his own. He hand-tinted about 40 copies of Beale's lantern art, and then sold or otherwise merchandised them. He does not seem to have claimed them to be original color art by Beale, though they are sometimes presented as such in today's markets.

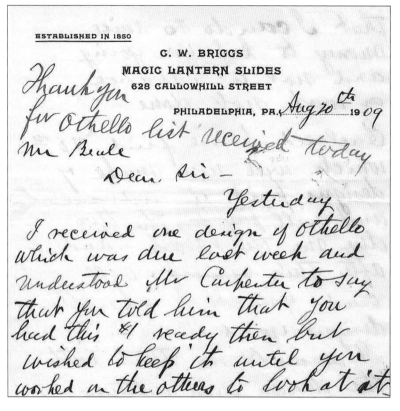

ESTABLISHED IN 1850

G. W. BRIGGS
MAGIC LANTERN SLIDES
628 CALLOWHILL STREET
PHILADELPHIA, PA., Aug 20th 19 09

Thank you for Othello list received today

Mr Beale

Dear Sir —

Yesterday

I received one design of Othello which was due last week and understood Mr Carpenter to say that you told him that you had this #1 ready then but wished to keep it until you worked on the others to look at it.

Fig. 12. Portion of a 1909 letter from Briggs to Beale. Letters like this help give a sense of the working relationship between the two, and of the nature of the artistic considerations that went into producing a slide set. Here Beale has retained the first image of the set of *Othello* so that he can use it to establish <u>continuity</u> throughout the set, a concern that comes up often in their correspondence. [Beale Collection.]

provenance, attribution, and dating, requiring that they be backed with additional evidence.

Finally, though in this review "Beale" is referred to as the artist, it is important to remember that he was working under the art direction of Briggs. That art direction always began with the selection of the content, and then seems to have varied from very vague comments like, "Work up some designs on ____". which left the creative process almost entirely up to Beale, to much more detailed instructions, including occasional rough sketches, which left Beale little room for his own invention. For his part, Beale often provided Briggs with storyboards or sketches or letters to explain to him in advance what the finished designs would look like, and get his approval (Fig. 12).[42]

In addition to these general problems in assessing Beale's work, there are specific difficulties particular to each of the areas of provenance, attribution, and dating, which will be discussed in turn.

Determining the Provenance of Beale's Work

To understand Beale's oeuvre, and more generally that of the Briggs firm, it is essential to know where a given group of extant slides, drawings, sketches, or letters came from; how the various pieces came to be in one place; and how the group fits into the larger context. The *Catalogue Raisonné* summarizes the drawing provenance with the initials of the current location of each Beale master drawing, e.g. GEH for George Eastman House. The location of other materials (slides, sketches, etc.) is outlined in Fig. 13. While the full provenance of each image is not detailed in *The Catalogue Raisonné* (one of the reasons we call it a *Condensed Catalogue*), the general provenance discussed here under-girds image attribution, for many of the arguments for an image's attribution rest on the knowledge of which

42 A contemporary and very laudatory article about Briggs, written while he was still alive, claims that he "frequently" made preliminary sketches for the slide designs. This is very doubtful. While there is evidence that he did make some sketches (See note for Set #80), there is not a single example in all the mass of materials from the Briggs company offices, or from the Beale studio. There is, however, ample evidence of Beale working on his own (preliminary sketches for his own use, sketches sent to Briggs for approval, storyboards, letters concerning images that Briggs wanted changed or was rejecting outright, etc. Briggs certainly knew what he wanted and insisted on it, but it is unlikely that he would have promoted Beale's name so heavily if Beale were simply filling in sketches that Briggs himself had made. Marie Louise Patterson, "Cinema Chrysalis", *Arts in Philadelphia* (June–July, 1939) 11–22.

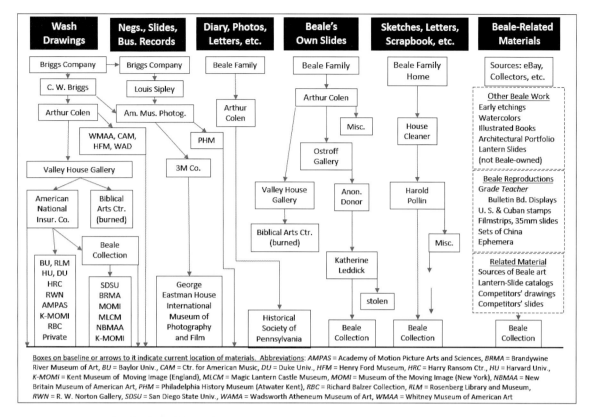

Fig. 13. Simplified Schematic of the Provenance of the Beale Materials.

institutions or individuals hold which Beale items, and the history of how they came to be where they are.

Tracking the provenance of the mass of Beale material is much easier than one might expect because, until recently, most of it changed hands in large batches, and 95 percent was in only a few sites, several of them private. (This concentration is one of the reasons Beale's work is not better known.) The following pages trace the transfer of the most important large collections of artifacts over the last 130 years.

A schematic (Fig. 13) may help orient the reader. The first five columns depict the provenance of artifacts that came directly from the Briggs Company or the Beale family. The sixth column depicts various types of artifacts related to Beale that were mainly sourced on eBay.

The schematic, though complicated, makes Beale's provenance look fairly orderly and clean, but, since provenance is a human story, lurking behind the neat boxes are a number of surprising twists and turns, a few mysteries, a little skullduggery, and some serious tragedies.

Beale's Drawings: *From Briggs to Colen to Valley House to Various*

The provenance of the Beale drawings, abbreviated "wd" in the *Catalogue*, begins with changes in the Briggs Company itself. In 1917 Casper W. Briggs took into the C.W. Briggs Company as partners his son, L. Warren Briggs, and nephew, Casper B. Carpenter, and a year later sold his share of the company to the two partners, though he continued to be somewhat involved.[43] Several times over the next ten years he suggested that he would forgive some of the debt that his relatives owed him if they would give him ownership of the company's engravings and original lantern-slide designs, including Beale's designs. Though the transaction is not documented, he apparently succeeded in making such an arrangement, leaving with the company those over-painted engravings and lantern designs that he considered un-saleable.[44] Briggs kept most of the drawings, but apparently gave the Beale drawings of *Marley's Ghost* to the Dickens House in London, though they are not now able to locate them.[45]

In 1935, nine years after Beale's death, Briggs sold to Arthur Colen, the Philadelphia art dealer, about 1,700 wash drawings, most of which were by Beale. (Briggs apparently retained about 700 drawings.) Colen immediately began promoting the images heavily, obtaining, among other things, an exhibit at the Whitney Museum of American Art (WMAA) in New York (Fig. 14), to which he sold *Bridget's Dream* and two other drawings.[46] He also sold "Jonah cast forth by the whale" to The Wadsworth Atheneum Museum of Art (WAMA);[47] the drawings and some of Beale's slides for *Swanee Ribber, Old Kentucky Home*, and *Old Black Joe* to The Center for American Music (CAM);[48] and *Mr. Spurt* to The Edison Institute (now The Henry Ford Museum, HFM).[49] Colen seems to have sold about 100 other drawings and a few slides to other institutions and individuals,[50] but he kept the vast majority himself. He marketed the images vigorously throughout the 1940s, and licensed the reproduction rights to various enterprises.

Colen's most important licensing connection, probably made in the early 1940s, was with The Bettmann Archive, the largest stock-picture house in the country. Bettmann prized pictures that were "clearly reproducible", and went "to the heart of the subject without gratuitous digressions". In 1966

43 Agreement of February 28, 1917 and October 12, 1918 between Casper W. Briggs and C.B. Carpenter and L. Warren Briggs, the Sipley Collection, GEH. It is unclear whether Beale continued to freelance for the company.

44 Letters from C.W. Briggs to C.B. Carpenter and L. Warren Briggs, May 24, 1924; May 30, 1924; and December 10, 1926, with an undated response from C.B. Carpenter, probably about May 26, 1924. Sipley Collection, GEH. The same collection of letters makes it clear that Briggs was not interested in any over-painted engravings.

45 The gift of *Marley's Ghost* is discussed in "Cinema Chrysalis", note 42. The same article says that Briggs gave *The Raven* to the Poe Museum in Baltimore, but this is unlikely to be true as Colen later exhibited it at the Whitney Museum (note 46), listing his own Modern Galleries as the owner.

46 Arthur W. Colen, "Introduction, *Paintings by David Blythe: Drawings by Joseph Boggs Beale*", (New York: Whitney Museum of American Art, 1936). This catalog lists 13 Beale drawings as from "The Collection of the Whitney Museum of American Art", for an exhibit from April 7 to May 7, 1936. An article in 1937 announces a separate exhibit of "new acquisitions" on Jan. 19, 1937 that includes Beale's drawings. *Brooklyn Daily Eagle*, January 17, 1937, C9. The Whitney currently has only image 4 of *My Mother's Bible* (Set 95) in its collection. It is unclear what happened to the other images it owned.

47 Described in a promotional brochure for Colen's art gallery, "The Modern Galleries", Beale File, Pennsylvania Academy of the Fine Arts. "Jonah and the Whale", is included in Judith Barter, ed., *American Drawings and Watercolors – From the Wadsworth Atheneun* (New York: Hudson Hills Press, 1987) 27.

48 Also described in the Colen brochure, ibid. Two email messages from Kathy Haines of CAM to the authors on March 12, 2001 note that the three sets of Beale material came to CAM through Harry Stone, a rare book dealer in New York. Since Colen was based in Philadelphia, he probably asked Stone to sell material that was related to the exhibit of Beale's work in New York at the Whitney Museum of American Art.

49 *Mr. Spurt* was exhibited at the Whitney Museum after being sold to the Edison Institute. The complete set was reproduced in *Ford Times* in June, 1946 in celebration of the 50th anniversary of the Ford Motor Company.

50 Some sets or images that Colen once owned are now owned by others, including Beale family members. They seem to have come from Colen, though there is no direct evidence of that.

he featured Beale in *The Bettmann Portable Archive*, a book of images that highlighted the company's holdings, displaying more pictures by Beale than by any other artist in history.[51] As a result, Beale's wash drawings were widely reproduced by print media from the 1940s through the 1970s, and continue to appear today on TV and in magazines, credited to Bettmann's new corporate name of Corbis, but almost never to Beale.

In 1973, Colen, then elderly, sold about 1,550 drawings to Valley House Gallery in Dallas, Texas. The connection for the initial sale of 700 drawings was made through another California art dealer, Marty Abram, who received a commission on the sale. Though Abram was a friend of Colen's, he considered Colen an "old pirate", especially when he learned that Colen did an end run around him to sell the additional 850 drawings to Valley House without paying a commission. Abram kept about 100–200 drawings himself, which he gradually sold off.[52]

Valley House Gallery in turn sold about 850 designs (primarily Americana and religious), plus some other artifacts to the American National Insurance Company (AN) in Galveston, Texas, for its corporate fine-art collection. American National gave about 130 religious images to Baylor University (BU), and transferred about 60 to branch offices or sold them to employees.[53] Valley House sold the remaining 440 religious drawings and about 120 Beale-Owned Slides to the Biblical Arts Center (BAC), a museum in Dallas. In 2005, the Biblical Arts Center was destroyed by fire (Fig. 15), and all of the Beale material was lost.[54] (BAC was rebuilt and is now called The

Fig. 14. A color slide from Beale's 1894 set of Edgar Allen Poe's *The Raven*. The black and white drawings of this set were among the images exhibited at the Whitney Museum of American Art in New York in 1936. As Musser points out, almost every image in the set is presented from a different perspective – "moving in" and "panning", to give a sense of the protagonist's emotional turmoil. [Beale Collection.]

51 Otto L. Bettmann, ed., *The Bettmann Portable Archive: A Graphic History of Almost Everything ... Presented by Way of 3,669 Illustrations Culled from the Files of the Bettmann Archive. . .Topically Arranged and Cross-Referenced to Serve as an Idea Stimulator and Image Finder.* (New York: Picture House Press, Inc., 1966) 81.

52 Authors' phone interview with Marty Abram, April 4, 2012 and April 5, 2012. Abram had met Colen by responding to an ad in the paper: "artist looking to sell paintings". He knew Colen well, describing him as "a lovely sweet guy, but if he had a chance to screw you, he would". At the time of our interview, Abram was selling, through another dealer, some of the material he purchased from Colen. The BC purchased one Beale drawing, and several lantern drawings by others – probably by Nisle (see p. 65) and Augustus Tholey (see p. 69).

53 Authors' personal interview with Kevin Vogel of Valley House Gallery, July 16, 1986. See also Donald Stanley Vogel, *Memories and Images: The World of Donald Vogel and Valley House Gallery* (Denton, Texas: The University of North Texas Press, 2000) 200–202. Also authors' personal interview with John Ferguson, Vice President, American National Insurance Co., July 15, 1986. The purchase included some color copies of drawings that Colen had created, and a lantern that was purported to be Beale's. (Both this lantern, and that mentioned in the BC, note 68, fit the available information about Beale's lantern, so either or both could have been his.)

54 Associated Press, June 28, 2005; BAC website, 2005; authors' phone message from a BAC curator, January 12, 2013.

Fig. 16. The American Museum of Photography in Philadelphia. From 1940 to 1968 it displayed a major collection of Beale/Briggs material. [Beale Collection.]

Fig. 15. The Biblical Arts Center in Dallas, Texas housed a large collection of Beale drawings and slides which was completely destroyed in a 2005 fire. [AP Photo/Donna McWilliam.]

Museum of Biblical Art.) Luckily, copies of the original BAC curator's notes were detailed enough to be used for attribution. These survived the fire in the authors' collection, hereafter called the Beale Collection (BC). In the course of the 1980s the Beale Collection also obtained about 300 drawings from Valley House, American National, and other sources, and exchanged some with various institutions. In 2011–12, American National de-accessioned several hundred Beale drawings, donating or selling the following: six story sets to the Rosenberg Library and Museum (RLM), one set to Baylor University (BU), several sets to The Harry Ransom Center (HRC), a set to The R.W. Norton Gallery (RWN), the Spanish American War drawings to The Academy of Motion Picture Arts and Sciences (AMPAS); a set each to Harvard and Duke Universities (HU, DU); several drawings to the Kent Museum of the Moving Image (K-MOMI), several sets and individual drawings to the BC; and other sets and drawings to various institutions and private collectors, including the Richard Balzer Collection (RBC). The Beale Collection in turn, sold or donated sets to San Diego State University (SDSU) and The Brandywine River Museum of Art (BRMA); and individual drawings to the Museum of the Moving Image in New York (MOMI), the Magic Lantern Castle Museum (MLKM), the New Britain Museum of American Art (NBMAA), and The Kent Museum of the Moving Image. (K-MOMI).[55]

Beale Drawings, Negatives, Slides, Briggs Business Records: *From Briggs Co. and C.W. Briggs to Sipley to American Museum of Photography to 3M to George Eastman House*

Despite the large number of drawings that Colen purchased from Briggs, a great deal of material was still in the Briggs Company factory. In 1930, Louis Walton Sipley purchased the Briggs Company (without most of the Beale designs) from the Briggs cousins.[56] Sipley was a trained engineer with a long-standing interest in magic and education. At the time he bought the company, the contract specified that the inventory included 12,000 glass negatives, 30,000 completed glass slides, and 12,000 slides that had been exposed but not completed. Though not specifically mentioned, the inventory probably also included the company's negatives and about 450 lantern designs, largely over-painted engravings, that C.W. Briggs had left with the firm. Sipley ran the company on a much-reduced basis, concentrating on the education market until 1939, when he closed the business.[57]

In 1940, Sipley opened the American Museum of Photography (AMP) in Philadelphia, the nation's first museum specializing in photography (Fig. 16). Because of Sipley's previous business activity with Briggs, the Museum's collection began with a large number of Briggs negatives (including almost all of Beale's work), and Briggs slides (including at least 500 copies of Beale slides), plus Briggs catalogs, business records, etc. Presumably included were also the 450 over-painted engravings and designs.[58]

Probably about 1941, Briggs, who was on the Museum's Board of Directors, gave the Museum a trunk of about 700 additional magic-lantern drawings- – those that he had not sold to Colen.[59] The AMP total of drawings was then about 1150, and included some of the pictures that Beale copied from other artists, some of his original Secret Society images, and some original and copied work by other Briggs artists.

Once AMP was established, Sipley ran it on a limited but vigorous basis. As part of his outreach efforts he gave four designs and some slides to the Atwater Kent Museum in Philadelphia (now The Philadelphia History Museum, PHM), and hosted an exhibit and celebration of the 100th

55   The Beale Collection obtained 222 drawings from Valley House, 70 from American National, and eight from the Schwarz Galleries of Philadelphia, which probably obtained them from Colen in 1976. (In a 1976 letter Colen tried to sell Schwarz 137 lantern slides. The efforts of Colen to sell slides at this time may be the source of the Beale's Own Slides that the Beale descendents now own. Colen probably sold the Schwarz Gallery some wash drawings at about the same period, when Beale was receiving a lot of attention in Philadelphia because of a 1976 touring Beale exhibit sponsored by American National Insurance Co. Authors' personal telephone interview with Robert Schwarz of Schwarz Galleries, September 26, 2007.
      Several Beale Collection drawings were traded with George Eastman House Museum to improve both collections. A few drawings were transferred to individual collectors and four to the Magic Lantern Castle Museum in San Antonio, which, according to the authors' May 21, 2010 personal conversation with Jack Judson, curator, also obtained 31 from other sources.
      Several of the 2011–12 American National transfers were arranged through the authors' personal calls and emails with Michael Henderson and Gay Massengill, representing American National, and representatives of the various interested organizations. Unfortunately, despite our best efforts, it is unclear exactly which wash drawings remain at American National.
      See page 88 for further information on the receiving institutions, and the *Catalogue Raisonné* for ownership of specific wash drawings and sets.

56   "Agreement of Sale between C.W. Briggs Co., and Louis Walton Sipley", May 26, 1930. Sipley Collection, GEH.

57   David Vestal, "Louis Walton Sipley, A Biography", *Popular Photography* (April, 1968): 22–24.

58   Louis Sipley (?), "The First Museum of Photography", *Pennsylvania Arts and Sciences 5* (1941): 37–66.

59   "700 Old Pictures Found in Trunk", undated and unsourced newspaper article, Sipley Collection, GEH.

anniversary of the Briggs Company.[60] When the American Museum closed at Sipley's death in 1968, the contents were sold to the 3M Company in St. Paul, Minnesota, which intended to create its own photography museum. In time the 3M Company changed its mind, and in 1977 donated the entire collection of 60,000 items to the George Eastman House (GEH), now the George Eastman House International Museum of Photography and Film.[61] The Sipley Collection, as it was called, formed the basis for a major exhibit at the Eastman House in 1978.[62]

Beale's Diary, Letters, Scrapbook, Photos: *From the Beale Family to Colen to The Historical Society of Pennsylvania*

At about the same time that Colen purchased the drawings from Briggs, it is likely that he approached the Beale family and obtained Beale's boyhood diary, some pictures of him, and a few letters from his early manhood.[63] (Colen left in the Beale attic a mass of other Beale sketches, paintings, business letters, etc. We believe that was almost certainly an oversight.) Colen used the material he did obtain as background to help merchandise the images. In 1973, he gave all of this material to the Historical Society of Pennsylvania.[64]

Beale's Own Slides: *From the Beale Family to Colen to Valley House Gallery to Biblical Arts Center; also from Colen to Ostroff Gallery to Anonymous Buyer to Leddick to Beale Collection*

When Colen obtained the Beale Diary and other material from the Beale Family, it is likely that he also purchased from them about 1,300 of "Beale's Own Slides" – slides that Beale himself had bought, one-by-one, from Briggs as he completed the drawings.[65] These slides are capitalized as "Beale's Own Slides" to distinguish them from the thousands of other slide copies of the same images that were sold to the general public. "Beale's Own Slides" are abbreviated "bos" in the *Catalogue*.[66]

In the late 1940s, Colen abruptly had to leave Philadelphia for California under a death threat from the husband of his mistress. He took the drawings and apparently 120 Beale Owned Slides with him, and, as mentioned

60   Sipley, "100th Anniversary", note 22.

61   Authors' October 5, 2005 interview with Andrew Eskind, Assistant Director at GEH in 1977.

62   Robert A. Sobieszek, *An American Century of Photography, 1840–1940; Selections from the Sipley/3M Collection.* (Rochester: George Eastman House, 1978).

63   Though there is no direct evidence of this source, the Beale family seems the only possible way Colen could have obtained this material.

64   Beale file, Historical Society of Pennsylvania, Philadelphia.

65   As with the purchase of the diary (note 63), there is no direct evidence of Colen's purchase of Beale's Own Slides from the Beale family, but the family seems the only possible source for this material.

66   Evidence that Beale purchased slides from Briggs as they were completed comes from a Sept. 12, 1890 entry in the *Briggs 1890–92 Ledger*, Sipley Collection, GEH. Evidence that he continued to do so comes from a letter, Casper W. Briggs to Joseph Boggs Beale, July 18, 1908, and from Beale's notes on some slides produced later in his career, both in the BC.

earlier, sold the slides to Valley House Gallery, which in turn sold them to The Biblical Arts Center, along with many of Beale's religious drawings. The slides were lost along with the drawings in the 2005 Biblical Arts Center fire. Before Colen left Philadelphia, however, he sold most of Beale's Own Slides to the Ostroff Antique Gallery there.[67] Ostroff sold almost all of them to an anonymous buyer, an admirer of the work of Katherine Leddick. Leddick ran a small hotel in Whitehall, New York and gave lantern shows there to supplement her income. Though she never knew for certain who had donated the Beale slides to her, she used them to give more elaborate shows over the course of many years (Fig. 17).[68] Thirty six of the American History slides were stolen from her during a show in the 1970s. In 1984, Leddick sold the remaining 1,265 slides and a Beale lantern to the authors, where they formed the foundation of the Beale Collection.[69]

Beale's Own Slides also served as the basis for the shows of The American Magic-Lantern Theater, directed by Terry Borton. AMLT is the nation's only professional theater company re-creating magic-lantern shows. (Leddick had insisted that the Beale slides should not be hidden away in a museum or private collection, but shared in public shows as Leddick herself had done, and she made this a condition of the sale.) At first we used Beale's Own Slides in AMLT's performances, but then shifted to same-size film copies of the originals. Since 1991, the company has toured nationally and internationally with 12 different lantern shows, reaching over a quarter- million people with Beale's magic-lantern entertainment.[70]

Sketches, Paintings, Letters: *From the Beale Family Home to a House Cleaner to Pollin to Beale Collection*

About 1965, the Beale family home was closed. A house cleaner hired to clear out the place found a large and messy collection of artistic materials in the attic (Presumably this was the material that Colen had not obtained from the Beale family when he originally purchased the diary and slides.) The house cleaner called an artistic friend of his,

Fig. 17. The Liberty Eatery in Whitehall, New York, where Katherine Leddick gave lantern shows for 30 years using Beale's slides.
[Beale Collection.]

---

67 Authors' phone interview with Paul Colen, son of Arthur Colen, March 16, 2005.

68 Katherine Leddick, notarized statement, October 26, 1983, in the BC. Leddick believed that a wealthy patron of the Liberty Eatery had purchased the slides for her because she was already giving small lantern shows. The Leddick collection included a lantern that was purported to be Beale's. See also Katherine Leddick Hill, "'The Liberty' and Lantern Shows", *The Magic Lantern Bulletin* (October, 1982); reprinted in *The Magic Lantern Gazette* 21, (Fall, 2009): 9–10.

69 Of course, since millions of copies of Beale's images were originally manufactured, there are also thousands of copies of his slides still extant in public institutions, private collections, and basements and attics around the country. These "non-Beale's Owned Slides" come up for sale on eBay almost every week. They have played a major role in attributing Beale's work because they provide an image where previously we may only have had a written comment, such as a catalog or curator's description.

70 For further information on The American Magic-Lantern Theater see www.MagicLanternShows.com.

Harold Pollin, to see if he might be interested in the materials, as indeed he was. Pollin sold some of this collection to various parties over the years. In 1986 the authors purchased from Harold Pollin two Beale scrapbooks, and several hundred sketches, story boards, oil paintings, annotated etchings, photos and letters, and added them to the Beale Collection.[71]

Beale Related Materials: *From eBay, Lantern Collectors, Antique Shops, Art Galleries, etc., to Beale Collection*

In addition, the Beale Collection (BC) secured, at various times over the years, a wide variety of material designed to provide greater context to Beale's work. Since most of this material came from eBay, its provenance is not well documented.

The material includes Other Beale Work such as a portfolio of Beale's Chicago architectural renderings that contains his explanatory notes, a partial portfolio of his other engravings, and miscellaneous non-slide paintings and watercolors.[72] (Some of these may have had a Pollin provenance, but that is not certain.) The BC also obtained a half-dozen published illustrations from Beale's early career as a commercial artist, and 15 books that Beale illustrated during this period. Regular scouring of eBay has added to the BC about 400 Beale lantern slides in unusual formats, variant uses, or from different companies, etc. Of critical importance are an additional 700 lantern slide images that Beale created but that were not included in the BC's original collection of slides, the ones that Beale himself owned. As a result of these additions, the BC now includes copies of 94% of Beale's magic-lantern slide images.

The BC also obtained a wide range of materials from 1936 to today that were Reproductions of Beale's Work – 45 monthly bulletin board displays carried in *Grade Teacher* magazine, the leading journal for elementary school teachers; a set of 48 Beale American History Drawings for classroom use; U. S. and Cuban stamps; 30 educational and religious filmstrips containing Beale pictures; several thousand 35mm Biblical slides, of which about 25% were Beale images; 30 pieces of china dinnerware illustrated with Beale images; and about 100 pieces of Beale-illustrated ephemera such as "news cards", song sheets, magazine or encyclopedia articles, etc.

Finally, the BC obtained a wide range of Related Material – 130 sources that Beale may have used in preparing his drawings; 20 lantern slide catalogs containing Beale images; 10 lantern drawings by those Beale worked with at the Briggs Company; and about 650 slides directly related to Beale's work – slides by other artists illustrating the same subjects, life-model sets, etc.

This broad range of materials has been helpful in attributing and dating Beale's work, and is essential for understanding the context in which he worked and how he impacted American culture long after his death.

---

71 Authors' interview with Harold Pollin, September 13, 1986. Pollin may have sold a number of Beale oil paintings that are quite crude, and were probably done while he was a student. Two male nudes, a landscape, and one portrait have come up for sale in auctions over the last 15 years. Similar oils are in the BC.

72 BC purchased the portfolio from a Chicago art collector in 1999.

Provenance Summary

Beale-related material springs from three major sources – the C.W. Briggs company, the Beale family, and eBay. Most of the Beale artifacts have moved in large collections from one person or institution to another, and most of those transfers can be well documented. Though some of the materials have been lost over the years (stolen, or destroyed by fire), the vast majority of it is still extant, and provides a unique basis for research into Beale's work; the American magic-lantern industry; and, more broadly, American visual and popular culture.

Attribution, and the Production Process

Though understanding the provenance of a group of Beale materials is very helpful in attributing the items to him, it is far from definitive. Many non-Beale drawings are mixed in with the Beale drawings; some of the slides from Beale's home are not by him; Beale images exist for which there are no known drawings or Beale Owned Slides. Multiple sources of attribution are necessary to establish what images Beale in fact created. In addition to provenance, seven other sources of attribution must be considered. In rough order of certainty they are: signature, catalog references, documentation, wash drawings, negatives, Beale's Own Slides, and artistic style. These are discussed below, each accompanied by the abbreviation that is used to identify it in the *Catalogue*. These abbreviations allow readers of the *Catalogue* to understand how attributions for each slide were determined, and to make their own judgments about the degree of confidence that Beale created a particular set, or a given slide. (Attribution also includes a decision about which images go in which sets. This requires examining the combined image artifacts together with the many lantern catalogs that listed how they were presented for sale to the public.)

The thousands of artifacts on which the attribution is based allow an in-depth look into the production process behind Beale's screen art. Hence, the following discussion of attribution is organized to trace that story – from Beale's first creative efforts on the drawings, to the final marketing of the slides.

Wash Drawings, designated "wd" or "wd★") in the *Catalogue*, represent the first well-documented step in the creative process, and are strong evidence of Beale's work, but are not definitive.[73] What makes the existence of a wash drawing less than definitive is the fact that there are many similar drawings made by artists other than Beale. In general, most credence should be placed in drawings with a Colen provenance, since Colen did get them directly from Briggs, and claimed that they were all "Beale art". Unfortunately, however, not all of them were in fact by Beale. Though Beale was by far the most prolific artist used by Briggs, he was not the only one, and there are a dozen sets of drawings with a Colen provenance that contain at least some images done by other artists in the Briggs company. The drawings in the

---

73   In a few cases artifacts exist from earlier in the creative process – sketches, storyboards, letters, etc. Because these are relatively rare, they are treated as "documentation", abbreviated as "d" in the *Catalogue*.

GEH collection are a mixture of several artists' productions, and so are particularly difficult to attribute.[74]

Aside from using Beale's wash drawings for determining attribution, the study of this first creative step in production is rewarding in its own right. It is important to remember that Beale never meant the public to see these drawings. They look as they do because they were the first step in the production of color screen images. When Beale began to work for Briggs, he dropped the style he had developed in his earlier career as a magazine illustrator, and gradually developed a number of new artistic approaches that would work much better when projected – primarily in the areas of design and tone. He became a real master of the controlled design and tonal range necessary to depict three dimensions convincingly in monochrome without interfering with the final color tinting (Fig. 18). He often used six or seven different planes of light over dark to give a sense of depth and drama. Careful examination of his drawings leads to a real appreciation for his skill – part of the style that made his pictures so successful on screen.

Signature, designated as "s" in the *Catalogue*, is the most definitive attribution, confirming without any doubt that it was Beale who originated the creative process. An "s" for signature appears in the *Catalogue* whenever there is a Beale signature on a drawing, slide, or negative. Signed images

74 Many attribution issues arise with the 1,147 drawings in the collection at The George Eastman House. As explained in the discussion of provenance, seven hundred of these came to GEH through The American Museum of Photography, by way of Briggs, after he had already sold the "Beale" drawings to Colen. The remaining 450+/- were presumably left by Briggs in the company's archive when Briggs swapped drawings for his relative's debt; were then sold with the company to Sipley, became part of AMP, and hence made their way to GEH.

About 221 of the designs in the GEH collection are in fact by Beale, though many are not original conceptions. Forty-three of them are over-paintings, either very close copies of other artists' works (e.g. Darley's *The Legend of Sleepy Hollow* and almost all of the Shakespeare), or over-paintings with significant changes to the original. (It is likely that there are so many Beale over-paintings and matched-out images in this collection because Colen did not want them when he reviewed the holdings of Briggs, believing they would be difficult to sell or merchandise as "original Beales". Very few of the pictures Colen selected are over-painted, though not all are original conceptions.) In the *Catalogue*, any image that Beale worked on is counted as "by Beale", since it is difficult in a summary form to make distinctions about degrees of originality. However, when all of a set is copied, and the source is known, it is discussed in the *Catalogue* endnotes.

About 916 wash drawings in the GEH collection are not by Beale, as determined by lack of his usual grey paper of a standard 13" x 13" size, marginal notes, and their artistic style. Many of these images use different colored paper (often brown) or cardboard of non-Beale sizes, or different artistic techniques. (These "non-Beale" formats pop up in other collections however, and sometimes they are clearly by Beale, especially those done in the early years like *Two Paths of Virture and Vice*, which is on brownish-grey paper, and includes one signed image.) Some of the GEH designs are obviously the work of other known Briggs' artists (see Chapter 4); most are unidentified. Some of the original GEH pictures, particularly the Secret Society images, are so limited in content (e.g. Masonic symbols) that it is impossible to make a judgment based on artistic style.

We were never able to examine closely the wash drawings at the Biblical Arts Center, and so in that case are relying on the detailed curatorial descriptions, not an inspection of the designs themselves, which have now been destroyed.

suggest a high degree of originality, and also suggest that Beale probably created the complete set, though some non-signed images in a set may be closely copied from the work of others.

But even the signatures have difficulties as a source of attribution. First, Beale only signed about 35 per cent of his wash drawings. There is no particular pattern to these signatures other than that he never signed over-paintings or direct copies; very rarely signed while he was a freelancer; and omitted signatures if they would interfere with the image, as in a snow scene or aerial view. Other than that, he sometimes signed most designs in a set, sometimes one, sometimes none. There is a similar lack of consistency among individual images. For instance, of those *New Testament* and *Parable* slides that the *Briggs 1917–20* catalog describes as being "By Beale unless otherwise stated", less than half are signed.[75] In short, we have found Beale's pattern of signatures arbitrary and frustratingly capricious.

The second difficulty with using signatures for attribution is logistical. Beale usually hid his signatures – hid them so effectively that it is easy to miss them in reproductions of the drawings or on the slides themselves (Fig. 19).[76]

Still, there are 721-signed Beale images that provide definitive evidence that Beale created the signed works. The presence of so many signed images is in itself an indication of Beale's special status in the magic-lantern field. Only three other American lantern artists had their signatures projected on screen – Herman Tholey, John McGreer and Xanthus Smith. The three of them together signed only nine images.

Artistic Style, designated with an "as" in the *Catalogue*, is the least certain form of attribution, in contrast to the certainty of a signature. It is our judgment that an image is by Beale, based on the artistic style of a wash drawing or slide. It is used only 14 times in the *Catalogue*, and then only

Fig. 18. On the facing page, the original black-and-white Beale wash drawing on grey paper for a scene from John Greenleaf Whittier's *Maud Muller* (1894) – the first step in the production process. Above is the slide image as it would be seen on screen after the slide made from the drawing had been tinted. Beale's tonal control in the original monochrome drawing provides the sense of depth essential for this rich <u>mise-en-scène</u>, and allows the colorists to create its brilliant chromatic quality. [Beale Collection.]

75 C.W. Briggs, *Catalogue of Economic Series Lantern Slides* (Philadelphia, C.W. Briggs Co., 1917–20). (See note 24 for the dating of this catalog.)

76 Though we tried to examine each image for a signature in one of its different formats of drawing or negative or slide that was not always possible. The drawings were sometimes in frames or protective museum glassine which we were not allowed to remove – obscuring the signature, as well as marginalia and writing on the back of the design. Negatives do not exist for some images. Signatures do not always appear on round slides, because they were sometimes written in the corners of a square "design", or they may be obscured in a matted rectangular slide. It is likely that more signatures will be discovered.

Fig. 19. This image from Beale's 1885 *The Visit of Saint Nicholas* emphasizes how the moon gave a "luster of mid-day to objects below". It also suggests the challenge of finding some of Beale's hidden signatures. (The signature is on the brick, top right, directly under the center icicle.) At lower right is a more easily read Beale signature in its typical block-letter format. [Beale Collection.]

when there is a supportive context such as evidence that Beale created the set in which the image appears.

Negatives, designated "n" in the *Catalogue*, represent the next step in the production process after the drawings. Briggs made "wet plate collodion" negatives and positives, a complicated chemical process that was able to capture microscopic detail – perfect for revealing Beale's elaborate images, and holding their detail when they were magnified by 60 times onto a 15' screen. Almost all the Briggs negatives used to print the slides are still extant at GEH. Usually they show the same information as the front side of the wash drawing, but sometimes the marginalia have been masked out, or the original image has been altered on the negatives themselves so that the negative, and hence the eventual slide image, is different from the wash drawing.[77]

The negatives are useful for attribution because they demonstrate that the image was part of the Briggs offering, though of course the existence of a Briggs negative does not in and of itself indicate that an image was by Beale.

77   Masking the sky or some other area of the negative is quite common. A few negatives are used directly to make dissolves by superimposing a second glass negative on the base. (*Ascension.*) A few negatives, for instance some of those for *Illuminated Hymns*, are composites made by simply pasting or taping two smaller negatives – one for the image and one for the text – onto a clear glass pane in order to make a single image.
In addition to selling slides to distributors, Briggs also sold negatives, presumably with an arrangement that the distributor would reimburse him for any slides made from the negatives. This arrangement would have cut down on the expense of shipping glass from one place to another.
Some negatives held by other companies appear to have been pirated. A number of Beale negatives in the BC from the Moore Bond Company were not made from original drawings. The Briggs slide labels can be clearly seen in the Moore Bond negatives. It is difficult to believe that someone as punctilious about negative quality as Briggs would have allowed second generation negatives to be used if he had known about them. Moore Bond also appears to have had some of Beale's Secret Society images redrawn with slight changes. Examples are in the BC.

Negatives are essential to determine attribution in those cases where the drawings or slides are not available.[78]

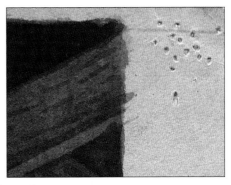

Fig. 20. The enlarged corner of a Beale drawing from image 1 of *Curfew Must Not Ring Tonight*. Fifteen tack holes suggest that *Curfew* was a popular Set.   [Beale Collection.]

Related to the preparation of the negatives is a method of estimating which Sets were "most used" in Beale's time, based on the "tack holes" in the wash drawings (Fig. 20). These holes were made when the drawings were tacked on the wall to be photographed in order to create the negatives. Because negatives could break, or darken as the silver in the collodion tarnished, or because Briggs wanted duplicate negatives to sell to others, popular Sets were photographed multiple times. As a result, some drawings have one hole; others have as many as fifteen. (Some drawing corners are so chewed up by re-tacking that they are worn off entirely; some drawings have had the margins cut off completely, perhaps by Colen because he thought they looked "tacky".) These tack holes do not serve as a source of attribution, but they are helpful in suggesting those sets most used in Beale's time, denoted with an italic "m" in the Set description. Because we thought of "counting tack holes" late in our research, we have been able to examine only a small fraction of Beale's drawings for their existence, but we have marked with an "m" those we have seen that have five or more holes. Another, broader source for a judgment of which Sets or Groups were "most used" is based on an estimate that at least one of the slides from the Set currently appears on eBay one or more times a year. (Some appear as often as monthly.) The estimate of "appearance on eBay" is not an exact tabulation – only a general impression – but yields useful information nonetheless. There are 45 Sets designated with an "m", generally from the Religion and Secret Society areas, but there are also a number of story and song Sets.

<u>Documentation</u>, designated "d" in the *Catalogue*, is another source of definitive attribution, and refers to outside evidence that Beale was involved in the creative process. The largest sources are the business records of the creative process – the *Briggs 1890–92 Ledger* at GEH; copyright records at The Library of Congress and GEH; and letters from Briggs to Beale – the latter in the BC and GEH collections.[79] (These materials are also one of the few sources of explicit information about the Briggs production methods, and the only source of information about the working relationship between Briggs and Beale.)

A major additional source of attribution, and a fascinating glimpse into the production process, is the GEH collection of paper sleeves originally used to store the negatives from which the slides were made. These negative sleeves offer many clues for attribution: subject or other information stamped on the sleeve, category titles (such as "Beale's Bible"), set titles, and the handwritten notes by Briggs identifying the slide artist – "Beale",

78 In addition to the negatives, some "lights" of positive slides images represent the next step in the production process. These are glass plates on which four slide images have been printed at once, like the "lights" of a windowpane. Examples are at GEH and BC. Because these lights are essentially regular black-and-white slides that have not yet been cut apart, they are not used for attribution.

79 Briggs *1890–92 Ledger*, Sipley Collection, GEH. The *Ledger* provides detailed records of all the Briggs transactions in this period, including sales to distributors, and payments to Beale. Unfortunately, it generally does not specify which slides were sold. Beale's working sketches, storyboards, etc. in the BC are characterized as "documentation" since there are relatively few of them.

Fig. 21. Beale's Own Slides – the ones he himself owned – sometimes have his handwritten notes on them, adding to their use for attribution, and for understanding his artistic process. In this case, Beale lists the portraits he painted of the various signers to the Treaty of Ghent, possibly simply as identification, or perhaps because he was proud of being able to capture so many likenesses at such a small scale.
[Beale Collection.]

"Tholey", etc. In addition, many of the sleeves contain dated and initialed notes by Briggs that make clear how much care was taken in printing slides from the negatives – for instance timing the negative's exposure to suggest a certainly quality of light such as daybreak or mid-day.

Beale's Own Slides, designated "bos" in the *Catalogue*, are another indication that an image is Beale's work. They also represent some of the finest examples of the finished product from the lantern-slide production process. All of Beale's Own Slides were made in the wood-framed 4" x 7" format, even after 1900, when most images he created were sold in the unframed "Economy" 3-1/4" x 4" format. All are beautifully colored, and stand in sharp contrast to some of the same images where the slide color was applied in a slapdash fashion.[80]

Beale's Own Slides should not be confused with the same pictures on slides offered by Briggs to the general public. They were once Beale's personal property, and are sometimes labeled or otherwise marked with his handwriting (Fig. 21).[81] (Beale also owned about 100 slides that he himself did not draw. They are primarily sources that he used as the basis for his images, or slides of statuary, and are now in the BC.)

Beale's Own Slides are an important indicator of attribution because they were not a "gift" from Briggs. Beale had to buy them himself, at half price, or $.75 per, a charge of about $8 per slide in today's dollars, or $64 for an eight-slide set. It is unlikely that he would spend so much to buy a set with which he did not have significant involvement.[82]

Catalog Attribution, designated "ca" in the *Catalogue*, is another definitive source of attribution, and represents the final stage of the production process – the marketing of the slides by promoting Beale's name in the slide catalogs themselves.

Starting in 1893, the McAllister catalog began specifically attributing slides to Beale, though only three pictures were listed in that year. By 1897 the practice was well established, with an additional 92 images, and continued in the catalogs of McAllister, McIntosh and others for many miscellaneous pictures in the "Religious" and "Artistic Gems" categories, though not often

---

80 Secret Society and Religious images are particularly likely to appear with minimal coloring – sometimes only a few splashes of color. Almost certainly, these slides were not colored in the Briggs factory. They may have been produced late in the lantern era, and be either pirated images, or the result of some arrangement in which the Briggs company allowed other companies to print and color their own slides.

81 Beale's Own Slides have a Colen provenance, often have Colen's inventory coding in the format "Fa–85, 27–4" written on them, and often are stamped "Beale" in purple ink, presumably by Colen. If there is documentary evidence – e.g. 35 mm copies or curatorial records – that other Beale's Own Slides existed, they are counted as "bos" even if they have disappeared, as is the case of the slides stolen from Leddick, or those lost in the fire at The Biblical Arts Center.
Almost all of the extant examples of Beale's Own Slides are in the BC, at a storage facility. About 120 others were destroyed in the BAC fire. Of the 36 that were stolen from Katherine Leddick, one has been recovered. A Beale descendent has the Beale-Owned Set of *John Gilpin's Ride*.
Almost all of the round slide images in this volume are reproductions of Beale's Own Slides.

82 See note 66.

in other subject areas. In fact, as already indicated, some entire sections of the catalogs were marked, "By Beale unless otherwise stated".[83]

The decision to limit the use of Beale's name to certain sections of the catalogs was probably a conscious marketing strategy. It is likely that Beale's name was listed only for the *"Religious"* and *"Artistic Gem"* categories because in these categories his images were mixed in with other slides by Old Masters or famous Victorian painters (Hoffman, Doré, Tissot, etc.). To leave Beale's pictures un-attributed would have been to diminish their appeal. But to put Beale's name on thousands of slides spread over the entire catalog would have cheapened the very cachet that came from listing him with famous artists.

Still, despite the limits placed on Beale attribution, the magic-lantern catalogs themselves supplied documentation that about 300 images were by Beale, and in about 50 cases it is the only evidence that Beale created the work.

Summary: The Creative Process, and Attribution

The artifacts used for attribution discussed here and summarized for each slide in the *Catalogue* allow one to follow the production process from Beale's wash drawings, through negatives to finished slides and on to the marketing of the images. They make clear that great care was taken at each step of the process, and that the whole was carefully coordinated to produce screen entertainment that was of high quality and reached a broad audience.

The multiple sources of attribution discussed – signature, catalog references, etc. – have allowed us to increase the number of Beale images from our own earlier estimate of 1,700 in the 2001 *Encyclopaedia of the Magic Lantern*, to 2,073 here, about a 20 percent increase.[84]

Dating Beale's Slides

Once the provenance and attribution of Beale's work is established, dating it is the next critical step in understanding his work.

The dating information in the *Catalogue* is derived from tracking each of Beale's slides through a matrix of 31 magic-lantern catalogs from 1880 to 1920. The process and its results are complex, producing multiple forms of dating (e.g. 1890~, 1890 i) that require the detailed explanation available in the *Introduction* to the *Catalogue*. The dates are usually accurate for sets to within a year or two. They provide the basis for analysis of a given image in the context of its time, and of changes in the style that Beale developed in his early years for handling projected images (Fig. 22). Dates also provide the data to show the way his work altered in response to economic conditions such as the Panics of 1893 and 1907, social conditions such as the influx of immigrants, current events such as the Spanish American War, and competitive pressures – especially the emerging competition from the movies.[85]

83 McIntosh Stereopticon Company, *Projection Apparatus, Accessories and Slides* (Chicago, 1895).

84 See note 3.

Multiple Formats

Beale's images did not necessarily appear in only one set or format. The same image in the standard slide formats of 4" x 7" woodframe or 3-1/4" x 4" Economy might be used in several different sets, and there were several important alternate formats, most notably children's slides, and filmslides (filmstrips).

Multiple Use in Standard Slide Formats

The multiple use of images in different sets was an obvious way to reach different markets without additional creative work, and was most effective in the Religious and Secret Society areas, where the market was divided into clearly distinct niches. For instance, the members of the Oddfellows would be unlikely to see some of their images used in the rituals of the Knights of the Mystic Chain. For this reason, multiple use is most striking in the Secret Society category, where 56 percent of the slides were first used elsewhere.[86] Altogether, there are 354 images with multiple uses, employed in 545 different places, so multiple use is a common occurrence.

These multiple uses are tracked in the *Catalogue* with a system that cross-references the slides from one set to an-

---

85 Once Beale's dates are established, it is also possible to date magic-lantern catalogs that are otherwise difficult to date. *See Appendix 5.*

86 The 170 slides listed as "New Images" under Secret Society in Fig. 7, *Subject Organization of the Catalogue*, were all created specifically for Secret Society sets, though some of them may have been used by several Societies. Most of the Multiple-Use images in the Secret Society catalog come from the Religion subject area.

other (designated with "E's" and "F's"), so that the reader can immediately see where a given image was first used. The multiple uses of Beale's drawings are not included in the tally of Beale's total oeuvre as 2,073 individual slide images. But if the multiple uses of his designs were included, his oeuvre would expand to 2,617 slides.

Just because a set contains images that are being used a second time does not mean that the set itself is of secondary importance. Some of Beale's most widely-seen slides – those in *The Photodrama of Creation* (Set 159), which was viewed by 9–11 million people in a single year – were all images first created for a different purpose (Fig. 23).[87]

Children's Slides

Many of Beale's images were produced in special smaller formats for use in children's lanterns. These lanterns were a very popular toy in the Victorian period; so popular that a half-dozen can be found for sale on eBay at any given time today. The children's slides, indicated by a small "c" in the *Catalogue*, came in two basic forms:

"Gem" slides were an inexpensive format that Briggs produced for children.[88] They usually consisted of three black-and-white images on a single all-glass slide measuring 8½" x 2½". What we call "toy" slides were a similar format, made for smaller toy lanterns. They came in various sizes, but the Beale images appear only in the 7" x 1-1/2" size. "Toy" slides had four images

Fig. 22 (facing page). Dating Beale's work allows an examination of changes in his style. Examples are two scenes from the six-slide Set of *Father, Dear Father*, 1887, one of Beale's early efforts. A third slide (see Fig. 43) also shares this exact "stage set", a theater-like approach to the screen that was typical of Beale's work at the beginning of his lantern career. Within a few years, his presentation became much more cinematic, often shifting the point-of-view with every slide, so that he could show new details to sustain attention to the story and increase its drama. [Beale Collection.]

Fig. 23 (below). This Beale image of Noah's flood was first used in *Noah* (Set 119) and later used in *The Photodrama of Creation* (Set 159). For the *Photodrama*, the slide and at least three others were also made into postcards like this, which were available for sale to the millions of people who saw the show. [Beale collection.]

87   Nelson, Richard Alan, "Propaganda for God: Pastor Charles Taze Russell and the Multi-Media *Photo-Drama of Creation* (1914)" in Roland Cosandey, André Gaudreault, Tom Gunning, eds., *Une Invention du Diable? Cinema des Premiers Temps et Religion* (Lausanne: Editions Payot, 1992), 234.

88   In the summary of the Briggs company's history contained in "Celebration", note 22, Sipley says that Briggs began producing Gem slides in 1890, but Gem slides were being offered in the catalogs, with Beale images, as early as 1886. Much of our information about Gem slides comes from catalog references. It is likely that more Beale children's slides will be found over time.

Fig. 24. A toy slide (top) and a "Gem" slide (bottom) from Beale's *Uncle Tom's Cabin*. The toy lanterns that used such slides were probably almost as common in middle-class families of the 1890s as video games are in similar homes today. [Beale Collection.]

per slide. Both Gem and "toy" slides were distributed through the regular lantern catalogs, and also to the general public by the mass marketers Sears Roebuck and Montgomery Ward Co. – one indication of their popularity (Fig. 24).

Thirty six, or 14 percent of Beale Sets or Groups contain images that were used in Gem or "toy" slides, but only four non-religious stories appear in these formats – *Robinson Crusoe, Uncle Tom's Cabin, Paul Revere,* and *Visit of St. Nicholas* (*Night Before Christmas*). Children were much more likely to be exposed to Beale's magic-lantern Bible stories and History than to his entertainment.

Filmslides

Beale's images also appeared in filmslides, (sometimes written "film slides" and later called "filmstrips"), indicated in the *Catalogue* by a small "f". Filmslides were developed about 1920. They consisted of black-and-white, 35mm projected films containing a series of sequential pictures – sometimes as few as four, sometimes as many as 100. The filmslides were not advanced automatically and rapidly, as were the movies of the time, but manually, frame by frame, like lantern slides – hence the early name, "filmslides". Filmslides were used primarily in educational or religious settings, and gradually became so popular that by the 1970s almost every classroom in American middle-class elementary schools had its own projector, by then called a "filmstrip" projector.[89]

In 1924 – about four years after the development of the filmslide format – the lantern-slide companies Geo. W. Bond and J. E. Holley began making filmslides using Beale images (Fig. 25).[90] These filmslides were probably

---

89   For the history of filmstrips see Dorothy Dent *Landmarks in Learning: The Story of SVE* (Chicago: Society for Visual Education, 1969) 37–44.
     The advantages of filmslides over lantern slides were that they were much lighter, cheaper, and easier to manage; the disadvantage was that until mid-20th century they lacked color. The advantages over the movies were that they were much less expensive; and the projector was much lighter, quieter, and much, much easier to manage. (In fact, The Society for Visual Education (SVE), a major educational filmslide producer, began its business by making instructional films and almost went bankrupt pursuing the movie business before it discovered the benefits and popularity of filmslides.)
     Other advantages of the filmslide format for teachers were that the teachers could control the pace of instruction and stop to respond to questions. Advantages to preachers were that they could shuffle the short filmslides of hymns in any order they wished, and advance the images to match the cadence of the verses as they were being sung.

90   For example, Geo. W. Bond produced *Onward Christian Soldiers* (1924), and J. E. Holley produced *The Bible in Pictures* (1924). These and many other Beale filmslides are in the BC.

distributed though their own catalogs, but were more widely distributed by The Society for Visual Education (SVE), primarily to the education market; and by National Picture(s) Service (NPS), primarily to the religious market.[91]

In 1930, the C.W. Briggs Co. (now often called BriggsCo or Briggsco) itself began making film-slides, perhaps selling them on its own, but clearly through Bausch and Lomb, Brayco, and SVE. About 1940, BriggsCo produced a handsome catalog, featuring 95 Beale Sets in filmslide format covering United States History, World History, Literature, and Religion.[92] Colen may also have produced filmstrips, but the evidence is inconclusive.[93]

Altogether, images from about half of Beale's Sets or Groups – 133 in total – were made into at least 135 different filmslides. Almost all of Beale's story and song entertainment Sets were transferred to film, as were most of the religious sets and groups. Most of the filmslides were black and white, but a few, such as the Bond Company's *The Other Wiseman* and *The Ninety and Nine*, probably produced in the 1940s, were in stunning color, and retain their appeal today.[94]

Fig. 25. Two frames from a 1940s Geo. W. Bond color filmstrip of *The Story of the Other Wise Man*, using Beale images. (Photo enlarged for visual readability.) Beale filmstrips extended the projected life of his work to mass audiences for another two generations beyond the magic-lantern era. [Beale Collection.]

35mm Slides

Beginning around 1936, when a stable Kodachrome color process was introduced, various companies began issuing sets of color Bible slides in 35mm format. A major such producer was J.E. Holley (Holley Bible Studies), who had earlier produced lantern slides, filmslides, and books using Beale images. Holley's 1,250 slide set (Fig. 26), was probably begun in 1937, and expanded in 1952. The set consisted of 500 photographs by Eric Matson for *The Bible Lands in Pictures*, coordinated with 375 illustrations for *The Old Testament in Pictures* and 375 illustrations for *The New Testament in Pictures*. Of the 750 illustrations, 145, or about 20 per cent, were by Beale – an impressive percentage considering that Holley could choose from the

91 National Picture(s) Service (NPS) sold its filmslides along with "The Great National No. 1 Stereopticon", an electrified, combination lantern-slide and filmslide projector that came in a sturdy case. A compartment in the lid could hold 15–30 filmslide canisters, enough for up to 100 filmslides. All five of the combination NPS projectors we have seen contained religious filmslides with Beale images. In 1932, NPS was selling its slides of *The Bible in Pictures* for $.10, and its "film slides" for $.03. (NPS advertisement, *International Journal of Religious Education* (June, 1932): 46. NPS referred to itself as both "National Picture Service" and "National Pictures Service".
The last published Beale filmstrip we have found was SVE's 1942 production of *The Life of Christ*, now in the BC. See also, Society for Visual Education, *Combined Catalog of Film Slides* (Chicago: Society for Visual Education, 1930s?) 10–17.

92 Louis Sipley?, *Briggsco Filmslides*, (Philadelphia: C.W. Briggs Co., 1940?) 1–7. See also, Louis Sipley, "New Literature Filmslides" (Philadelphia, C.W. Briggs Co., 1940s?).

93 Ninety-three color lantern slides that Beale himself owned are marked with a label in the format "FS 1 17" – presumably standing for "Filmstrip 1, #17. Colen is the most likely person to have selected and marked these slides, apparently as contributions to American History filmstrips on the Colonial Period, The Revolution, the Young Nation, The Civil War, and the Spanish American War. Colen did produce 35mm slides on these subjects, stamped, "Beale Collection, Modern Galleries, Philadelphia". Samples in the BC.

94 Because we have not seen the actual contents of many of the filmslides listed in the SVE and BriggsCo catalogs, we have used our judgment in about a half-dozen of these attributions. The Beale images in a given filmslide were sometimes drawn from a variety of different Beale Sets or Groups, and were mixed with a variety of images from other sources, so the names of the filmslide Sets do not necessarily match those in the Beale *Catalogue Raisonné*, though they are generally close.

Biblical art of every Western artist who ever lived.[95] Spread out on a light table – dozens of 35mm Beale and non-Beale slides side-by-side at the same time – Beale's appeal is evident. His designs are strong and varied; he tells the story with flair; his pictures "read" well, even in such a tiny format, and would read even better when projected at a larger scale on screen.

~ ~ ~

Ironically, while it was film, in the form of the movies, that killed the commercial appeal of Beale's lantern slide entertainment, it was film in the form of filmslides and 35mm slides that extended the mass use of Beale's projected imagery to new generations. The large sets of 35mm color Bible slides were popular, showing up regularly today on eBay, and were produced by various companies and groups. The BC contains an unattributed 500-slide Bible 35mm set in excellent color, probably from the 1950s, that is 50 per cent Beale, and likely extended the use of Beale's Bible imagery into the 1960s and '70s.[96] In the Literature area, SVE published Beale's work in 2" x 2" Kodachrome slides and filmslides in the 1940s. The nation's major reference guide for educational filmstrips emphasized Beale in 1948, making it likely that his SVE filmslides would continue in schools for yet another generation, into the 1970s.[97] In the Secret Society area, the Masons of the Victorian period were heavy users of Beale's lantern slides for their rituals, and in 2013 some of the 2.5 million modern Masons are still using those same Beale images in the 35mm format, or in PowerPoint presentations based on them.[98] Thus, several of Beale's intended mass audiences were watching his images on screen from the 1890s until the 1970s, and in the case of the Masons, are still watching today – 130 years after Beale created them.

Fig. 26. This set of 1952 35mm color slides, conveniently packaged for the minister or missionary, contained 750 Bible history illustrations, of which about 20 per cent were by Beale. Such sets may have been used into the 1980s and '90s. [Beale Collection.]

95 J.E. Holley and Carolyn F. Holley, *Bible Lands in Pictures: A Syllabus* (Title uncertain; title page is torn.). (Los Angeles: Holley Bible Studies, 1952.) and Carolyn Fizzell-Holley, *Visserslides: The Bible in Pictures, The Old Testament Visualized, A Syllabus* (Los Angeles: Fred Visser Co., 1937?). Both of these scripts and the accompanying chest of 35mm slides are in the BC.

96 The Victor Animatograph Company also published Beale images in the 35 mm format; samples are in the BC. The unattributed 500 slide set in 35mm is made with film sandwiched between two thin pieces of glass.

97 The SVE Kodochromes were light-weight, easily managed slides that were an intermediate step toward the later 35 mm slides. See *SVE Library of Kodachromes*: Unknown, News Item, *Motion Pictures – Not for Theaters*, Installment 23, January (1941) 42. In 1948, Verna Falconer compiled a 572-page book indexing 3,400 available educational filmstrips. She described some of the Beale strips in detail, and, in a very rare credit, listed Beale by name as the illustrator. This was probably in recognition of his standing in the classroom during the 1940s due to a monthly feature using Beale images in *Grade Teacher*, the leading professional magazine for elementary teachers. See Vera M. Falconer *Filmstrips: A Descriptive Index and User's Guide* (New York: McGraw-Hill Book Company, Inc., 1948) 171, 173, 187–90.

98 In the Secret Society area, an *Entered Apprentice* set of 34 slides, offered by a major modern supplier of Masonic materials, and purchased in October, 1913, had about 25 per cent Beale images. George Lauterer, 2011–2012 Masonic Buyers Guide (Chicago: George Lauterer Co., 2012). The evidence for the PowerPoint presentations is anecdotal. Not included in this review of recent use of Beale's slides are the "re-created" lantern shows by Katherine Leddick in the 1960s and '70s, or those of The American Magic Lantern Theater from 1991 to the present, since they were not marketed for presentation to mass audiences.

Chapter 3

The Larger Context of Beale's Work

Foreign Sources of Screen Entertainment in America

Beale was not alone in producing magic-lantern entertainment for the American screen. There was a great deal of imported material, as well as a few original sets created by other American artists. This chapter documents the magic-lantern stories and songs available in the period before the movies, from 1859 (the earliest catalog found) through and including 1895, just before the movies arrived in America. To cover this period, 56 different catalogs from 17 different American companies were surveyed, plus the leading American trade journal of the time (*The Magic Lantern*), and archival records at GEH and elsewhere. The Sets uncovered were then divided into Foreign and American-made.

In fact, foreigners – primarily the British – were supplying the majority of stories and songs to the American screen in the early years. Foreign-made entertainment slides that were available on the American market are presented alphabetically in *Table 1, Foreign-Made Story and Song Sets in American Catalogs, 1859–1895.* [99]

The definitions of the columns in *Table 1* are similar to those presented earlier in the discussion of the *Catalogue*. The most critical information in *Table 1* is the Name of the Set, and the evidence that a Set is Foreign. Detailed definitions of the columns are given in Fig. 27. [100]

---

99 Most of the catalogs used for *Table 1* and *Table 2* were copied early in our research, before we had such a broad survey in mind, and hence are not as complete as we would wish. In addition, because in both *Tables* we are looking at Sets that may be offered by only one company and may lack multiple years of that company's catalogs, we cannot be as confident in dating as we were in Beale's work, which was offered by many companies, and could be tracked across time with the catalogs of different companies. Consequently, unless there are Multiple Listings ("M" under Use), we limit our dating to the single company listed, which means that the Last Date listed may simply be our last pre-1896 issue of the company's catalog that includes the Set.

Besides reviewing the catalogs, we also examined the following: all issues of *The Magic Lantern* (ML), the American trade journal of the period; the Sipley collection of magic-lantern drawings at GEH, which has almost all of the extant non-Beale work produced by Briggs; and the curatorial records of the Biblical Arts Center (BAC) in Dallas, Texas which, before its fire, had about 440 Beale and non-Beale slide drawings.

With these multiple sources, we are confident that we have found most, if not all, of the relevant foreign Sets, though the dating is not as tight as that for Beale, and the indication of Single and Multiple Use may be somewhat shaky.

100 In selecting "story and song" Sets we obviously excluded history, science, travel, etc. Temperance or Religious Sets that had no narrative line were excluded. We also excluded biographies – "Life of ____" Sets such as *Mary, Queen of Scots* and *Joseph* and Bible Stories, since in this period they tended to be made up of previously existing images, rather than created as original cohesive works.

We did not include single "Art Slides", even if they were "genre" pictures that implied a story and were accompanied in the catalogs by a snippet of poetry. These seem to have been used for what was called "emblematical" presentations – evocations of a moment, rather than narratives. (Twice in the *Catalogue Raisonné* we have treated single slides as a Beale "Set" because the slides illustrated a popular short "Parlor poem", *Barbara Freitchie*, or a song, *The Blue and the Gray*.)

In *Table 1*, we have also avoided two-slide dissolves unless they were clearly intended to illustrate a story, as was *Abou Ben Adhem*, one of only a few such dissolves to have "readings" sold with them. We have not included two-slide pairs illustrating novels, since

Fig. 27.
Table 1, Column Headings and Explanations; followed by Table 1, Foreign-Made Story and Song Sets in American Catalogs, 1859–1895

Name of Set. The title of the Set.

in Set. Number of slides in the Set in the period studied.
Multiple numbers indicate changing numbers in the Set.

Artist. Artist, if known, who did the original engravings or other art from which the slide Set was made.

Foreign Evid. (Foreign Evidence) "Foreign" Sets are defined as those created outside of America and imported, or derived (e.g. copied) from foreign work without any direct American artistic involvement, not even over-painting, though the Sets may have been physically printed in the 3-1/4"x4" American format. Evidence for "Foreign" Sets, in rough order of certainty, includes: British slide format (3-1/4" square); Life Model slides which were rarely made by Americans in this period; British readings in the on-line database of the (British) Magic Lantern Society (http://www.magiclantern.org.uk/srlhome.html);foreign authors or foreign terms; foreign artists, art motifs or art styles; a very early offering in our period, which suggests an import; positioning in the catalogs next to other Foreign sets; and offerings in only one catalog, or a very short run in several catalogs, which suggests a marketing test using foreign imports,
A database of American-made slide Sets (*Table 2*) was also established, which will be discussed shortly. It is sometimes difficult to tell if a Set is foreign or American. However, the degree of possible misplacement is not large enough to affect the conclusions of this study.

Yr. Intro. (Year of Introduction) First year that the Set appears in the catalogs during the period 1859–1895.

1st Cat. (First Catalog) Name or initials of the catalog or periodical in which the Set was first listed.

Use. S = Set appeared in only one **S**ingle company's catalogs.
M = Set appeared in **M**ultiple companies' catalogs.

Last Cat. (Last Catalog). Last year that the Set appears in the catalogs Reviewed, 1859–1895. (Many Sets continue in the catalogs after the end of the study period, both those in the Last Catalogs of 1894-95, and those in the Last Catalogs of earlier dates.)

Notes. Related information of interest, especially additional evidence of foreign creation. If a Set was replaced by Beale or other Briggs artists, that is indicated.

obviously these were not enough slides to support a narrative. We have included three and four-slide dissolves only if they seemed to tell a "story", and were not primarily intended to create an "effect", which is how most of them seem to have been used.

We have not included children's stories or nursery rhymes that were presented as such in the catalogs (*Elephant's Revenge; Cinderella; Jack and the Beanstalk; Little Red Riding Hood; Peter, Peter Pumpkin Eater; Pied Piper; Sing a Song of Sixpence*) though we have included stories that appeal to all ages, such as *Visit of St. Nicholas*. If we do not know if the story was primarily for children (e.g., *Funny Little Boy*), we included it.

Following, listed alphabetically, are the catalogs cited in *Table 1*, and the initials used to identify them if initials rather than the names appear. The year in the citation is for the specific catalog title given. Other years examined for our period follow in parentheses; company names and catalog titles may vary over time. Benerman and Wilson (Ben&Wil), *Illustrative and Descriptive Catalogue of Magic Lantern Slides, Magic Lanterns, Sciopticons and Lantern Appliances* (Philadelphia, 1875) (1875, '77, '80 [in an ML ad.]); J. B. Colt & Co., *Optical Lanterns and Views* (New York, 1893) (1893, '95); James F. Hall, *Illustrated Catalogue of Optical Lanterns, Photographic Transparencies and Colored Views for Luminous Projection* (Philadelphia, 1887) (1867, '87); Theo. J. Harbach, *Illustrated Catalogue and Price List of Magic Lantern Slides, Sciopticons, Stereopticons, Photographic Transparencies and Artistically Colored Views*, [etc.] (Philadelphia, 1880?) (1880?, '92); Langenheim Brothers (American Stereoscopic Co.) (Lang), *Catalogue of Langenheim's New and Superior Style of Colored Photographic Magic Lantern Pictures for the Dissolving View and Stereopticon Apparatus, Carefully Selected From the Best Pictures of the Old and New Masters for Educational, Private and Public Exhibitions. . .[etc.]* (Philadelphia, 1861) (1861, '66, '67); L. Manasse (Man), *Illustrated Catalogue of Sciopticons, Stereopticons, Magic Lanterns and Views, Mechanical Novelties, etc.* (Chicago, 1893) (1887, '93); T. H. McAllister (McA), *Catalogue of Stereopticons*, note 34; C. T. Milligan (Mil), *Illustrated Catalogue of Stereo-Panopticons, Sciopticons, Exhibitors' Lanterns, and Every Form of First-Class Magic Lantern Apparatus and of Photographic Transparencies and Artistically Colored Views in Great Variety, Imported and Manufactured* (Philadelphia, 1892); James W. Queen & Co., *Priced and Illustrated Catalogue of Optical Lanterns, Stereopticons, Photographic Transparencies and Colored Views* (Philadelphia, 1884).

Table 1. Foreign-Made Sets

Name of Set	# in Set	Artist	Foreign Evid.	Year Intro	First Cat.	Use	Last Cat.	Notes
Ancient Mariner	38	Dore	Artist	1880	Ben&Wil	M	1893	Beginning 1885 McA, individual slides not listed.
Baron Munchausen	17	Dore	Artist	1892	Har	S	1892	
Bashful Man	6		MLS reading	1895	Mcl	S	1895	
Beautiful Snow	5		3-1/4" sq.	1881	McA	S	1892	
Billie's Rose	10		3-1/4" sq.	1888	McA	S	1892	Life Model
Birth of the Water Babies	?		MLS reading	1880	Ben&Wil	S	1880	
Bottle, The	8	See note	MLS reading	1861	Lang	M	1879?	Foreign art is Cruickshank. New Briggs version, 1880+.
Buy Your Own Cherries	10		MLS reading	1887	Hall	M	1892	
Buy Your Own Goose	6		MLS reading	1895	Mcl	S	1895	
Careless Maggie	6		3-1/4" sq.	1887	Hall	S	1887	"First time published in this country."
Chimes, The	24		3-1/4" sq.	1885	McA	M	1893	Life Model
Christiana, Bunyan's Pilgrim's Progress	32, 12		See note	1881	McA	M	1895	Beside Brit. Mus. slides; New Briggs art. version, 18??.
Christie's Old Organ	24		3-1/4" sq.	1885	McA	S	1885	Life Model
Course of True Love Never Did Run	6		See note	1892	Mil	M	1893	Different from Am. set. French empire.
Cricket on the Hearth	24		3-1/4" sq.	1890	McA	S	1892	Life Model
Curfew Must Not Ring Tonight	9, 10		3-1/4" sq.	1888	McA	M	1892	Life Model. New Beale version, 1894.
Dan Dabberton's Dream	18		Life Model	1895	Mcl	S	1895	
Dante's Inferno	76	Dore	Artist	1867	Lang	M	1879?	New Briggs artist version, 1880+.
Dora	11		3-1/4" sq.	1890	McA	S	1892	Life Model
Drunk as a Brute	14		MLS reading	1893	Manasse	S	1893	
Drunkard's Children	8		MLS reading	1893	Colt	S	1893	
Emigrant Ship	6		Only 4 years	1890	McA	S	1894	"Dissolves"; 4 of 6 are "moveables"; made-up story?
Enoch Arden	20		3-1/4" sq.	1890	McA	S	1892	Life Model
Faust	13	Mayer	Artist	1893	McA	S	1894	
Fondly Gazing	2	Brooks	Early use	1867	McA	M	1894	New Beale version of # 1 in 1903.
Friendless Bob	18		3-1/4" sq.	1885	McA	S	1892	Life Model
Frolic, The	6?		Very early	1869	Queen	M	1869	1879, Mil: "Original designs, this house". Then on Am.
Funny Little Boy, The	30		MLS reading	1895	Mcl	S	1895	"With reading."
Gabriel Grub	17		3-1/4" sq.	1885	McA	M	1893	Life Model
Gin Fiend	4		3-1/4" sq.	1885	McA	S	1892	Life Model
Gin Shop	12		MLS reading	1893	Colt	S	1893	
Girl and the Butterfly	?		Single co. list	1880	Ben&Wil	S	1880	
Girl Who Would Like to Marry	12		Only 3 years	1889	McA	S	1893	
Gossips, The	12		MLS reading	1895	Mcl	S	1895	Life Model
Heart and Its Inmates	9		MLS reading	1892	Mil	S	1892	Religious allegory
Home Again	3		See note	1893	Manasse	M	1894	Probably import; polished academic engravings.
Honey Stealers, The	8		MLS reading	1895	Mcl	S	1895	"With reading."
Ill Fated Ship/Life of a Ship	6	See Note	Artists	1866	Lang	M	1895	Foreign artist: M. Fatio. New Briggs artist version, 1880.
Jack Holiday	14		3-1/4" sq.	1887	Hall	S	1887	"First time published in this country."
Jack the Conqueror	12		MLS reading	1895	Mcl	S	1895	"With reading."
Jackdaw of Rheims	13		3-1/4" sq.	1885	McA	S	1892	"Original Designs." McA did not usually do originals.
Jane Conquest	18, 11		3-1/4" sq.	1881	McA	M	1893	Life Model. 1885 McA "rewritten".
John Tregenoweth, His Mark	18		MLS reading	1885	McA	M	1895	
Johnny Sands	4		MLS reading	1887	Hall	S	1887	
Kate Maloney	6		3-1/4" sq.	1888	McA	S	1892	Life Model
Level Crossing	9		MLS reading	1890	McA	S	1890	Life Model

Table 1. Foreign-Made Sets

Name of Set	# in Set	Artist	Foreign Evid.	Year Intro	First Cat.	Use	Last Cat.	Notes
Life Boat	7		3-1/4" sq.	1885	McA	S	1892	Life Model
Life of a Horse	8	V. Adams	Artist	1866	Lang	M	1876	
Little Bird Catcher	?		See note	1880	Ben&Wil	S	1880	Listed in only one company.
Little Jim, the Collier Boy	6		3-1/4" sq.	1885	McA	M	1892	Life Model. British term in title.
Man Who Wanted to Marry	12		Only 5 years	1889	McA	S	1893	
Marley's Ghost	25		3-1/4" sq.	1885	McA	M	1893	Life Model. New Beale version, 1908.
Mary, the Maid of the Inn	10		3-1/4" sq.	1888	McA	S	1892	Life Model
Matt Stubb's Dream	13		MLS reading	1889	Queen	S	1889	
Miller's Daughter	12		See note	1892	Mil	S	1892	Poem by Tennyson.
Mistletoe Bough	4		MLS reading	1887	Hall	S	1887	
Mother's Last Words	12		MLS reading	1895	Mcl	S	1895	
Mrs. Giles Runs with the Hounds	8		3-1/4" sq.	1887	Hall	S	1887	"First time published in this country."
Nellie's Dark Days	14		3-1/4" sq.	1889	McA	S	1892	Life Model
No Cross, No Crown	4		Early	1877	Mil	M	1895	GEH labels cutouts as NCNC; but prob. Rock of Ages.
Ocean Waif	12		See note	1892	Mil	S	1892	1879 story by C.E. Broad, published in Glasgow.
Old Coaching Days	10		Only Mcl	1895	Mcl	S	1895	"With reading."
Old Curiosity Shop	24		3-1/4" sq.	1885	McA	M	1893	Life Model
Origin of the Moss Rose	4		With reading	1875	Ben&Wil	M	1892	"Four slides. With the poem." But no MLS reading.
Paradise Lost	12, 50	Dore	Artist	1867	McA	M	1895	New Briggs version, 1880.
Pilgrim's Progress (22, 36, 40, 50)	Various	Dore, etc.	See note	1861	Lang	M	1895	Unknown, Life Model, *Art Journal*, New Beale version, 1896–97.
Prodigal Son	3	Dubufe	Artist	1885	McA	M	1894	New Beale version, 1893.
Prodigal Son	72	H.C. Selous	Artist	1892	Mil	S	1892	New Beale version, 1893.
Progress of Intemperance	6		Very early	1859	McA	S	1859	
Reynard, the Fox	15	Kaulbach	Artist	1866	Lang	M	1876	Very early. Engravings. MLS reading.
Road to Heaven	8		3-1/4" sq.	1890	McA	S	1892	Life Model
Road to Ruin	5		Engravings	1885	McA	M	1894	Engravings, appear to be British. Not at GEH.
Robinson Crusoe	17		MLS reading	1893	Manasse	S	1893	New Beale version, 1894.
Roger Ploughman	12		See note	1887	Hall	S	1887	British term in title.
Ruined Cottage	10		3-1/4" sq.	1891	McA	S	1892	Life Model
Sam Bowen's Dream	12		See note	1889	Queen	S	1889	Next to Matt Stubb in catalog which has MLS reading.
Seven Ages of Man	8	D. Maclise	Artist	1893	Manasse	S	1893	Irish painter. New Beale version, 1896–97.
Spiritual Manifestations	4		Only 2 years	1885	McA	S	1886	Dissolving set
Tale of a Tub	6		MLS reading	1869	Queen	M	1894	New Briggs' artist version, 1875 called "New Tale ...".
Tobbit and His Son	6		Only 1 year	1866	Lang	S	1866	
Tommy's First Photo	12		With reading	1892	Mil	S	1892	But no MLS reading.
Trap To Catch a Sunbeam	15		3-1/4" sq.	1885	McA	S	1885	Life Model
Uncle Tom's Cabin	20		See note	1893	Manasse	S	1893	"Original Illustrations." New Beale version, 1882.
Vat You Please	6		MLS reading	1887	Hall	S	1887	
Village Blacksmith	4, 7		3-1/4" sq.	1889	McA	M	1892	Changes in 1892 to 7. New Beale version, 1896–97.
Wandering Jew	12	Dore	Artist	1867	Lang	M	1894	Individual slides not listed in some catalogs.
Wedding Bells	10		3-1/4" sq.	1888	McA	S	1892	
Women of Mumbles Head	8		3-1/4" sq.	1888	McA	S	1892	Life Model
Wreck of the Hesperus	10		3-1/4" sq.	1889	McA	S	1894	New Beale version, 1894.

Comments on *Table 1, Foreign-Made Story and Song Sets in American Catalogs, 1859–1895*

The first thing that struck us about *Table 1* was the large number of foreign story Sets that appeared. (There were no song Sets.) Altogether, at some time in the period 1859–95 inclusive, 90 foreign Sets of stories were available in the American market. (In addition, though we have not seen the relevant catalogs, Riley Brothers, a British firm, opened short-lived American offices in the mid-1890s and carried story slides. Benerman and Wilson imported a large number of slides from the French firm, J. Levy and Company, but these Levy slides were primarily travel Sets.)

While the number of foreign-made lantern story Sets was substantial, the proportion of such Sets compared to American-made Sets changed dramatically over time. In the 1859–69 catalogs, for instance, 60 percent of the 17 stories carried in the catalogs were foreign. The proportion of American work increased steadily in the next decade, as 18 new American Sets were gradually introduced – most of them made from photographed engravings. But then in 1885, McAllister, the major lantern-slide distributor, introduced 14 new foreign Sets, all at once. He must have felt there was a positive response, for beginning in 1888 and over the next four years he added 21 more foreign Sets, for a total of 35, or again about 60% of his story offerings. Other companies followed suit, either picking up some of the same Sets that McAllister was offering, or introducing their own.

The surge of new foreign McAllister Sets that began in 1885 consisted primarily of direct imports of existing lantern slides. They were in the British (3-1/4" square) format, rather than the American (3-1/4" x 4"), required a special slide changer, and were primarily Life Model slides – that is, slides that were produced by photographing live models in front of a stage set. The subject matter was a mixture of famous authors' stories such as Dickens's *Marley's Ghost* and Longfellow's *Village Blacksmith*, children's stories such as *Jack and the Beanstalk* (not counted here), and temperance stories such as *Buy Your Own Cherries*. Gradually, however, this mix changed, and the total dropped, perhaps because of the quantity and quality of Beale's work, both in replacing foreign imports, and, as we shall see, in creating new story Sets. Of the 91 stories from foreign sources found in all the catalogs summarized in *Table 1*, 17 were eventually replaced by Briggs artists, ten by Beale, and seven by others.

It is curious that while McAllister's earlier foreign offerings contained some Temperance stories, they were a small fraction of the hundreds of such tales that were commonly sold in England. There are also comparatively few American-made Temperance stories. This relative paucity of Temperance stories in America may be accounted for by the fact that while the English Temperance movement remained largely educational, requiring new lantern stories, the American movement became heavily political, culminating in the passage of the Prohibition amendment. It could be that Temperance moral tales were not as important to the American movement as were parades and protests.

Life Model Sets in general do not seem to have been particularly popular in America. In England, they were offered over a long time, including

Fig. 28. The climatic scene of Rose Hartwick Thorpe's *Curfew Must Not Ring Tonight* in an English Life Model set (top), and in Beale's 1894 version (bottom). Because Beale was illustrating rather than photographing such scenes, he could give them a much greater sense of energy, and, paradoxically, of life and realism – qualities that characterize most of his work. Aerial perspective provides this "crane shot" with additional drama. [Beale Collection.]

relatively late in lantern history, and today are ubiquitous in English antique markets. Yet, early life model slides (as opposed to the later "illustrated songs", p. 63) are rarely seen in America today on eBay, or in museums or private collections, suggesting that comparatively few such Sets were sold in the States. Perhaps this is because the Life Model Sets were often grim in their subject matter and static in their portrayal (Fig. 28). Or, perhaps it is because the British slides, particularly the Temperance Sets, all sounded alike and all sounded depressing. For instance, in 1898 the catalog of the British firm Riley Brothers that was prepared for the American market contains a long defensive note to customers trying to explain that the Temperance Sets really were different from each other; really did have a humorous side; and really did "rise above the level of the penny dreadfuls".[101] The British Life Model format for telling stories may have simply developed a bad reputation in America. Indeed, even some

101 Riley Brothers, *Catalogue of Stereopticons, Magic-Lanterns, and Lantern Accessories* (Riley Bros., New York, 1898) 33.

British lanternists joked that rather than calling these Sets "Taken from Life", they should be called "Taken from Death".[102] Perhaps, over the course of Beale's career, his "livelier" illustrated stories, with their artistic drama and energy, simply pushed the British slides aside.

American "Mass-Market" Magic-Lantern Artists

In addition to Beale, a number of other American artists were producing stories and songs for mass-market screen entertainment. *Table 2, Story and Song Sets by American Magic-Lantern Artists Other Than Beale, 1859–1895,* contains all the stories and songs by non-Beale American magic-lantern artists for this period found in the catalogs, *The Magic Lantern* trade journal, and museum archives. In order to facilitate attribution, the data is organized by date of first appearance, with the listings broken by sub heads that indicate which artists were working for Briggs at the time.[103]

The definitions of the columns in *Table 2* are similar to those in *Table 1* and are listed in Fig. 29.

There is quite a range of confidence concerning the information in *Table 2.* The survey of American catalogs is large enough to have found most of the then-available stories and songs, and it is reasonably clear when each was first introduced, when it was dropped, and how much it was used. But questions remain: These Sets appear to be by Americans, but sometimes the evidence is not conclusive. It is often unclear which artist created the Set, beyond the fact that an artist worked for a certain company at certain dates, buttressed by an analysis of paper types and artistic styles. Attributions to these artists are often much less definite than that for Beale and so many are followed with question marks. However, as will be seen later, the uncertainty is not large enough to make a difference in the final analysis of Beale's role.

Comments on *Table 2, Story and Song Sets by American Magic-Lantern Artists Other Than Beale, 1859–1895*

Focused as we are on Beale, the first thing that struck us when we examined the data in *Table 2* is how many non-Beale American stories and songs were available or developed from 1859–1895 – a total of 56 Sets. In the first seven years of this study (1859–1866), however, there were only five, almost all

---

102 A Cambridge Reader, "My Clerical Lantern Work", *The Optical Magic Lantern Journal and Photographic Enlarger* 6 (October, 1895): 161. In the later magic-lantern period (1920s?), there were a number of Life Model religious sets made by several American manufacturers, and a few story sets by the lantern manufacturers William H. Rau and Moore, Bond and Co., but they are outside the purview of this study. The illustrated song slides, though Life Model, were a whole other order of artistic creation with their jazzy colors and fantastic montages. They were wildly successful.

103 Following, listed alphabetically, are the catalogs cited in *Table 2*, and the initials used to identify them if initials rather than the names appear. Short titles are used if the full titles are given in note 100. The year in the citation is for the specific title given. Other years examined for our period follow in parentheses; company names and catalog titles may vary in these years. Benerman and Wilson, *Illustrative and Descriptive Catalogue*; J.B. Colt & Co., *Optical Lantern*; N.H. Edgerton (Edg/Q), *Priced and Illustrated Catalogue of Magic Lanterns, Stereopticons, Photographic Transparencies and Colored Views* (Philadelphia, 1876) (1876) [Edgerton took over Queen for a short period.]; Langenheim Brothers (American Stereoscopic Co.) (Lang), *New and Superior; Magic Lantern, The* (ML) (Philadelphia, 1874) (1874–1886); L. Manasse, (Man), *Illustrated Catalogue*; McAllister (McA), *Catalogue of Stereopticons*; Milligan (Mil), *Illustrated Catalogue*; Geo. H. Pierce, *Illustrated Catalogue of Stereopticons and Magic Lanterns of the Best Quality and of Every Variety of the Best Lantern Views and Lantern Novelties* (Philadelphia, 1887) (1887); Queen, *Priced and Illustrated Catalogue.*

Fig. 29.
*Table 2, Column Headings and
Explanations; followed by
Table 2, Story and Song Sets by
American Magic-Lantern Artists
Other Than Beale, 1859–1895*

Set Name/Note #. Title of the Set. The "(#)"after the name indicates a note at
        the bottom of the chart. It is possible for a Set Name to appear in both
        Table 1 and *Table 2*.
in Set. Number of slides in the Set in the period studied.
        Multiple numbers indicate changing numbers in the Set.
Copied? "O" indicates a Set is original.
        "C" indicates a Set directly copied from engravings.
        "C?" indicates that the Set was probably copied.
Engrav. Artist. (Engraving Artist) Artist, if known, who did the
        original engravings from which the slide Set was made.
Pub./Artist(s). Publisher or Artist(s) who over-painted or adapted the
        original engravings to make lantern designs, or who created original designs for slides.
        See Chapter 4 for a discussion of these artists.
        "Artist's Name/Beale" indicates that Beale (or another named artist) replaced or expanded
        a Set originally worked on by someone else, but not necessarily that he revised it in the
        study period. Beale replacements are detailed in the column, "Last Cat./Beale."
Am. Evid. (American Evidence) Evidence of American creations such as
        the presence of American flags, American authors, 3-1/4"x4" American format, the
        Location of known drawings, etc. The Location is the one that contains the largest number
        of drawings from the Set, and that number is indicated after the Location abbreviation:
        GEH = George Eastman House; AN = American National Insurance Co.; BC = Beale
        Collection; RLM = Rosenberg Library and Museum.
Yr. Intro. (Year Introduced) First year that the American-made Set appears in the catalogs or *The
        Magic Lantern* in the period 1859–1895, inclusive. As in the *Catalogue Raisonné* a range
        of dates indicates the Set was created during the range. The last date in the range indicates
        the first catalog to carry the Set, and we use that date as the time of introduction. A "?" in
        the column indicates we have not seen an earlier catalog of this company in our study
        period.
1st Cat. (First Catalog) Name of catalog or periodical in which the American-made Set
        was first listed.
Use.   S = Set appears in only a **S**ingle company's catalogs;
        M = Set appears in **M**ultiple companies' catalogs.
Last Cat./Beale (Last Catalog/Beale) Last date, 1859–1895, in which
        the Set appears in the catalogs examined. The years 1894 and 1895 should
        both be considered as indicating that a Set ran through to the end of this
        study. It may well have continued longer.
        If the Set was Expanded (E) or Replaced (R) by Beale, this is noted, with the year.

of which were on religious or Temperance themes. More stories and songs that were secular were developed after 1867. This trend accelerated when Briggs bought the Langenheim Brothers company in 1874, and developed his vision of creating a repertoire of story and song entertainment for the American screen.

The second feature that stands out in *Table 2* is how much of this work came from the Langenheim/Briggs artists. This one company among the 17 reviewed created 36 Sets, or about 65 percent of the total. Even without counting Beale's new work (not tabulated in *Table 2*) Briggs was responsible for most American magic-lantern story and song Sets. Just as important, his slides were much more heavily used, as can be seen by comparing the Multiple/Single Usage column of Briggs Sets with the Sets from other companies. The greater number of Multiple uses occurs because, as a wholesaler, Briggs distributed his slides throughout the industry. Most of his Sets appeared in most of the catalogs examined.

The third thing of note about *Table 2* is how much of the Briggs output by non-Beale artists was simply over-painting or matching out previously existing engravings or British slides – as indicated in the Copied column. Nineteen Sets are copied and fifteen are probably copied, about 60 percent of the total. The only potentially original works are two by Blue, three by McGreer, one by Xanthus Smith, and perhaps one by Beard. There was not

Table 2. Sets by American Artists Other Than Beale

Set Name/Note #	# in Set	Copied?	Engrav. Artist	Pub./Artist(s)	Amer. Evid.	Yr. Intro.	First Cat.	Use	Last Cat./Beale
1859–1873+: NISLE BEGINS WORK FOR LANGENHEIM IN 1860									
Drunkard's Career/ Progress	8, 12	C	Seymour?	Briggs Art: Nisle/Tholey	GEH 12	1859	McA	M	1894
Pilgrim's Progress (1)	12, 27	C		Briggs Art: Nisle?/Tholey?/Beale	BC 24	?–1861	Lang	M	R. by Beale, 1897
Christiana and Her Children	12, 27	C		Briggs Art: Nisle?/Tholey?	GEH 12	?–1861	Lang	M	1894
Life of a Slave	8	C?		Lang Art: Nisle?	Am. Subj.	1862–66	Lang	M	1892
Gambler's Career/ Progress	6	C	Cruickshank	Briggs Art: Nisle?/Tholey?	GEH 6	1862–66	Lang	M	1895
Brave Drummer Boy & Father	3			McAllister Art?	Am. Civil War	1867	McA	M	1892
Life of Country Boy (Scenes)	4	C		Briggs Art: Nisle?/Tholey	GEH, 4	1870–74	Queen	M	1894
Seven Ages of Man	7	C?		Briggs Art: Nisle?/Beale	BC 7	1870–74	Queen	M	R. by Beale, 1897
Rip Van Winkle	6	C	Darley	Briggs Art: Nisle?/Beale	AN 6	1870–74	Queen	M	R. by Beale, 1893
1874–1876: BRIGGS BUYS LANGENHEIM IN 1874									
Tam O' Shanter	6	C	John Faed	Briggs Art: Nisle?/?	GEH 6	1868–75	McA	M	1895
Cotter's Saturday Night	6	C	John Faed?	Briggs Art: Nisle?/?	GEH 8	1868–75	McA	M	1895
History of Johnny Short	12	O		Beard	Am. Author	1868–75	McA	S	1891
Drake's Ode to Am. Flag (2)	6	C	various	Briggs Art: Nisle?/Beale	AN 1	1868–75	McA	M	R. by Beale, 1893
Voyage of Life (Not Cole)	4	C?		Briggs Art: Nisle?		1868–75	McA	M	1894
Course of True Love Never Did Run (3)	5	O		JE Blue		1875	ML	M	1893
My First Segar & What It Did	4	O		JE Blue		1875	ML	S	No catalog listings.
New Tale of a Tub (4)	6	C?	British set	Briggs Art: ?	GEH 6?	1875–76	Ben&Wil	M	1894
Ten Nights in a Bar Room (5)	12	C?		Briggs Art:?/Beale	Am. Flag	1875–76	Edg./Q	M	R. by Beale, 1893
Abu Ben Adhem	2	C?		Edgerton/Queen Art?	no MLS read	1876	Edg./Q	M	1895
1877–1879+: BRIGGS HIRES FABER TO FREELANCE IN 1877									
How Persimmons. . . Baby (2)	4	C/O	Champney	Briggs Art:/Faber?/Beale	BC 4	1877	Ben&Wil	M	R. by Beale, 1???
Heathen Chinee	3	C?	Eytinge?	Milligan artist?	Am. Author	?–1877	Mil	M	1892
Hiawatha	4	C		Milligan/Briggs Art: ?/Beale	AN 22	?–1877	Mil	M	R. by Beale, 1900
Sentimental Toastmasters	6			Milligan artist	"Orig. Design"	?–1877	Mil	S	1892
Visit of St. Nick (A) (6)	5			Milligan artist	"Orig. Design"	?–1877	Mil	S	1892
Prodigal Son	8	C?		Milligan/Briggs Art: Faber?/Beale		?–1877	Mil	M	R. by Beale, 1893
Flight of Mercury	5			Bennerman and Wilson artist?		1877	Mil	M	1892
Rock of Ages	4, 12	C?	Ortel (1)	Briggs Art: Faber?/Beale	AN 2	1876–78	McA	M	R. by Beale, 1887
Flight of Time	?			Bennerman and Wilson artist?		1878	ML	S	No catalog listings
Journey of Aurora	12			Bennerman and Wilson artist?		1878	ML	S	No catalog listings
The World	11			Bennerman and Wilson artist?		1878	ML	S	No catalog listings
Ghostly Adventure	4, 3			Bennerman and Wilson artist?		1878	ML	M	1893
How Jones Became a Mason	4			Briggs Art:?/Beale		1878	ML	M	R. by Beale, 1891
A Common Occurrence	3			Platt (H.C.)		1879	ML	S	?
Way of Salvation	4	C?		McAllister Art?/Briggs Art?		1878–79	McA	M	1894
The Frolic (7)	6	C		Milligan artist?	"Orig. Design"	1878–79	Mil	S	1892

Set Name/Note #	# in Set	Copied?	Engrav. Artist	Pub./Artist(s)	Amer. Evid.	Yr. Intro.	First Cat.	Use	Last Cat./Beale
Table 2. Sets by American Artists Other Than Beale									
1880–1891: BRIGGS HIRES THOLEY (1880–81?) AND BEALE (1881) TO FREELANCE (Only Beale revisions indicated)									
The Bottle	8	C	Cruickshank	Briggs Art: Tholey	GEH 8	1879–80	Mil	M	1894
Visit of St. Nicholas (B) (8)	5, 4, 6	C?	Nast	Briggs Art: Tholey?/Beale	RLM 6	1879–80	McA Feb.	M	R. by Beale, 1885
Cole's Voyage of Life	4	C	Cole	Briggs Art: Tholey?		1879–80	McA	M	1894
Ill-Fated Ship (New)	4	C?		Briggs Art: Tholey?	Am. Flag	1880	Queen	M	1895
Paradise Lost	12	C	Dore	Briggs Art: Tholey	GEH 13	1880	McA	M	1894
Dante's Inferno	12	C	Dore	Briggs Art: Tholey?	GEH 18	1880+	McA	M	1894
Champagne to the End (9)	4	C?	Puck?	Milligan Art?/Beale	"cents"	1882	Mil	S	1895
Road to Ruin	5	C?		McA Art?/Briggs Art:Tholey?		1883–85	McA	M	1894
Last Voyage, Ocean Steamer	4	0	X. Smith	Briggs Art: X. Smith	Am. Artist	?–1887	Pierce	M	1894
House on Fire	4			McAllister Art:?		1890	McA	S	1891
Diana or Christ?	4	C?		McA Art:?/Briggs Art:Tholey?		1890	McA	M	1894
Judith and Holofernes	4			McAllister Art:?		1891	McA	S	1894
1892–1895: BRIGGS HIRES BEALE TO WORK FULL TIME, 1892— (Beale's original work listed in Catalogue Raissone, not here)									
Vagabonds	5	C	Darley	Briggs Art: Tholey?	GEH 5	1888–92	Mil	S	1892
Soldier's Return	6	C	John Faed?	Briggs Art: Tholey?	GEH 6	1888–92	Mil	S	1892
Photographing the Baby	4	0		John M. McGreer/Briggs Art	$ sign in pix	1892	Mil	S	1892
Family Prayer	4	0		John M. McGreer/Briggs Art	style	1892	Mil	S	1892
Fishing	4	0		John M. McGreer?/Briggs Art	style	1892	Mil	S	1892
Uncle Tom's Cabin (10)	20			Manasse Art?	"Orig. Illust."	1893	Man	S	1893
Faust	14	C	Kreling	Briggs Art: Tholey	GEH 10	?–1893	McA	M	1894
An Engineer's Love	16			Lubin photographer		?–1894	Lubin	S	1894
Forgotten	12			Lubin photographer		?–1894	Lubin	S	1894
1896: MOVIES ARRIVE IN AMERICA									

Notes to Table 2

1. Pilgrim's Progress – Original 12 by Nisle? Probably re-done by Tholey, 1880–93. In 1896–97 Beale expanded by 12 to 24, with 12 old remaining.

2. Drake's Ode – in this and "How Persimmons", both marked with note "2", Beale revised the Set but the date of revison is uncertain, so the "Last Cat." column has a question mark.

3. Course of True Love – *The Magic Lantern* mentions a Set by Blue in 1875, which never appears in the catalogs. A Set based on academic engravings appears in 1892. We assume the two are different Sets, the first American, the second a foreign import.

4. New Tale of a Tub. "The Tale of a Tub" (no "New") appears in 1869. "The New Tale of a Tub" appears in 1875. We count the first as foreign, the second as American. The Tale may have been redrawn after the study period by Herman Tholey, as the drawings at GEH look like his.

5. Ten Nights – Set appears in 1876, before Beale, so counted here as "Briggs Art", but Beale wd and bos exist of a slightly different version which Beale presumably reworked or replaced in 1881–93.

6. Visit of St Nicholas (A) – One of 2 sets by unknown artists, the 'sketchy set'. By Milligan artist. See note 8.

7. The Frolic – Assume early 1869 appearance is a test and so counted as foreign. Milligan 1878–79 "Orig. Designs" counted here as American.

8. Visit of St Nicholas (B) – One of 2 sets by unknown artists, later revised by Beale. See note 6.

9. Champagne to the End – Rather than being a separate Milligan Set, it is possible that "Champagne to the End" has the same images as those in Beale's "William Jackson's Treat", with only the title and line descriptions changed. WJT was introduced in 1885 and is the name used in other catalogs.

10. Uncle Tom's Cabin – This is a Set of 20, so is not the same as the 1882 Beale Set of 12.

much competition from these American slide artists for Beale's outpouring of original work.

Finally, it is striking how many of the Briggs Sets were revised or expanded by Beale at some point – 11 of the 36 Briggs Sets, or about a third. Beale spent a good part of his time fixing up the work of others. (During the pre-movie period, Beale also revised 22 pre-viously-existing slides by the most popular artist of the 19th Century, Gustave Doré.[104] These slides are not simple over-paintings to enhance projectability. Though the Doré source is clear, Beale re-conceives most of the subjects. As in his original designs, his control of cinematic tech-niques makes his image dra-matic as well as "readable" on screen (Fig. 30).

Fig. 30. A slide from James Russell Lowell's *The Courtin'* (1894) shows Beale's ability to manage the detail that filled his slides. The room is cluttered, but the scene is carefully controlled with a <u>closed-form</u> design to highlight the story-telling drama. Three items – her red dress, his black coat, and the black cloak on the chair – create a triangle with the kiss at the top. <u>Backlighting</u> from the off-screen fire at left produces a huge cat's shadow that, together with the cat's tail and the cloak, creates a second larger triangle – again with the kiss at the apex. The mantle, the top-left vertical line of the sideboard, and the framing of the slide's left edge create a third triangle. This triple triangulation leads the eye through the clutter, right to the kiss that is the "defining moment" of the story. [Beale Collection.]

---

104 Dan Malan, "Gustave Doré's Magic Lantern Slides", *The New Magic Lantern Journal 9* (Winter, 2001): 3–6.

Chapter 4

Other American Magic-Lantern Artists

The survey of Beale's work, and overview of foreign imports and of other American artists, now allows a more detailed assessment of Beale's importance. He has previously been called America's "Premier Magic-Lantern Artist", and "A Great Magic-Lantern Artist".[105] But can he also be considered "America's First Great Screen Artist" – a description that would not only honor his role in magic-lantern culture, but also place him in the larger context of cinema history? It is already obvious that Beale meets the underlying criteria for this rubric: He was an American screen artist working before the movies, and hence before movie artists. But were there any other American lantern artists working at Beale's time or earlier who might also be considered "great" – artists who also produced a significant amount of work, or more work, or work of higher quality?

There are two types of artists who might be considered: first the many American magic-lantern artists documented in *Table 2* who were producing slides for mass use and sale through the catalogs; and second, several individual showmen who produced slides for their own exclusive use, and who were not represented in the catalogs. Both groups contain artists of fascinating backgrounds, and unique talents.

The slides of the artists listed in *Table 2* who were not working for Briggs will be presented first. Omitted from this discussion are all Sets that were over-painted or "matched out" from engravings. (Beale did some of this work too – they are listed Sets in the *Catalogue* with special notes – but his over-paintings are not included here when comparing him here with other artists.)

Artists Who Did Not Work for Briggs

There are six artists, or types of slide artists, who did not work for Briggs, but who made significant contributions to the magic-lantern culture of story and song entertainment:

J.E. Blue

The November 1874 issue of *The Magic Lantern* (ML) introduced the comic work of J.E. Blue, produced by Benerman and Wilson – 30 comic slides

---

105 Premier: Permanent exhibit, The Magic-Lantern Castle Museum, San Antonio, Texas. Great: "Speaking of Pictures. . . These Are By A Great Magic-Lantern Artist", *Life 8* (January 8, 1940): 4–6. (Arthur Colen wrote a letter to *Life* the next month, (February 5, 1940): 4, giving his version of the story of Beale's "discovery", and asserting his copyright for the images that *Life* had printed.)

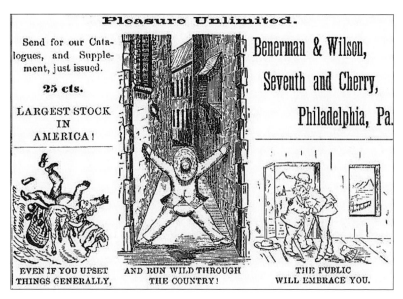

Pleasure Unlimited.

Send for our Catalogues, and Supplement, just issued.

25 cts.

LARGEST STOCK IN AMERICA!

Benerman & Wilson,

Seventh and Cherry,

Philadelphia, Pa.

EVEN IF YOU UPSET THINGS GENERALLY, | AND RUN WILD THROUGH THE COUNTRY! | THE PUBLIC WILL EMBRACE YOU.

Fig. 31. An advertisement for the Benerman and Wilson lantern company, carried on the back of the trade journal, *The Magic Lantern*. It uses three cartoon images, probably by J.E. Blue, to create a joke about the trials of a traveling lantern showman. [Beale Collection.]

related to travel (Fig. 31), and a nursery-song Set. In January 1875, ML described another nursery rhyme by Blue, and *The Course of True Love Never Did Run Smooth*. In July 1875, ML discussed Blue's *My First Segar and What it Did*.[106] Of these story Sets, only *Course of True Love* survived in the catalogs. *My First Segar* did not even make it to the 1880 catalog of Benerman and Wilson.

However, by 1881 Blue's original 30 comics had expanded to 100 black-and-white "crayon caricatures". (Some of these images appear to be by Blue, some by other artists.) The "crayon caricatures" appeared in a number of different catalogs over the years, and may have been adapted from cartoons that ran in *Harper's Weekly*, to which Blue was a regular contributor during the Civil War.[107] Blue's lantern cartoons are nicely drawn, and even today retain some of their humor. (Beale re-worked 42 "crayon-transparency" comic lantern slides in 1894 [See Groups 238–242], but the original artist remains unknown. Since most of these revisions are not stories or songs, they are not included in this study.)

Blue definitely had talent, but it seems to have been for the individual comic scene, rather than stories. None of the latter found an audience, and all but one was quickly dropped.

Daniel or Frank Beard

In 1875, McAllister (McA) listed a story by "Beard", *The History of Johnny Short*. There are two likely candidates for the illustrator of this story, Daniel or Frank Beard. Daniel is best known as the co-founder of the Boy Scouts, but he was also a talented illustrator, including in his illustration credits the pictures for Mark Twain's *A Connecticut Yankee in King Arthur's Court*, and presidency of the Society of Illustrators.[108] His brother, Frank Beard, was less well-known and was primarily a cartoonist. The *History of Johnny Short* is a temperance tale and since Frank specialized in cartoons, especially the "moral cartoons" that appeared in *The Ram's Horn*, a religious magazine, it is likely that the *History* is his (Fig. 32). The *History* continued to run in the magic-lantern catalogs for many years. Later, *The Ram's Horn* created its own magic-lantern catalog of Beard's moral cartoons. The cartoons also appeared

---

106 Edward L Wilson?, "Blue's Lantern Comicalities", *The Magic Lantern I* (November, 1874): 25–26; "Blue's Comics" (January, 1875): 5; and "New Slides" (July, 1875): 11. The nursery rhymes (not counted in *Table 2*) were *Sing a Song of Sixpence* (1874) and *Peter, Peter, Pumpkin Eater* (1875).

107 Barber, note 6, 153. Samples of Blue's Civil War cartoons can be found by searching for his name on http://www.sonofthesouth.net/.

108 Walt Reed, *The Illustrator in America* (New York: Society of Illustrators, 2001), 48.

under *The Ram's Horn* name in the McIntosh Stereopticon catalog of 1901, and the Chicago Projecting Company's catalog of 1908.[109]

Both Beards were accomplished artists, so we can assume that whichever one was the illustrator of the *History*, he did a good job, though perhaps making no particular attempt to depict the subject in a style suitable for projection. For whatever reason, there are no more stories illustrated by "Beard", though a few individual slides by that artist's name do appear.

Benerman and Wilson Artist

In January and February 1878, *The Magic Lantern,* published by Benerman and Wilson, touted several new Sets of dissolving views that seem to have enough narrative so that they might to be considered "stories", and thus are included here. All but *Ghostly Adventure* were carried only in the 1880 Benerman and Wilson catalog.

> *The Flight of Mercury* – Seems to have been first projected by the lanternist John Q. Manard. It remains in the Benerman and Wilson catalog, and others. The zoom-like technique was new at the time and received warm praise (Fig. 33).
>
> *Ghostly Adventure* – Appears as both a three and four-slide Set. Continues in the catalogs.
>
> Three other Benerman and Wilson Sets, *Flight of Time, Journey of Aurora*, and *The World* do not appear in other catalogs.

These slides were probably created by Benerman and Wilson's staff, possibly by one artist, unnamed. Perhaps it was J.E. Blue, mentioned earlier, or H.C. Platt, mentioned later, but this seems unlikely, as the work of both was comic, and these Sets

Fig. 32. A "moral cartoon" by Frank Beard (above left), and a comic trade card, also by him (right), show that he had a broad range of comic style. Beard's moral cartoons were later offered as a group of slides called *The Ram's Horn Cartoons*. He is the most likely artist for the lantern Set, *The History of Johnny Short.*
[Beale Collection.]

Fig. 33. *The Flight of Mercury* (1877) created a type of zoom effect by using a series of dissolves of Mercury increasing or decreasing in size, inter-cut with clouds to hide the transitions.
[Beale Collection.]

109 Frank Beard, *Lantern Slides of 100 Great Cartoons* (Chicago: Ram's Horn Press, 1900?). McIntosh *Projection Apparatus*, 1901. Chicago Projecting Co., *Chicago Projecting Co's Entertainers Supplies* (Chicago, 1908).

are serious. Whoever the "Benerman and Wilson artist" was, with the exception of *Mercury* and *Ghostly Adventure*, he or she does not seem to have created a lasting body of work.

Milligan Artist

At various times, the C. T. Milligan company offered new Sets that were sometimes presented as "original designs, available only from this house" – an obvious attempt to establish a sense of house art separate from that of Briggs. The following were all in the Milligan 1892 catalog, but did not appear in the catalogs of other companies.

> *Visit of St. Nicholas (Version A)* – "Original designs". Introduced in 1877. Replaced in all catalogs, including Milligan, by Briggs/Beale art revision of Version B.

> *Sentimental Toastmasters* – "Only this house". Introduced 1877, and *The Frolic* – Temperance – "Only this house". Introduced 1878–79. Both in Milligan only.[110]

> *Champagne to the End* – Introduced in 1882. No claim of, "Only this house". Probably the same as Beale's *William Jackson's Treat* carried by other catalogs. See *Table 2*, note 9.

Whoever the Milligan artist was, if he was a single artist, his offerings lasted through the study period, but were confined to the Milligan catalog.

Single-Shot Artists, and Short-Term House Artists

In a fashion somewhat similar to Milligan's "Only this house" strategy, a number of houses, using named or unknown artists, made periodic small attempts to create unique stories using the term "Original design". The phrase did not imply "Only from this house". It was used to indicate that a Set of designs had been prepared especially for screen projection. The phrase dropped into disuse once Beale began full-time production in 1892 and story Sets were no longer copied directly from engravings.

Most of these single-shot attempts did not last much beyond the originator's catalog, and none led to any sustained attempt to create a repertoire of screen entertainment.[111]

---

110 Barber, note 6, 155 credits this Set to Briggs, as an Americanization of an English Set. If so there must have been an arrangement that it was for the use of Milligan only.

111 "Single shot" attempts included:
Benerman and Wilson: H. C. Platt, artist, *A Common Occurrence* – Introduced with a description in
   The Magic Lantern 5 (Jan. 1879). It did not even appear in Ben&Wil 1880.
Manasse: *Uncle Tom's Cabin* – "Original designs". 1893, 20 slides, so not by Beale.
Queen: *Heathen Chinee* – "Original designs". Little used outside Queen.
Edgerton/Queen: Abou Ben Adhem – Introduced, with reading, in 1876. No evidence of Briggs involvement.
   Carried by multiple catalogs.
McAllister: *Judith and Holofernes* – McAllister catalog only; no longer in McAllister in 1897.
McAllister: *House on Fire* – stays in McAllister catalog only.
McAllister: *Brave Drummer Boy and His Father* – in McAllister and others to 1892. No evidence of Briggs involvement.

The following two Sets are listed as McAllister, since that is where they first appear, but they may have been developed by Briggs and broadly marketed by him, since they later appear in all catalogs, including Briggs, and two of them are represented by Sipley slides at GEH. However, there is no other evidence of Briggs involvement such as extant drawings.
Road to Ruin – Stays in McAllister catalogs and others.
Diana or Christ – Stays in McAllister catalogs and others.

Illustrated Song Slides

Two entries that come right at the end of *Table 2*, in 1894, are the leading edge of what would become a major form of lantern screen entertainment, illustrated songs:

> Sigmund Lubin:
> *An Engineer's Love*
>
> Sigmund Lubin: *Forgotten*

"Illustrated" song Sets were in fact not illustrated, but were usually made photographically, using the "life model" technique, though they looked nothing like the drab and stilted British images. They rapidly became a dramatic art form of their own, and were sold to theaters to be "illustrated" (i. e., performed) by a local vocalist singing solos and

leading "sing alongs". Elaborate photographic collages, contemporary imagery, and vibrant colors all combined to make song slides extremely popular, especially in America (Fig. 34). Often the publishers of piano sheet music provided the slides to theaters, hoping audiences would rush out to buy the sheet music after hearing the song. When the movies arrived, song slides were often used between the short reels of film, and became a major attraction in their own right, often receiving higher billing than the films themselves. Their popularity lasted until about 1917.[112]

Fig. 34. Illustrated Song Slides like this one often used striking photo montages, and vibrant colors. Interspersed with films, they became an important part of the early cinema experience. The firm of Scott and Van Altena was the leading producer of such slides. [Beale Collection.]

Though credit for the creation of life-model Illustrated Songs is usually given to George H. Thomas for his 1894 *The Little Lost Child*, the two Sets from Lubin are the first to appear in catalogs, and certainly signal the start of a significant cinematic trend. However, so few song slides were created in the next year that they do not constitute a significant amount of magic-lantern art in the period before the movies. (Lubin himself was one of the few lantern slide manufacturers to also shift over into the production of movies.)

A small number of later illustrated song slides employ Beale images, often in situations when a character in the song was remembering the "olden days". The Beale images appear among the photographic slides, or were sometimes used as a "thought balloon" (Fig. 35). These illustrated songs did not generally appear in the traditional lantern catalogs, but were

---

112 Richard Abel, "That Most American of Attractions, the Illustrated Song", Richard Abel and Rick Altman, eds., *The Sounds of Early Cinema* (Bloomington: Indiana University Press, 2001), 143–155. See also, Rick Altman, *Silent Film Sound* (New York: Columbia University Press, 2004). ~~ An August 1895 ad in *Metropolitan Magazine* for McAllister promotes "Illustrated Songs", so the 1895 McAllister catalog may well have had a good selection, but we have not seen it so we cannot be sure.

Fig. 35. A slide from the illustrated song Set, *Hello Central, Give Me Heaven*, produced by the Chicago Transparency Co., combines a photograph of a little girl trying to call Heaven, and a Beale image of a heavenly city. [Beale Collection.]

marketed directly to theaters. A list of Illustrated Song Sets Containing Beale Images may be found in *Appendix 6*. Additional Sets may well emerge.

Artists Who Worked for the Langenheims or Briggs

As already described, Briggs was the major source of magic-lantern screen entertainment in the pre-movie period, and Beale was his chief artist. But there were six other artists besides Beale who worked for the Langenheims or their successor, the C.W. Briggs Company. Their contributions will be considered next.[113]

It was not always easy for us to tell some of these artists apart. While it is relatively easy to be certain of an attribution to Beale if enough sources are used, little of the work of his colleagues was signed or attributed in the catalogs. Adding to the difficulty is the fact that Sets were often re-done several times by different artists. For instance, a surviving Langenheim catalog, one that includes pictures of the slides, shows a Set of *Pilgrim's Progress* done in a very sketchy style – probably a direct photograph of pre-existing line drawings. These same 12 images were re-done in a more projectable style at some point before 1893 – probably by Briggs freelancers Tholey or Faber. Beale later expanded the Set to 24 by interlarding 12 new images among the original 12. Similar revisions make a number of other Sets difficult to attribute, and difficult to date.

Accepting these problems and the lack of certainty that comes with them, assessments are made primarily on the basis of Artistic Style (type of paper, technique, skill, habitual motifs or ways of presentation), combined with the time period in which the artists were working. To a certain extent the attribution is a process of elimination, beginning with the easiest to pick out, Nisle and Tholey, and then working down to the most difficult to determine. Since the time period when the work was done often became the critical factor in the attribution process, the following discussion is organized chronologically, using the same headings as appear in *Table 2*.

113 See Louis Walton Sipley, "The Pictures of Casper W. Briggs", *Pennsylvania Arts and Sciences* 1 (1936): 228–231, and "The Magic Lantern", *Pennsylvania Arts and Sciences* 4 (1937? '39?): 39–43. See also Elizabeth Shepard, "The Magic Lantern Slide in Entertainment and Education, 1869–1920", *History of Photography* 2 (April–June 1987): 91–108. Drawings cited in the following text by Nisle (Neslie), Herman Faber and Augustus Tholey are courtesy of the Atwater-Kent Museum, Philadelphia, now The Philadelphia History Museum at The Atwater Kent. The drawings, along with one by Beale, were given to the Museum by Louis Sipley in 1940 to form a representative collection of the work of the Briggs Company's major artists. Since Sipley was communicating regularly with Briggs at the time, it is reasonable to assume that his attributions were correct, despite his 1936 mistake of attributing *The Bottle* to Beale in "The Pictures of C.W. Briggs".

1859–1873+ Nisle Begins Work for Langenheim in 1860

Nisle (Neslie)

Nisle is the most mysterious of the artists considered. He was hired in 1860 by the Langenheim Brothers, whose business Briggs bought in 1874. Nothing is known about him personally; even his name is uncertain – first written as "Nisle" by the Langenheims, yet McAllister and others refer to him as "Neslie", or sometimes "Nislie" or "Nesle" or even "Nesler". There are a half-dozen individual Nisle slide drawings at GEH, which are easy to distinguish from those of other artists. One appears to be signed (spelled "Nesle"), or perhaps the "signa-

Fig. 36. Nisle's awkward anatomy and hard-edged drawing sometimes gave serious subjects the aura of "crayon caricatures". But his Civil War slides, though not numerous, were the first especially designed to bring the War to the screen. [Courtesy of the Philadelphia History Museum at the Atwater Kent.]

ture" is simply a notation by someone else. At any rate, it puts a name to the group of images. They are on white paper, generally much smaller (7"–10" square) than other art prepared for Briggs, and often circular, presumably because at the time Nisle was working, only a circular wood-framed aspect ratio was being used (Fig. 36). Nisle's sense of perspective, anatomy, and tonal control are uneven. He had particular trouble with heads; sometimes his figures appear to have their necks broken. His views are often so close to the action that legs and arms are cut off by the framing, and they frequently have a cartoon quality because of the hard outlines. There are no existing full Sets of original drawings in Nisle's style.[114]

Nisle is the only named artist that the Langenheims used, so it seems likely (though by no means certain) that any original Langenheim illustrations appearing before 1874 are by him. (If the designs have not survived they are referred to here as "Langenheim Art"; if they do, then "Briggs Art".) Altogether there are eight Langenheim/Briggs Sets listed in the 1859–1874 period. If Nisle continued after the Briggs purchase, there are an additional four, for a total of 12. Nine of Nisle's Sets are direct copies of engravings (marked "C" in column three of *Table 2*), so they are excluded from this analysis. Three Sets from this period marked "C?" may be copies or may be original work:

114 We use the "Nisle" spelling because it is the one used first, by the Langenheims, who actually employed him. Other spellings appear in various catalogs or on slides. It is unclear how many History or Civil War pictures Nisle did. In "One Hundredth Year" ("In Celebration", note 22), Sipley says that Langenheim issued 960 slides of the Civil War in 1866. Clearly Nisle created at least a few of these, but not many. To judge from the remaining pages of the Langenheim's catalog that shows the actual slide images, almost all are engravings or lithographs: American Stereoscopic Co., *Langenheim's Magic Lantern Pictures* (Philadelphia: 1870's?) in the Sipley Collection, GEH. Similarly, of the 27 non-Beale Civil War slides in the GEH Sipley Collection, only one is by Nisle. Nineteen are clearly etchings or lithographs; three are overpaintings. Fifteen of the etchings or lithographs are credited on the slides themselves to either the Faulkner and Allen Company or the Kurz and Allison Company.

Life of a Slave (C?) – No known examples of slides. Very little used in catalogs.

Seven Ages of Man (C?) – No known examples of slides. Promoted as "well-colored" which suggests copies of master paintings. Later redone by Beale.

Voyage of Life (C?) – Different from *Cole's Voyage of Life,* but very closely related. Appears after Briggs bought Langenheim, and is described in the catalogs as "From Langenheim". Slides of it are similar to Nisle's work. Remains in the catalogs. Three drawing are in the Beale Collection.

Nisle can also be credited with creating some American History slides, 60 Bible slides, and some comics. He is an intriguing figure. Whoever he was, he created a fairly large number of individual slides and several non-story Sets, but at best only three story Sets that may have been original. So far as can be told, he was the first American artist to create any significant amount of work for the screen, but his art showed little skill or originality, and little appreciation for how to use the medium of projection. In addition to the crude aspect of his drawings, he lacked the qualities that could give screen stories a cinematic feel – continuity, dramatic use of light, control of mise-en-scene, changing perspective points, etc.

1874–76: Briggs Buys Langenheim in 1874

When Briggs purchased Langenheim in 1874, it might seem natural that he would make changes in the company's artists. It appears that Briggs did not admire Nisle, because almost all of Nisle's Sets were eventually re-done by other Briggs artists except perhaps *Voyage of Life,* and *Life of a Slave,* which were simply dropped. Even the early Nisle story Sets that were copies of engravings were all re-done, most by Augustus Tholey, whose work will be discussed shortly. Beale completely re-conceived the non-story Nisle Set, *The Lord's Prayer,* and another Set that may have been by Nisle, *The Ten Commandments.* The relentless revision process is most evident in the Bible area, where about 60 slides were originally presented under the rubric, "By Neslie" or "By Nisle". In 1897, his name was dropped from the title and moved to individual slides. By 1908 Beale had replaced about half of the slides, and only seven were attributed to Nisle. Meanwhile, various catalogs were listing either the Old Testament or the New or both as "By Beale unless otherwise stated".

It is possible that Briggs kept Nisle on for a while after the 1874 purchase, or he may have let him go immediately. The latter seems more probable, so we have labeled the last two Sets in this section (1874–76) as by an "Unknown Briggs Artist". It seems unlikely that Nisle did them. Since they are probably copies, it makes little difference to this exploration of original screen art work, though both were widely used in the lantern catalogs.

New Tale of a Tub (C?) – May have been originally copied from a British Set. Existing designs at GEH look as though they may have been done much later by Herman Tholey, son of Augustus.

Ten Nights in a Bar Room (C?) – Perhaps originally photographed from engravings and then later re-worked by Beale, since the designs' paper is reported to be his, and Beale's Own Slides of the Set exist. As a result, *Ten Nights* is included in the list of Beale Sets as well as here. It remained very popular.

1877–1879+: Briggs Hires Faber to Freelance in 1877

Herman Faber

In 1877, Briggs hired Herman (Hermann, Harmon, Harman) Faber to work for him on a free-lance basis. Faber was born in Germany in 1832, attended the University of Giessen there, and migrated to America in 1854. He studied at the Pennsylvania Academy of Fine Arts (as did Beale), and

Fig. 37. Herman Faber's drawings for the magic lantern (1870s) demonstrated a refined technique, especially in the handling of faces and landscapes, but their sketchy quality made them ill-suited for projection.
[Courtesy of the Philadelphia History Museum at the Atwater Kent.]

was a student of Thomas Eakins. He specialized in medical illustration, and during the Civil War worked for the Surgeon General's Office documenting injuries, treatments, and results. Many of his illustrations were published in a medical history of the war. Faber is best known for his pencil drawings of President Lincoln on his deathbed. Though he was not actually present at Lincoln's death, Faber did sketch the room immediately after the President was removed, and since his drawing was checked for accuracy by one of the attending physicians, it has become an important historical document. Thirty-nine of Faber's medical drawings, including the Lincoln sketch, are at the National Museum of Health and Medicine. Faber died in 1913.[115]

Faber's training gave his art a classical feel, and his experiences during the Civil War must have provided unparalleled opportunities to study anatomy. The one Briggs original design that Sipley directly attributed to Faber demonstrates his artistic skill (Fig. 37). A study of some of his medical images and some engravings in the Beale Collection shows a clear command of anatomy and perspective, and a delicate drawing line.

It is not clear how long Briggs employed Faber. He appears to have been the lone Briggs' artist from 1877 to 1880, so assume that he produced all Briggs material from that period, except for *How Jones Became a Mason*, which will be discussed shortly. Attribution is uncertain because most of

---

115 Michael Rhode, "Drawing on Tragedy", *Hogan's Alley 6* (Winter, 1999): 50–53, and authors' phone interview with Rhode, Archivist of the National Museum of Health and Medicine, September 25, 2005. Also Gil E. Farr, "Three Medical Illustrators: The Fabers of Philadelphia", *Fugitive Leaves from the Historical Collections, Library of the College of Physicians of Philadelphia 3* (Spring, 1987): 1–5.

Fig. 38. This bizarre image is from the early version of *How Jones Became a Mason*, later re-drawn by Beale. New initiates to Masonic lodges were sometimes blindfolded, and put astride a stuffed goat attached to poles, which could then be jerked back and forth to simulate the pounding that would have been delivered by the real beast. [Beale Collection.]

Faber's work seems to have been over-painting or matching-out existing engravings. Perhaps he was the artist who over-painted many images that Briggs notes simply were "re-drawn" without noting by whom. *Hiawatha*, one of the seven works produced by Briggs during this period, is certainly a copy. Four others from this period may be copies, or may be originals, at least in part:

How Persimmons Took Cah Ob Der Baby (C?) – Story written in 1874 by Elizabeth Champney for *St. Nicholas Magazine*. The drawings for two slides are copies of the story's illustrations by her husband, J. Wells Champney. Two other slides in the Set were drawn in a sketchy manner; later re-drawn by Beale.

Rock of Ages(C?) – Based on a single image by Johannes Oertel; Set later re-drawn and expanded by Beale.

Prodigal Son (C?) – Probably based on engravings. Set re-drawn by Beale in 1893 and added to in 1902–03.

Way of Salvation (C?) – No GEH designs. Remained in catalogs.

Faber seems to have done relatively little work for Briggs. Among the thousands of extant drawings and negative sleeves, there is not one that Briggs identified as by "Faber", though he identified many as by "Tholey" or "Beale". To judge by the image at The Philadelphia History Museum, Faber's work is much less detailed than Beale's, and much less dramatic. However, he is technically much more accomplished than Nisle, and his medical and landscape work shows great skill. What he seems to have lacked was the flair for creating art designed specifically for projection. Though *Way of Salvation* and some individual images may have remained in the lantern repertoire, it is striking that three fourths of what may have been his original productions were re-done by Beale. He made no significant contribution to magic-lantern art, yet he and his two sons had a major impact on the medical illustration of the time.[116]

116 Faber may have gone on to play another minor role in cinema history. Sometime during the period that Eadweard Muybridge was sponsored by the University of Pennsylvania in Philadelphia to create animal locomotion studies (1883–85), he probably hired Faber to over-paint some of his photographic slides in order to make them better suited for projection. Certainly Faber was well versed in the over-painting technique, the Muybridge slides show its use, and there is evidence that Muybridge visited Faber's studio. Stephen Herbert, ed., *Eadweard Muybridge: The Kingston Museum Bequest* (Hastings, England: The Projection Box, 2004), 136.

Unknown Briggs Artist

How Jones Became a Mason – Redrawn by Beale (1891); greatly expanded by him in 1905. It was a popular parody.

The parody, *How Jones Became a Mason* is from 1878 when Faber was working, but before Beale and Tholey were hired (Fig. 38). While it appears to be original, the images are so crudely drawn that it is difficult to believe they are Faber's, even if they are cartoons. Perhaps they were actually produced earlier, or perhaps Nisle was still working, or perhaps they are by someone else, who might be called a naïve artist.

1880–1891 – Briggs Hires Tholey (1880–81) and Beale (1881?) to Freelance

Augustus Tholey

Fig. 39. Augustus Tholey's lantern slides had a sense of action, but lacked control of tonal values, making them difficult to "read" on screen, as in the lower left area of this image.
[Courtesy of the Philadelphia History Museum at the Atwater Kent.]

In 1880–81?, at about the same time that Briggs hired Beale on a free-lance basis, he also hired Augustus (August) Tholey, an artist born about 1844 who emigrated as a child from Germany to Philadelphia. Tholey was trained by his father in engraving and lithography, and executed a number of historical lithographs that are now in the Library of Congress. Later in his career, Tholey turned to pastel portraits. He died sometime before 1898. After the turn of the century, Briggs also employed Tholey's son, Herman, who created several cartoon Sets.[117]

At some time, perhaps after Briggs gave the GEH designs to Sipley, Briggs marked a number of Sets as "Tholey", or "Redrawn by Tholey". Three of these Sets are ones already mentioned that were presumably made first by Nisle (*Drunkard's Progress, The Bottle, Country Boy*). Three other copies (*Faust, Christiana,* and *Pilgrim's Progress*) appear to be by Tholey. In addition, Tholey created at least a few original designs such as "The Battle of Crecey" that are attributed to him by Sipley. From these it is possible to get a better sense of his magic-lantern style than can be formed from those images that he simply re-worked. His designs are usually 14 inches to 15 inches square, and often but not always on white paper that is pasted to white board. He

117 George C. Groce and David H. Wallace, *Dictionary of Artists in America, 1564–1860* (New Haven: Yale University Press, 1957). Sipley, in "One Hundredth Year", ("In Celebration", note 22) says Briggs hired Herman Tholey in 1880 and that "Tholey's son" was "employed into the 20th Century". In 1880 Herman Tholey was only three years old; it was surely his father, Augustus, whom Briggs hired in 1880. Herman was hired later, after his father's death, which occurred sometime around 1898. Herman Tholey is the one who signed four of the slides in the Set of *The Farmer and the Calf*, published by Briggs in 1902–03.

frequently used an airbrush technique or a very light gouache to get the tonal gradations that Beale achieved by starting with gray paper and then moving up and down the tonal scale. Generally, Tholey's images are dark, without as much tonal variation as Beale's (Fig. 39). While he has a better sense of anatomy and perspective than Nisle, he is not as good as Beale at either, and his images are not as full of detail as Beale's. In particular, objects in the distance tend to be very crudely and hastily drawn, rather than rendered in the soft atmospheric detail that is characteristic of Beale.

Even if one assumes that Tholey created all the non-Beale work from Briggs in the period 1880–81 through 1895, six of the nine Sets are clearly direct copies (*The Bottle, Cole's Voyage of Life, Paradise Lost, Dante's Inferno, The Vagabonds, Soldier's Return*) and two are probably copies (*Road to Ruin, Diana or Christ*).[118] Only one Set from 1880–1895 may or may not be an original production by Tholey:

> *Visit of St. Nicholas (Version B)* – Based on Thomas Nast illustrations. Re-done by Beale in 1885 and expanded by Beale from four slides to six in 1901.

Briggs seems to have used Tholey primarily to do the over-painting and matching-out of existing images, either engravings or lantern stories of previous artists such as Nisle, or biographies (*Napoleon, Luther*). Tholey's successes in other fields of art were substantial, but his lantern work was not, though he made the most significant contribution of any Briggs artist other than Beale.

John McGreer

John M. McGreer was born about 1839, and grew up in Mercer County in western Illinois. In the 1880s (possibly 1870s–1880s) he set himself up in business in Chicago as the Cartoon Publishing Company.[119] He specialized in trade cards – lithographic images, sometimes in single cards, but often produced as a series of two to eight pictures. The cards presented a comic story, and advertised some product either within the story itself, or on the backs of the cards. They were usually numbered, and had a caption that was either explanatory or part of the joke.[120] McGreer's trade-card humor was broad, physical, and often ethnic. Huge heads and melodramatic gestures characterized his drawings – common features of the genre (Fig. 40).

From creating a sequence of trade-card images it was an easy jump to creating a sequence of lantern slides. Three Sets of McGreer comic stories, each with four slides, appear in the Milligan 1892 catalog and again in the Briggs illustrated 1893 catalog that was sent to distributors, which is why we consider him a "Briggs Artist", though he did seem to work as a freelancer.[121] The McGreer Sets are in the same artistic style as the trade

---

118 We have already listed two of these Sets (*Road to Ruin, Diana or Christ*) under "McAllister Art", but they may have been produced either by McAllister, or drawn by Tholey for Briggs, and then distributed by McAllister. There is no clear evidence for the later, except that they were widely available in many catalogs, not just McAllister, including the Briggs catalog itself. We count them as Briggs in this part of our analysis to give Tholey the benefit of the doubt. Even if they are by Tholey, these three Sets are probably all copies, and if so that would account for the fact that Beale did not change them later. Tholey may also have created a Set of *The Wreck of the Hesperus* (1894), but if so it was never issued, so far as we know, and was immediately re-done by Beale, with the exception of slide # 7. Because we believe the Set was never issued, we have not counted it here as a Tholey production.

119 *Lake View [Illinois] Directory*, 1885–89, 178.

120 Samples of McGreer's trade cards are available on line at The Trade Card Place, http://www.tradecards.com/scrapbook/f97.html.

cards, and include the same kind of numbered captions. They were probably direct copies of the cards.

> *Photographing the Baby* – Signed by McGreer. Makes fun of a common middle-class mishap.
>
> *Family Prayer* – Lampoons a Black family.
>
> *Fishing* – Done in a more restrained style and possibly not by McGreer. Follows a fisherman into the water after his fish.

Milligan and Briggs also offered a number of individual comic slides and comic dissolves from McGreer.

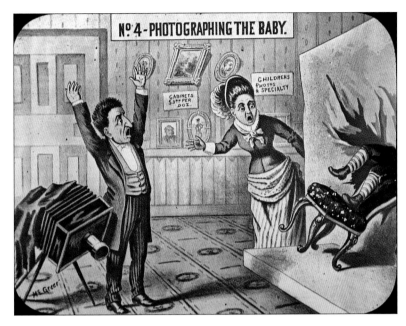

Fig. 40. John McGreer's comics were crudely drawn, but made their point. The on-screen labels were probably a holdover from McGreer's earlier work creating trade cards. McGreer's signature is visible under the camera. [Beale Collection.]

In spite of being promoted by Briggs, McGreer's Sets do not appear in catalogs other than Milligan during the study period. Perhaps there was little response. Or, perhaps there was a positive response, and Briggs saw that there was a market for more modern cartoons than the hoary "crayon transparencies" and decided to market comics that he himself owned, rather than pay McGreer a royalty. In any case, just a year after promoting the McGreer Sets in 1893, Briggs had Beale re-conceive and re-draw about 40 of what were probably the most popular comic crayon transparencies. Briggs promoted them for the rest of the lantern era, and seems to have dropped McGreer, though he apparently held the rights to the three sets mentioned, as they appear again in the Milligan 1913 catalog and in the expanded *Briggs 1917–20* catalog.

No other McGreer work appears in any of the pre-movie catalogs studied, but in 1906–08, three Chicago-based lantern companies all introduce an "entirely new list of comic slides", both singles and dissolve Sets, illustrated in all three catalogs by two sample McGreer images. The three catalogs do not contain the McGreer stories that Milligan and Briggs had carried in 1892–93.[122]

In terms of story entertainment during the study period then, McGreer seems to have been a short-lived phenomenon, limited to Milligan for at most three years. For whatever reason, Briggs stopped promoting him, and introduced his own line of Beale comics. That double punch kept McGreer from reaching a wider market until late in the lantern era.

121 Milligan, *Illustrated Catalogue* (note 100); Briggs, *(1893) Untitled Picture Catalog*, (Philadelphia, 1893). The latter, the only Briggs catalog to show pictures of the slides, is at GEH.

122 Chicago Projecting Co., *Entertainers Supplies*, 1906?) 151–155. Sears Roebuck & Co. *Catalogue of Motion Picture Machines, Magic Lanterns, and Stereopticons. Slides, Films and Supplies* (Chicago, 1907?) 97–101. Amusement Supply Co. *Catalog of Lantern Slides for Motion Picture Theatres and Traveling Exhibitors* (Chicago, 1907–08?) 79–86. All three companies promoted McGreer with identical copy and pictures. All three also used Beale images to promote other sets, especially those in current events like the Spanish American War. (These companies are the only ones to promote Sets by showing sample slides.)

71

Fig. 41. A slide from Last Voyage, The Ocean Steamer by Xanthus Smith. Smith specialized in marine art, and became a well-known American painter. His "XS" initials are barely visible on the barrel lying on the dock.
[Beale Collection]

Xanthus Smith

Xanthus Smith was born in Philadelphia in 1839, the son of a well-known stage scenery and panorama painter who also produced an impressive body of fine art. Xanthus studied medicine at the University of Virginia for two years (1856–58), painting on the side. Probably encouraged by his father, he began exhibiting his paintings at The Pennsylvania Academy of the Fine Arts, where, like Beale, he also studied. (Beale was an acquaintance; possibly a friend.[123])

Smith continued his art studies at the Royal Academy in London, and during a stint in the navy paid particular attention to ships and the sea. He became one of America's most respected marine painters. He died in 1929, just three years after Beale.[124]

Briggs hired Smith to paint one story Set, *Last Voyage, The Ocean Steamer* (Fig. 41). It is handsomely done, and remained in the catalogs for many years. Though Smith did not do other story Sets, and so contributed little to screen entertainment, Briggs seems to have admired his work, and brought him back later to create a non-story Set called *Natural Phenomena*, also very striking, and a few other individual slides.

The drawings for neither of the Sets are extant. It is possible that Smith, who probably considered himself a "fine artist" rather than an "illustrator", demanded that he be able to keep his original art. Briggs would probably not have been enthusiastic about such a position, and that may account for Smith's very limited lantern-image production, despite his evident talent.

Lantern Showmen Who Created Their Own Slides

A few non-Briggs early artists were also showmen, and created images for their own shows or hired artists to create a special Set of slides for their performances, rather than for sale through the catalogs. Most of these, such as Edward Wilson of Benerman and Wilson, were photographers who gave their own lectures. Henry Heyl of Philadelphia exhibited an 1870 "phasmatrope", a magic-lantern equipped with photographic slides on a wheel to simulate movement, and gave at least one public show. In the

123 A photograph from Beale's effects, now in the BC, is marked on the verso, "Taken with my camera by Mr. Xanthus Smith".

124 Vose Galleries, *The First Exhibition in Fifty Years of Oil Paintings by Russell Smith and his son Xanthus Smith* (Boston: Vose Galleries, 1979).

1880's Eadweard Muybridge created genuinely sequential photographs for his "Moving Animals" show, and helped reinforce the concept that continuous motion on screen was possible with his "magic lantern gone mad". Other lecturers may well have used illustrated images for their shows. In all of these cases, however, the presentations were lectures, and not stories or songs.[125]

One artist stands out from these and many other lecturers. He not only created his own images, but also his own stories and his own unique form of presentation:

Alexander Black

Alexander Black was a journalist, literati, and photographer who in 1894 created what he called "picture plays" (Fig. 42). Using a script written by himself (of no great literary merit, as he freely admitted), Black created slides to fit the script by photographing live actors. What distinguished Black's work from the Life Model slides common in England was that he used many slides to tell a single story that made up an entire evening's entertainment, and that the slides changed every 20–30 seconds, creating a kind of stop-motion effect. (The idea of a relatively rapid sequence of images was not new in the magic-lantern world – for instance in 1892 the Frenchman Émile Reynaud gave 15-minute shows of illustrated images that changed every two or three seconds. In America Muybridge and others had previously shown short rapid-action sequences, and Beale's 1885 *Leap for Life* has a three-slide action sequence in which three images change rapidly. But Black extended the concept much further than had any American. He was also aware of some of the properties of a good cinematic presentation, for instance taking great care to pose his actors against a carefully registered and unchanging background in order to enhance the sense of their movement, and lighting them to good effect. His first production, *Miss Jerry*, premiered in October of 1894. After its success, Black presented a number of other shows in the succeeding years. He toured with his productions, primarily to lyceums, through the rest of the 1890s.

Black's picture plays make an interesting contrast with the creations of the artists examined so far. Rather than working in relative anonymity in a shop,

Fig. 42. Alexander Black's "picture play" of *Miss Jerry* used a series of life-model photographs, projected at 20–30 second intervals, to suggest motion on screen.
[From the novel of Miss Jerry.]

125 Some showmen used drawn illustrations rather than photographs. For example, Ezra Ripple used drawings by James E. Taylor about 1900 (after our study period) to create a lecture on the horrors of the Southern prison at Andersonville during the Civil War. Taylor was a colleague of Beale's when Beale worked as a young illustrator at *Frank Leslie's Weekly*. Ezra Hoyt Ripple, *Dancing Along the Deadline: The Andersonville Memoir of a Prisoner of the Confederacy*, ed. Mark A. Snell (Novato, CA: Presidio Press, 1996). For descriptions of other lecturers, see *The Magic Lantern Encyclopaedia*, and note 14.

he was a solo artist and showman, and presented himself as such. He was in many ways one of the most original of the artists examined so far, creating a new form of magic-lantern presentation, at least new in America. He was successful in his efforts, reached significant numbers of people with his performances, and became well known for them.

But Black came to his art late. *Miss Jerry* was Black's only continuing production before the movies arrived in America in April of 1896. His pre-film work was thus highly limited, and came 33 years after Nisle began work, 16 years after Faber began, and 13 years after Tholey and Beale. In the one year that Black worked before the movies, he could not match the reach of the substantial mass market that magic-lantern screen entertainment had already become.[126]

Summary

There were then, a number of other American artists besides Beale who were creating lantern-slide drawings before the movies. Several of them – Faber, Smith, Black – had a flair for dramatic story telling, and several – Blue, Beard, McGreer – had a talent for comic images. For a variety of individual reasons, none of them produced a sustained body of pre-movie Sets. Even if their output of original work is combined, it does not begin to equal that of Beale, despite the fact that he was only working for Briggs on a free-lance basis until 1892, and so had only three years of full-time lantern work before 1896. Even if the attribution to the others is not as solid as one would like it to be, there is no way to reshuffle the deck that brings any one of them anywhere close to Beale's production quantity. Additionally, Beale's story and song illustrations were not ephemeral, as were most the works of his contemporaries. The entire Beale repertoire was promoted in the catalogs of almost every major distributor until the end of the lantern entertainment era.

126 *Miss Jerry* premiered on October 9, 1894. It is unclear how often Black performed it from its premier to October of 1895, when he began a "Date Book" that lists 52 presentations from that date to April of 1896, the date we have used as the "start" of movies in America. To estimate the total size of his audience up to April of 1896, suppose we project his 1895 rate of nine shows a month over a period beginning in January 1895 (leaving the months of October and November of 1894 to get tours organized). If we carry that rate right through the summer (which seems optimistic) until April of 1896, that would be 144 performances in total. If we assume 400 people at each performance (generous, since Black was playing the Lyceum circuit, not major theaters), that would mean a pre-April 1896 audience for *Miss Jerry* of 58,000 – substantial, but nowhere near the size of the audience Beale was reaching every year through the distribution network organized by Briggs.

Black's second production, *A Capital Courtship* premiered at the Brooklyn Institute on April 15, 1896, just a week before the first public movie in America and had only five performances before the movies arrived. Alexander Black, "Date Book, Oct. 1895–Dec. 1899" Alexander Black Papers, Rare Books and Manuscripts Division, New York Public Library. See also, Burnes Hollyman, "Alexander Black's Picture Plays: 1893–1894", *Cinema Journal* 16 (Spring, 1977): 26–33. (Hollyman's title seems to suggest that Black was performing in 1893, but what Hollyman is actually describing in 1893 is the gestation period.) See also Terry Ramsey, *A Million and One Nights: A History of the Motion Pictures Through 1925* (New York: Simon and Schuster, Inc., 1926): 91–103; Alexander Black, "Photography in Fiction: 'Miss Jerry,' The First Picture Play" *Scribner's Magazine* 18 (1895): 348–360; Alexander Black, *Miss Jerry: With Thirty-Seven Illustrations From Life Photographs by the Author* (New York: Charles Scribner's Sons, 1895).

Chapter 5

Assessing the Screen Art of Joseph Boggs Beale

While Joseph Boggs Beale was clearly the most prolific of the magic-lantern illustrators, he also demonstrated the highest level of original cinematic presentation. Specifically, in the period 1881 to the end of 1895, inclusive, Beale created or contributed to 35 Sets of original stories and songs, many of outstanding quality. Sample images from these Sets are presented in Fig. 43. In addition, and not presented in Fig. 43, he created two copied Sets (*Nellie's Prayer* and *Rip Van Winkle*), and two biographies (*The Life of Grant* and *The Life of Mary Queen of Scots*), plus five single-slide stories and songs, also not presented here because they do not meet the study's criterion of multiple images.[127] Beyond that, he created or contributed to 186 additional non-entertainment slides, including a 33-slide series of individual images for the nation's Sunday School programming; 21 slides for Secret Society rituals; 69 Comic Singles, Dissolves, and Artistic Gems; 36 American History slides, and 27 miscellaneous images.

Fig. 43 displays images from the Beale Sets of stories and songs, 1881–1895 (pre-1896). The captions give Set titles, Set numbers, dates, genres, and brief comments about the Sets' history or the cinematic techniques Beale employed to create them. Some titles and captions are elided for space reasons. The Sets are presented chronologically. Other images from these Sets may be found in the other Figures, and in the *Catalogue Raissoné*.

The Cinematic Quality of Beale's Screen Art

Beale's reputation – in the Victorian period and today – does not rest only on the quantity of his production or his commercial success. It is primarily a function of the cinematic quality of his images. Though Beale's earliest style in 1881–82 (e.g. *Two Paths of Virtue and Vice*) is very similar to that of his colleagues, and shows strong traces of his own earlier approach to magazine illustration, he rapidly developed a new presentation format that was dramatically different from his earlier commercial illustration, and that was specifically created for screen projection. He became a master of "the defining moment" and used bold dominant images to drive the story forward. The backgrounds of his pictures were packed with detail to sustain attention while the slide was on screen, so that the viewer could mentally

127 *Life of Grant* was largely original; *Life of Mary Queen of Scots* was largely copied from engravings. The single-slide story (narrative poem) is *Barbara Freitchie*; the songs are *The Blue and the Gray*, and the three single slides listed under *Comic Songs*.

Fig. 43. Beale Story and Song Sets Before 1896, [Beale Collection.]

Uncle Tom's Cabin, #8, 1882 – Novel. Beale often made use of the circular form of slides to <u>frame</u> his designs in order to focus attention.

Two Paths of Virtue and Vice, #200, 1882 – Temperance. Story uses split screen images for contrast. Pole and hat here line up to split the screen.

The Drunkard's Daughter, #194, 1882 – Temperance Story. Beale often used <u>associational forms</u> – contrasting images in one slide.

William Jackson's Treat, #202, 1885 – Temperance Story. Clothing becomes a <u>metaphor</u> for life – wealthy drinker, bum, suicide's hat in river.

Tramp, Tramp, Tramp, #61, 1885 – Song. Rescuers appear at the prison door when their image is rapidly <u>dissolved</u> from this one.

Leap for Life, #31, 1885~ – Poem. A striking arrow-like design points to the <u>off-screen space</u> atop the mast where a boy is paralyzed by fright.

The Visit of St. Nicholas, #43, 1885~ – Poem. The strong <u>side light</u> adds a warm glow, and clearly illuminates Santa and his toys.

The Drunkard's Reform, #195, 1887 – Temperance. The back-and-forth <u>screen direction</u> of the child in the bar drives the story line.

Father, Dear Father, #196, 1887 – Temperance. <u>Ideological</u> song often accompanied the ever-popular *Ten Nights in a Bar Room*. Cf. Fig. 22.

Rock of Ages, #101, 1887, 1891, 1906 – Beale adds <u>story value</u> to this mysterious hymn by depicting the symbolic rescue of two women.

Home, Sweet Home, #49, 1887, 1904 – Song. The Set grew over time. This slide of the boy returning home was revised to reinforce <u>continuity</u>.

A Christmas Hymn, #86, 1887~ – The "haughty senator" is lost in wealth, unaware of God's grandeur <u>symbolized</u> by the heavenly comet.

Pygmalion and Galatea, #15, 1890 – Play. <u>Realistic detail</u> helped sustain attention during the lengthy times that slides were projected.

Marching Thro' Georgia, #51, 1891 – Song. This "<u>long shot</u>" allows Beale to suggest the mass confusion of war amid the swamps.

How Jones Became a Mason, #78, 1891, 1905 – Story. <u>Campy</u> parody. Compare Fig. 38, another artist's conception of the scene.

Drake's Ode to the American Flag, 1881–93 – Poem. Beale's flag <u>iconography</u> often had to be revised as America added states, and stars.

Ten Nights in a Bar Room, #199, 1881–93 – Temperance. Melodrama made this <u>faithful book adaptation</u> one of Beale's most popular Sets.

Steamboat Race, #247, 1881–93 – Story. <u>High-contrast lighting</u> in this "wooding up" scene added to the drama of a race down the river.

America, #45, 1893 i – Song. Flag-waving was typical of Beale. The howling dog (right) adds <u>intrinsic interest</u> to the scene.

Swanee Ribber, #59, 1893 – Song. Though Beale did some comic caricatures of Blacks, many of his portrayals were sympathetic.

From Greenland's Icy Mountains, #87, 1893, Hymn – <u>Available light</u>, especially a sunset, was a favorite Beale technique to maximize color.

The Prodigal Son, #150, 1893~ – Parable. Images based on engravings. Beale's changes clarify the visual story-telling and emphasize emotion.

Knights of Pythias, #216, 1891–94, 1896–1902 – Secret Society. Story of *Damon and Pythias* was probably one of Beale's most widely seen.

The Courtin', #23, 1894 – Poem. This "<u>point of view shot</u>" is what the lover first sees through the window. (Cf. the lover, Set 23 *Cat. R.* pix and Fig. 30.)

Curfew Shall Not Ring To-Night, #24, 1894 – Poem. <u>Size diminution</u> of the distant scene reinforces the danger of the bell over Bessie.

Maud Muller, #33, 1894 – Poem. The <u>soft lighting</u> of this scene contributes to its gloom; contrasts with brighter lighting earlier.

The Raven, #37, 1894 – Poem. The pictures on the wall of this final scene, drawn in early scenes with sharp detail, are now lost in the <u>soft focus</u> of mental anguish.

The Wreck of the Hesperus, #44, 1894 – Poem. This tranquil <u>establishing shot</u> sets up the later tragedy of the little girl lost at sea.

Robinson Crusoe, #7, 1894 – Novel. Summarized in 12 slides. Specific details – the dog's mournful look – capture the novel's emotion.

Abide With Me, #84, 1894 – Hymn. This <u>deep space</u> scene emphasizes the loneliness of the old man as he stumbles toward his death.

Ben Hur, #64, 1894–95 – Novel. Beale cross-cuts between Ben Hur in the galleys, and the story of his mother and sister in prison.

Raid on the Moonshiners, #198, 1895 – Story. When this Set was presented as a slow <u>dissolve</u>, the revenuers seemed to creep forward.

Where is My Wandering Boy To-Night?, #201, 1895 – Temperance song. <u>Narrative form</u> follows Boy from baby, to bar, and home again.

Nearer My God To Thee, #97, 1895 – Hymn. When an angel like this was projected using a <u>fade-in</u>, she seemed to float into the sky.

The Sower, #151, 1895 – Parable. A low <u>angle of framing</u> allows us to see the seed by the wayside, as well as the sowing in the field.

"zoom in" to create "close ups" in his own imagination as the literary work was read. He organized that detail with bold designs that led the viewer's eye immediately to the most important element, and then through three dimensions of space to explore the rest of the image. His rendering was almost Pre-Raphaelite in its precision, yet he drew with a brush to avoid the hard outlines of pen and pencil that had made some of his predecessors' work look like cartoons. He used the full spectrum of the tonal range, off-set with small highlights – two qualities that Alfred Stieglitz, the famous photographer and avid promoter of lantern-slide art, considered the hall-marks of the best photographic slides of the time.[128] Not coincidentally, this broad tonal range was ideal as the base for the delicate coloring that was one of the hallmarks of the Briggs company's work.

Beale also developed a truly cinematic style that made full use of the projected medium. He employed about 75 percent of what are commonly thought of today as the techniques that make up the "art of the cinema". That is, if one examines the glossaries of today's leading introductions to film art, most of the roughly 300 terms found there can be effectively applied not only to film art, but to magic-lantern art as well, especially that of Beale.[129] (A sampling of these terms has been underlined in the Figure captions, and in the text throughout this book.)

While Beale may not have necessarily used the modern technical terms, if the concepts were described to him, we believe he would recognize them and be able to say where he had used them and why. These cinematic techniques not only include the mechanical lantern effects such as dissolves, fades, and superimpositions (Fig. 44). They also included artistic ways of creating a sense of depth with deep focus and aerial perspective; dramatic ways of lighting such as backlighting and key lights; ways to vary the audiences' point of view such as tracking shots and low angle views and medium close-ups; and ways to ensure continuity such as storyboarding, establishing scenes, and eye-line matches.

How can one know that Beale was using such techniques consciously, and that their appearance in his work is not mere happenstance? While obviously his thoughts cannot be "known", many elements make a strong circumstantial case for his intentional use: There is a record of the art courses he took and the art books he read, so it is possible to know exactly what techniques he was taught, particularly in the management of perspective and light. It is clear that his style shifted dramatically once he left his career with the illustrated newspapers to create lantern slides. He had to learn how to develop a format that would project well on screen – for instance, controlling the dominant contrast through tonal variation and design. Examples of his sketches, working drawings and storyboards allow one to "see" his mind at work, especially in managing mise-en-scene and blocking. Correspondence back and forth between Beale and Briggs discusses technical prob-

128 Alfred Stieglitz, "Some Remarks on Lantern Slides", *Optical Magic Lantern Journal*, 8 (1897): 204–06. See also Martin Wilson, "Lantern Slides", *The American Amateur Photographer* (1900): 440.

129 Louis Giannetti, *Understanding Movies, Eleventh Edition* (Upper Saddle River, NJ: Pearson Prentice Hall, 2008). David Bordwell and Kristin Thompson, *Film Art: An Introduction, 7th Edition* (New York: The McGraw-Hill Companies, Inc., 2004). The 300 terms mentioned are a combination from the two glossaries, concentrating on the artistic area of film production.

lems such as maintaining <u>continuity</u> and how to solve them.[130] And with thousands of Beale's images to study, one can observe him using the same techniques again and again to achieve certain effects – for instance, using symbolic <u>iconography</u> and areas of <u>intrinsic interest</u> to hold audience attention, and <u>parallel editing</u> to handle a double story (Fig. 45).

Such techniques did not necessarily move from the world of the magic lantern to the world of film – there is no evidence at this point that Ameri-

Fig. 44. This scene from Beale's *Tramp, Tramp, Tramp*, an 1885 Civil War song, depends on the lantern effect of the <u>dissolve</u>. The slides are in two different lanterns, with the images perfectly aligned. When the light is turned down in the first and up in the second, the victorious troops dramatically appear.
[Beale Collection.]

can movie-makers copied them or learned from them. Nonetheless, their use by Beale and others was certainly a significant reason for the success of magic-lantern shows. Of course, there were also techniques unique to the magic-lantern medium itself (phantasmagoric images in a field of black, matching-out, etc.), and Beale used over a hundred of these. But for our purposes here, Beale's use of the techniques shared by the lantern and film serves as an effective reminder of the continuity between them.

130 See note 42.

We will not attempt at this time to cover the details and caveats concerning the use of film terms to explore magic-lantern art, or to discuss how Beale adapted these techniques to the demands of different genres, or varied them over the course of his long career. These issues will be dealt with at length in the forthcoming book, *Cinema Before Film*.[131] But the pictures of Beale's work in the present volume, with some of the techniques underlined in the captions, provide a brief glimpse of the cinematic sophistication of his pre-1896

Fig. 45. In these slides from the Beale 1882 version of Harriet Beecher Stowe's *Uncle Tom's Cabin*, which are closely based on the book illustrations of Hammet Billings, a limited form of <u>parallel editing</u> is used to inter-cut the stories of two different contrasting slaves – the more accommodating Uncle Tom, and the rebellious George Harris.
[Beale Collection.]

style. It was a technical repertoire that he continued to use – consistently, consciously, and with clear indications that he knew exactly what he was doing – for the rest of his career, and one that became even more fluid after the advent of the movies.

An examination of the images reproduced here makes it clear that Beale had a real gift for storytelling on screen. The high artistic quality of his oeuvre ensured that his slides remained in the Briggs repertoire, that they were pro-

131 *Cinema Before Film: See note 4.*

moted nationally, and that they met with wide public approval. In a career that lasted until 1917–20, Beale went on to create or contribute to a total of about 122 stories, songs, plays, operas, parables, hymns and comic sketches, plus an additional 134 Sets and Groups on other subjects, for a total of 256 consisting of 2,073 separate lantern images.[132] His work was reproduced in millions of slide copies, and was seen in thousands of different venues.

Despite his pervasive impact on Victorian culture, Beale's art is not well known today. His work did not directly influence the filmmakers who came after him, at least in so far as can be determined from the existing record. They tended to re-discover on their own the cinematic techniques that Beale had been using, or they imported them from the fields of art and drama. Yet Beale certainly paved the way for screen entertainment in America. By the time the movies came along, his work had already taught millions of people that sitting together in the dark, watching pictures tell stories on the big screen, could be exciting, moving, scary, funny, and inspiring.[133]

Beale died in obscurity in 1926. But his star did rise again. New formats of filmstrips and 35mm gave his slides a new life into the 1960s and '70s, and mass audiences like the Masons continue to watch his lantern images to the present day – representing more than 130 years of continuous screen presence. When the master drawings that created those slides were re-discovered in the 1930s and promoted by Arthur Colen, the pictures created a national sensation, producing major articles in *Time* magazine and a later one in *Life* magazine.[134] The wash drawings were exhibited at the Whitney Museum of American Art in New York, the American Museum of Photography and the Atwater Kent Museum in Philadelphia, and elsewhere around the country.[135] During the 1940s and 1950s, reproductions of his work appeared in hundreds of newspapers, textbooks, and encyclopedias as well as in a U. S. postage stamp, and dinnerware sets.[136] In the 1970s, at the time of the Bicentennial, there was another resurgence of interest in Beale, with a touring exhibit of his Americana wash drawings that visited museums and other institutions in 13 cities, backed by a handsomely illustrated catalog, *Star Spangled History: Drawings by Joseph Boggs Beale*.[137] Today, Beale's work is held by about two dozen museums; slides of his stories and songs are highly prized by magic-lantern collectors around the world; and modern lantern shows featuring his work have captivated the imagination of more than a quarter-million people.[138]

132 The total of 122 Sets mentioned consists of 83 in the Literary categories, plus 20 Hymns, seven Temperance stories and songs and 12 Parables.

133 See Miriam Hansen, *Babel and Babylon: Spectatorship in American Silent Film* (Cambridge: Harvard University Press, 1991) 25, 29, 42. Hansen discusses the ways in which audience experience of lantern shows prefigured film spectatorship, but she concentrates primarily on lantern lectures, rather than on story-and-song entertainment.

134 *Time*, "Professor", note 40 and *Life*, "Speaking of Pictures", note 105.

135 Whitney Museum Exhibit: Note 46. American Museum of Photography Exhibit: Louis Sipley (?), "The First Museum of Photography", *Pennsylvania Arts and Sciences 5* (1941): 37–66. Atwater Kent Exhibit: "Professor", note 40. (The Atwater Kent Museum is now the Philadelphia History Museum.)

136 Examples are in the BC.

137 Frances Osborn Robb, David M. Robb, Jr., Dale Roylance, *Star Spangled History, Drawings by Joseph Boggs Beale, Magic Lantern Artist, 1841–1926*. (Galveston, American National Insurance Company, 1975).

Even in the first 14 years of Beale's magic-lantern career – before film, from 1881 through and including 1895 – Beale created a body of original work that was larger than the original production of all of his colleagues combined, and was much more sophisticated in cinematic style. Beale used his talents to fulfill Briggs's vision of establishing an American screen repertoire of literature and songs, as well as religious and temperance tales, hymns, and history. Beale's genius for visual storytelling helped Briggs become the nation's exclusive wholesaler of American-made magic-lantern entertainment during this period. Consequently, Briggs was able to mass-market Beale's slides through more than 100 lantern-slide distributors, including all of the largest. (See *Appendix 4*.) For practical purposes, this marketing monopoly made Beale's cinematic images the only American story and song entertainment that was available nationally on screen to the generation before the movies, and gave him an audience of millions of people a year.

Beale's dominance of the magic-lantern field, as represented in the catalogs, only increased during the 24 years he worked after the movies were introduced. By the end of his career, he had produced 62 percent of the secular stories and songs that were available in the catalogs, 80 percent of the religious stories and hymns, and 40 percent of all the images in the specialty Secret Society catalogs.[139] His work was pervasive in American culture – projected in theaters, meeting halls, churches, Chautauqua tents, fraternal lodges, schools, living rooms, and playrooms in almost every city and town in the country. Taking into account his entire lantern slide production, Beale created about 34 hours of screen programming, the screen-time equivalent of 17 full-length modern movies.[140]

138 The American Magic-Lantern Theater. See www.MagicLanternShows.com.

139 The percentage of secular and religious stories and songs presented in the lantern catalogs are both determined from *McIntosh 1913* catalog, which has the largest collection. The Secret Society catalog is *Briggs, 1917–20*. For this tally we broadened the definition of "story" to include biographies, and Bible stories, since by this time they were no longer patched together collections of slides, but had been created by Beale to have continuity.
Outside the traditional lantern catalogs, and to some degree within them, illustrated song slides became very popular. Also outside the catalogs, Alexander Black continued to give his photo plays to lyceum audiences through the 1890s.

140 Beale created 2,073 lantern images. Figuring one minute of screen time per slide (which is conservative, as the Victorians often had a slide on screen for two minutes) that would equal 34 hours of programming. Assuming that a movie today is two hours long (again conservative – many are shorter) that would be equivalent to 17 full-length movies.

Beale himself summarized his career by quoting his employer, Briggs, the leading producer of magic-lantern entertainment: "We never had any work done by any artist which [was] so well done and so suitable in style for projection…"[141] This review of Beale's work supports that assessment, and leaves little doubt that he has a legitimate claim to be recognized as America's first great screen artist.

Acknowledgements

We owe a debt of gratitude to many, many librarians, archivists, scholars and friends who have helped us with our work over the last two decades, but most especially to Charles Musser who generously agreed to write the Foreword; to Jack Judson, Curator of The Magic Lantern Castle Museum, whose library of catalogs and personal assistance was invaluable; and to the staff at the George Eastman House International Museum of Photography and Film, which over a twenty-year period was untiring in its efforts to give us access to the Sipley Collection.

Illustration Sources and Abbreviations:

Most illustrations are from the Beale Collection of the authors. Others are specified.

Abbreviations are explained in the Quick Key (p. 91), with a more detailed explanation available on p. 88.

Request for Assistance

This book is a beginning effort at media archeology in a largely unexplored field – the American magic-lantern culture of the 19th and early 20th century. No doubt we have missed important elements and made errors. We welcome corrections, suggestions, and comments.
Please contact Terry Borton: TBorton@MagicLanternShows.com.

Fig. 46 (facing page). Beale created magic-lantern paintings specifically for projection, and to dramatize famous literary works on screen for the generation before the movies. In this scene from *Ben Hur* by Lew Wallace, Beale's 1895 slide captures the moment when Ben Hur saves the tribune in his galley, which has been wrecked during a naval battle. The action of the present moment is clearly presented in the foreground – highlighted by the bright gold of the captain's helmet; framed above by the oars and ship's foam, and below by the curved edge of the slide. Behind the two struggling swimmers, a fantastically detailed galley symbolizes the power of Rome slicing through the water, about to the rescue them. And in the background, burning enemy ships cast an eerie key light, their destruction telling us the outcome of the battle, and Rome's triumph despite the loss of the tribune's ship. This use of multiple scenes in a single slide was part of Beale's story-telling technique – a way of compressing time – of presenting past, present, and future in one image. The technique helped him present an entire novel on screen with relatively few slides.
[Beale Collection]

141 Beale to Harper and Brothers, publishers, September 15, 1909, in the BC. In the letter, Beale quotes the praise of Briggs. Beale is seeking work after having been laid off by Briggs at the point when the movies finally and suddenly cut into the lantern entertainment business. Because Briggs worked regularly with Harper and Brothers and the reference could easily be checked, and because it specifically comments on his "suitability for projection" which would not have been apropos for any other employer, there is no reason to believe that Beale distorted or exaggerated Briggs's comment. Beale continued to work for the Briggs company on a part-time basis for another 8–11 years, until 1917–20.

Appendix 1

Notes to the Condensed Catalogue Raissoné of Beale's Magic-Lantern Slides

With *Chapter 2* as a background, readers can approach the *Catalogue Raisonné* of Beale's work at one of three different levels. Some may want to simply use the "Quick Key" as a reminder of the meaning of the various abbreviations in the *Catalogue*. Those who want a more in-depth understanding of exactly what each term implies will want to read this *Introduction*, especially the sections on Dating and Multiple Use, where the meanings of the abbreviations are not immediately self-evident from the "Quick Key." They may also want to get a sense of Beale's images in context by browsing the McIntosh Stereopticon catalog for 1895, which is now available on line by searching Google Books for "McIntosh Stereopticon." Those who want to understand the processes used to create the *Catalogue* should delve into the annotations for this section.

This *Introduction* follows the form of a typical entry, as presented in the "Pro Forma Sample" beside the "Quick Key," and the *Catalogue* Set entries themselves.

The Subject Categories

The Subject Category information (Literature, Religion, History, etc.) can be found in the *Catalogue Raisonné Table of Contents* immediately preceding the *Catalogue* itself. The Subject Category for each page appears as a heading in all caps, bold, and covers all "Sets" or "Groups" under it until the next designation. This heading indicates what the "Set" or "Group" is about. (The "Set/Group" distinction will be explained shortly.)

Information on Sets

The Name of the Set or Group appears as a title in bold face, preceded by an Identification Number. These titles are of Sets or Groups of slides in which there is at least one Beale image. Set names are from the catalogs.[1] Group names marked with an "★" are not from the catalogs, but have been created by us. Titles have sometimes been slightly altered: quotation marks may be added for consistency; clarifying words added (in parentheses) to the title, or a more

common title for the same work added below the catalog title, e.g. placing *A Christmas Carol* in parentheses below *Marley's Ghost*. A "+" after a title indicates that there are additional slides in the Group that are not suggested by its name. For instance, the Set, *American History – Revolution+*, includes miscellaneous slides covering the period after the Revolution and before the next Group, *The War of 1812*.

Sets and Groups are arranged alphabetically within their Subject areas, except when there is a more logical order, as in the case of the History or Bible Groups (chronological order) or Secret Society Groups (order of the rituals, as presented in the catalogs.) Unusual aspects of Sets or Groups are indicated after the title by numbered endnotes.

The Author information is the first item in the italicized listing under the Set Name. It indicates the last name of the original author of the script (or "reading" as it was often called) on which the slide "Set" was based – Dickens, Poe, etc. The full author's name may be found in the index. The actual magic-lantern reading may be a short summary of a long original work such as *Uncle Tom's Cabin*.[2]

The Number of Beale information is on the first line of italics under the Set name, following the Author, and is the first number in the slashed pair (e.g. 23/24). It indicates the number of slides in a Set or Group created by Beale.[3] This figure includes images Beale may have over-painted or copied from pre-existing engravings (e.g., by Darley) or "matched-out," so there are different degrees of originality obscured in this summary, but it is impossible to characterize this variety easily and consistently in a limited space. If the entire Set or a significant part of it consists of Beale over-paintings or copies, that fact is explained in the *Catalogue* notes for that set, provided the sources have been found.

The Number of Slides information appears as the second of the slashed pair of numbers (e.g. 23/24). It indicates the total number of images in a Set or Group. For Sets, the number of total slides given is usually the largest version of the Set, which may vary from one to 32, with the usual range being 4–12. Group numbers are more complicated to establish.[4] The Sets or Groups may also contain slides by artists other than Beale, but these are not listed. Thus the designation "23/24" should be read, "Beale created 23 of the 24 images in this Set." By comparing the "Number of Beale" with the total number, the reader can judge the proportion of the Set or Group done by Beale, which can vary widely, from one to all.[5]

The Set or Group information is indicated by an "S" or "G" in italics immediately after the slashed pair of numbers. It indicates how the material was presented in the catalog – either as a Set or a Group.

The Sets (S) were sold as a cohesive unit, had a title, generally had numbered slides (1–8, etc.), and generally had a description or line caption in the catalog for each listed slide. A Set with only one slide in it indicates that a single slide was used to present a complete story, poem, or song, e.g. *Barbara Freitchie*.

The Group (G) designation indicates slides that were usually listed together in the catalog, but were not necessarily a cohesive unit, nor necessarily divided into the Groups specified. The catalogs often provided long groups of slides under a topic such as "Old Testament." These lists usually break easily into the Groups presented here, and it was obviously expected that the lanternist pick out slides to make up smaller story Groups of 6-24 slides for such subjects as *Moses, David*, etc. We have created the smaller Groups used here, rather than leaving hundreds of slides in one collection such as *Old Testament*, to make it easier for the reader to see what specific subjects Beale was treating, to make clear the degree to which his work covers a subject, and to facilitate more precise dating. Since the size and configuration of Groups often changed over time, the *Briggs 1917–20 Catalog* was selected as the basis for Group listings unless otherwise indicated in the *Catalogue* notes.[6]

Children's Slides are denoted by a small italic "c" immediately after the "S" or "G" for Set or Group. This indicates that at least some of the images in the Set or Group appeared as Gem or "toy" slides.

Filmslides are indicated by a small italic "f" immediately after the "S" or "G" for Set or Group, or the "c" indicating children's slides. The "f" indicates that at least some of the images in the Set or Group appear in filmslides, also written "film slides" and later "filmstrips".

Those Sets Most Used in Beale's time are denoted with an italic "m" after the S or G, (or the after the "c" or "f" if they are included). This "m" designation is meant to give at least some sense of those Beale works that were Most Used 100 years ago. The judgment of which Sets or Groups were "most used" is primarily based on an estimate that some slides from a Set appear on eBay five or more times in a year.[7] A second source for estimating which Sets were "most used" is the frequency of "tack holes" in the wash drawings. Most Sets with an "m" are from the Religion and Secret Society areas, but there are also a number of story and song Sets.[8]

The Location information is in the italicized line under the slide Set name, following the Set or Group information, and the "c," "f," or "m" if they are included. The Location information indicates where the wash drawings are housed, if they are mostly in one place. It represents the end of the chain of provenance for wash drawings discussed in *Chapter 2*. (Often other materials such as slides, negatives, etc. are in these same places.) The locations for any drawings not in one place are indicated beside the slide names. If the drawings are in very different places, the location information is dropped from the Set or Group description, and given beside individual slides.

The location abbreviations are:

AMPAS = Academy of Motion Picture Arts and Sciences, Hollywood, California
AN = American National Insurance Company, Galveston, Texas
BAC = Biblical Arts Center, Dallas, Texas (As noted in the discussion of provenance, BAC burned to the ground in 2005, so a BAC notation is an indication of where Beale's Own Slides and wash drawings, once were, but also that they have been lost to fire. BAC was rebuilt and is now called The Museum of Biblical Art.)
BC = Beale Collection of the authors
BU = Baylor University, Waco, Texas
BRMA = Brandywine River Museum of Art, Chadds Ford, Pennsylvania
CAM = Center for American Music, Pittsburgh, Pennsylvania
DU = Duke University, Durham, North Carolina
GEH = George Eastman House International Museum of Photography and Film, Rochester, New York[9]
HFM = Henry Ford Museum, Dearborn, Michigan (Formerly the Edison Institute.)
HRC = Harry Ransom Center, Austin, Texas
HU = Harvard University, Cambridge, Massachusetts
K-MOMI = Kent Museum of the Moving Image, Deal, England
MLCM = Magic Lantern Castle Museum, San Antonio, Texas
MOMI = Museum of the Moving Image, Astoria, New York
NBMAA = New Britain Museum of American Art, New Britain, Connecticut
PHM = Philadelphia History Museum, Philadelphia, Pennsylvania (Formerly The Atwater Kent Museum.)
PR = Private Collection known to the authors
RBC = Richard Balzer Collection, private but available on the internet
RLM = Rosenberg Library and Museum, Galveston, Texas
SDSU = San Diego State University, San Diego, California

UN = Location Unknown to the authors
WAMA = Wadsworth Atheneum Museum of Art, Hartford,
    Connecticut
WMAA = Whitney Museum of American Art, New York,
    New York

Dating Beale's Slides

The Date of a Beale Set is the last item to appear under the Set name at the end of the italicized line of data. The date or date range indicates when most of the Beale slides in the Set or Group were created, as defined below. If the slides in the Set were not created at one time, exceptions are listed beside the slide names.

The dating of Beale's slides faces many of the same general issues outlined in *Chapter 2*, with the additional obstacle that, with two groups of exceptions, Beale did not "date" a single drawing.[10] Other than a few images that can be dated by copyright, or references in Briggs–Beale letters or the *Briggs 1890–92 Ledger*, magic-lantern catalogs have been the source of dating information.

When used for dating, catalogs present daunting obstacles of their own. The catalogs are rare bits of historical ephemera, though that is changing with the recent advent of catalogs on CD's and Google Books. No complete yearly set (or even partially complete set) of any one American magic-lantern company's catalogs yet exists, and most public institutions have only a few miscellaneous examples of catalogs from different companies. To track Beale's creative output over time we created a matrix of different catalogs covering the years 1859–1929. This database represented 121 catalogs from 37 different companies lodged in 25 different institutional and private collections.[11]

Thirty-one catalogs were then selected covering almost every year in the period bracketing Beale's work (1878–1920).[12] The first appearance of each Beale image was then tracked though these catalogs, and any changes were noted in the number of slides in a Set, titles, attribution, etc. The result gives a detailed and well-documented picture of what Beale created when, though a number of caveats apply.[13]

Because catalogs could not be found for some years, an exact date cannot be given for about 25 percent of the Sets, and so a range is used, usually of two years, though in a few cases the range is longer.[14] Thus, for instance, the date entry "1888–1889" should be interpreted as, "An 1887 catalog was reviewed and this Set does not appear in it. No catalog for 1888 is available. The extant 1889 catalog is the first one containing this Beale Set, so the Set was created sometime in 1888 or 1889." If a Set is given two dates or date ranges, that indicates two distinct periods of development.[15]

Groups are much more difficult to date than Sets because the slides were usually created over a period of years, and were often used in several different Groups. Individual slides that make up a Group are dated in a similar manner as Sets, following the same procedure just described.[16] When calculating the Group dates, only those Beale slides are counted where the slide's first catalog listing was in this Group. If there are slides that were first listed in some other Set or Group, they are not included in the dating to avoid double-counting, and to make it clear when Beale was creating slides for this particular Group. (See "First Used In," to be discussed shortly.)

For Groups with a narrow date range, that range is given, e.g. 1890–1894. For many Groups, the total range is so broad that it provides little useful information. In these cases we report the narrowest range in which at least 60 percent of the Beale slides in the Group were listed in the catalogs, again trying to indicate the timing of Beale's creative effort on the Group. The fact that the Group range has been calculated with the "60-percent" criterion is indicated by marking the date range with a "~." Occasionally, the "~" is added to Set dates to indicate that the same "60 percent" criterion was employed.[17]

In the case of a few Groups, the individual slides were created over a wide range of dates, but the Group itself was introduced all at one time, usually later than many of its constituent slides. In these cases, the 60-percent criterion is not applied, but a single date is given, followed by an "i" for "introduced" – e.g. 1914 i.

If a more precise date range cannot be given, the date range 1881–1920 is used, meaning that Beale created the listed slides at some unspecified time during his magic lantern career, which is bracketed by those dates.[18]

The Beale Method for Dating Catalogs

It is possible to use the tight dating of many Beale Sets as a kind of Rosetta Stone to determine the year of publication for those magic-lantern catalogs which have no date, or where the catalog dates are problematic, as they often are. See *Appendix 5* for details.

Individual Slide Descriptions

The information concerning individual slides is listed under the Set/Group data.

Numbers at the start of the line indicate the number of the slide as published in the catalogs, if there were numbers, and may not be consecutive if Beale did not do all slides in the Set. (Slides in Groups are usually unnumbered.)

Variant Images are indicated with a "v" or "v 1," or "v 2" before the slide name. A "v" shows that Beale created several alternatives for this slide that were not presented as choices in the catalogs. One image was simply substituted for another. Such variants are counted as Beale images, but not used in dating a Set. Variants were usually created to provide an "establishing shot," or to improve continuity.

The Slide Names are, in general, those given in the *Briggs 1917–20* catalog, or the *Briggs Secret Society* catalog of about the same date.[19] Additional names in parentheses () are alternative titles or parts of titles if capitalized; if not capitalized, they are our explanatory or clarifying comments such as "effect" or "dissolve."

Multiple Use of the same Beale image in different Sets or Groups is tracked by putting after the slide title an "E" for "Used **E**lsewhere" or a "F" for "**F**irst Used In" followed by the number of the related Set or Group.

The "E" for "Used Elsewhere" indicates that this Set is the earliest dated appearance of the image, and that it is also Used Elsewhere in another Set or Group. The number following the "E" provides the Set or Group identification number of this other listing. Thus "E 133" indicates that, "This Set is the first time this image was used, and it also appears in Set 133." Some images are used in several Sets, in which case all the different "E" numbers are given.

The "F" for "First Used In" is the reciprocal of the "E." It indicates that this appearance of the image is not the earliest dated use, and that it was First Used in another earlier context. As above, the number following the "F" provides the ID of that listing. Thus "F 176" indicates that, "This image was first

used in Set 176, and this Set is a later multiple use of it".[20]

The Location of the Wash Drawing for the image follows the "E's" and "F's" if the Set of drawings is not all in one place and hence the drawing location for a given slide has not already been indicated in the Set data.

The Date of the Image follows the location information. It indicates the date of the individual slide if that slide was not made in the year designated by the Set description.

Sources of Attribution

The Attribution information follows the date, and indicates seven possible sources of attribution for the image, in rough order of certainly:[21]

- "s" for "signature" indicates a Beale signature on some form of the image.
- "ca" for "catalog attribution" indicates that a lantern catalog specifically listed Beale as the creator of the image.
- "d" for "documentation" indicates that some outside source such as a letter or a ledger entry attributes the image to Beale.
- "wd" indicates the existence of a Beale "wash drawing" of the image.[22]
- "n" indicates the use of a "negative" to identify the image as by Beale.
  (Since almost all images have negatives, "n" is used only when the use of the negative was determinative.)
- "bos" indicates that one of "Beale's Own Slides" exist for the image. Beale himself owned these slides.
- "as" indicates that the authors made a judgment that the image was by Beale based on "artistic style." This criterion was used extremely sparingly.[23]

Other Slide Information

- A " ^ " indicates that this slide is illustrated by the picture for this Set. The pictures have the same numbers as the Sets, but may not be on the same pages.

Summary

The *Catalogue Raisonné* presents a wide range of information about each Beale Set, Group, and image, helping researchers to locate them, date them, assess their authenticity, and see how images were used in multiple contexts. It should provide the data necessary for a wide range of analyses of Beale's art and its relationship to many aspects of Victorian culture.

Quick Key
See text for detailed explanations

History – American = Subject Category

24. Name of Set[1] = set ID number, set title, endnote number

Alternate Title: e.g. *Christmas Carol* for *Marley's Ghost*

Author = creator of literary work illustrated

23/24 = number of Beale images/number in set
S = Set (G = Group)
"+" = additional slides in set
"★" = Set name created by us.
"c" = Set also produced as children's slides
"f" = images from set used in filmslides (filmstrips)
"m" = most used sets, 100 years ago

Abbreviations for Locations of Drawings

AMPAS = Academy of Motion Picture Arts and Sciences, Hollywood, California
AN = American National Insurance Company, Galveston, Texas
BAC = Biblical Arts Center, Dallas, Texas (As noted in the discussion of provenance, BAC burned to the ground in 2005, so a BAC notation is an indication of where Beale's Own Slides and wash drawings, <u>once were</u>, but also that they have been lost to fire. BAC was rebuilt and is now called The Museum of Biblical Art.)
BC = Beale Collection of the authors
BU = Baylor University, Waco, Texas
BRM = Brandywine River Museum of Art, Chadds Ford, Pennsylvania
CAM = Center for American Music, Pittsburgh, Pennsylvania
DU = Duke University, Durham, North Carolina
GEH = George Eastman House International Museum of Photography and Film, Rochester, New York[9]
HFM = Henry Ford Museum, Dearborn, Michigan (Formerly the Edison Institute.)
HRC = Harry Ransom Center, Austin, Texas
HU = Harvard University, Cambridge, Massachusetts
K-MOMI = Kent Museum of the Moving Image, Deal, England
MLCM = Magic Lantern Castle Museum, San Antonio, Texas
MOMI = Museum of the Moving Image, Astoria, New York

NBMAA = New Britain Museum of American Art, New Britain, Connecticut
PHM = Philadelphia History Museum, Philadelphia, Pennsylvania (Formerly The Atwater Kent Museum.)
PR = Private Collection known to the authors
RBC = Richard Balzer Collection, private but available on the internet
RLM = Rosenberg Library and Museum, Galveston, Texas
SDSU = San Diego State University, San Diego, California
UN = Location Unknown to the authors
WAMA = Wadsworth Atheneum Museum of Art, Hartford, Connecticut
WMAA = Whitney Museum of American Art, New York, New York

Alternate Dating Formats

1890 = date of set introduction. Second date: expansion of set
1890-1892 = date range of set introduction
1890~ = date by which 60% of slides in set were created
1900 i = date of group introduction if contains multiple slide dates

Individual Slide Information

"Beale slide in set" = title of individual slide
( ) = alternate title for this individual slide
F 222 = set where slide was First Used and associated set ID #
E 23 = set where slide is Used Elsewhere and associated set ID #
AN and other abbreviations = location of slide drawing, at left
Date in slide information = date of this slide if not covered in set
v = variant of previous slide

Sources of Attribution to Beale

s = signature exists
ca = catalog attribution exists
d = documentation exists
wd or wd★ = wash drawing exists or existed
n = negative of slide exists and is used for attribution
bos = Beale's Own Slide exists
as = authors' judgment based on artistic style
" ^ " = image depicted is of this slide

See a Full Magic-Lantern Catalog

The full McIntosh catalog for 1895 is now available on line. Search Google Books for "McIntosh Stereopticon".

Catalogue Raisonné

Table of Contents

The Condensed Catalogue Raissoné of Beale's Magic-Lantern Slides

Literature – Long Poems[24]

1. Courtship of Miles Standish, The
Longfellow, 23/24, S, f, HU, 1908

1. "Look at these Arms," he said. – *s, wd, bos*
2. "She was the first to die." – *s, wd, bos*
3. "A wonderful man was Caesar." – *s, wd, bos*
4. "Now to the bed of the dying." – *wd, bos*
5. "The name of friendship is sacred." – *s, wd, bos*
6. "Alden went on his errand." – *s, wd, bos*
7. "Saw the new built house." – *s, wd, bos*
8. "Silent before her he stood." – *s, wd, bos*
9. "Why does he not come himself." – *s, wd, bos*
10. "Why don't you speak yourself, John?" – *s, wd, bos,* ^
11. Alden alone by the sea. – *wd, bos*
12. "Long have you been on your errand." – *s, wd, bos*
13. "Up leaped the Captain of Plymouth." – *s, wd, bos*
14. "Here, take it, this is our answer." – *s, wd, bos*
15. The march of Miles Standish. – *F 164, GEH, 1885, d, wd, bos*
16. "Nearer the boat stood Alden." – *wd, bos*
17. "Priscilla was standing beside him." – *E 164, s, wd, bos*
18. Indian parleying with Miles Standish. – *s, wd, bos*
19. "Headlong he leaped on the boaster." – *s, wd, bos*
20. "The skein on his hands she adjusted." – *s, wd, bos*
21. "Pressing her close to his heart." – *s, wd, bos*
22. "Taking each other for husband and wife." – *s, wd, bos*
23. The Captain saluting Priscilla. – *s, wd, bos*

2. Evangeline[25]
Longfellow, 24/24, S, f, RWN, 1900

1. The forest primeval. – *wd, bos*
2. Pastor in street of Arcadia. – *wd, bos*
3. Evangeline going to church. – *wd, bos*
4. House and barns of Benedict. – *wd, bos*
5. Evangeline and Gabriel hunting eggs. – *wd, bos*
6. Indian Summer. – *wd, bos*
7. Basil and Benedict arranging betrothal. – *wd, bos*
8. Notary drinking to health of couple. – *wd, bos*
9. Merrymaking at the betrothal. – *wd, bos*
10. Women in churchyard – Arrival of soldiers. – *wd, bos*
11. English commander delivering order. – *s, wd, bos*
12. Priest in church subduing his people. – *s, wd, bos*
13. Parting of Evangeline and Gabriel. – *s, wd, bos*
14. Evangeline with her Father at seaside. – *UN, d, n, bos*
15. Burial of Evangeline's father. – *s, wd, bos*
16. Evangeline at the prow of the boat. – *UN, n, bos*
17. Boat on Mississippi with the bugler. – *wd, bos,* ^
18. Basil on horseback calling his cattle. – *s, wd, bos*
19. Evangeline in the garden. – *s, wd, bos*

20. Indian woman at tent of Evangeline. – *s, wd, bos*
21. Black-robed chief of the missions. – *wd, bos*
22. Hunter's lodge in ruins. – *s, wd, bos*
23. Evangeline in Philadelphia visiting the sick. – *wd, bos*
24. Evangeline Finds Gabriel at last. – *UN, n, bos*

3. Gray's Elegy
(. . . Written in a Country Churchyard)
Gray, 32/32, S, f, BC, 1900, 1904

1. "The curfew tolls the knell of parting day." – *1900, wd, bos*
2. "Now fades the glimmering landscape." – *1900, wd, bos*
3. "The moping owl does to the moon complain." – *1900, wd, bos*
4. "Beneath those rugged elms." – *1900, wd, bos*
5. "The breezy call of incense breathing morn." – *1900, wd, bos*
6. "For them no more the blazing hearth." – *1900, s, wd, bos*
7. "Oft did the harvest to their sickle yield." – *1900, wd, bos*
8. "Let not ambition mock their useful toil." – *1900, s, wd, bos*
9. "The paths of glory lead but to the grave." – *1900, s, wd, bos*
10. "Nor you, ye proud, impute …the fault." – *1900, s, wd, bos*
11. "Can storied urn, or animated bust." – *1900, wd, bos*
12. "Perhaps in this neglected spot is laid." – *1900, wd, bos, ^*
13. "But knowledge to their eyes her ample page." – *1904, wd, bos*
14. "Full many a gem, of purest ray serene." – *1904, wd, bos*
15. "Some village Hampden." – *1900, wd, bos*
16. "The applause of listening senates." – *1904, s, wd, bos*
17. "Forbade to wade through slaughter." – *1900, wd, bos*
18. "The struggling pangs of conscious truth." – *1904, wd, bos*
19. "Far from the madding crowd." – *1904, s, wd, bos*
20. "Some frail memorial still erected nigh." – *1900, wd, bos*
21. "Their name…spelt by the unletter'd Muse." – *1904, wd, bos*
22. "For who, to dumb forgetfulness a prey." – *1904, s, wd, bos*
23. "On some fond breast the parting soul." – *1900, s, wd, bos*
24. "For thee, who, mindful of the…dead." – *1904, wd, bos*
25. "Oft have we seen him at peep of dawn." – *1900, wd, bos*
26. "There at the foot of yonder nodding beech." – *1900, wd, bos*
27. "Hard by yon wood, now smiling." – *1904, s, wd, bos*
28. "One morn I miss'd him on the custom'd hill." – *1904, wd, bos*
29. "Slow through the churchway path." – *1900, s, wd, bos*
30. "Here rests his head upon the lap of earth." – *1904, wd, bos*
31. "He gave to misery (all he had) a tear." – *1900, s, wd, bos*
32. "No farther seek his merits." – *1904, s, wd, bos*

4. Hiawatha[26]
Longfellow, 24/24, S, f, RLM, 1900, 1907

1. The peace pipe. – *1907, wd, bos*
2. The four winds. – *1907, wd, bos*
3. Hiawatha's childhood. – *1907, wd, bos*
4. Hiawatha and Mudjekeewis. – *1907, wd, bos*
5. Hiawatha's fasting. – *1907, wd*
6. Hiawatha's friends. – *1907, wd, bos*
7. Hiawatha's sailing. – *UN, 1907, s, wd, bos, ^*
8. Hiawatha's fishing. – *1907, wd, bos*
9. Hiawatha and Pearl Feather. – *1907, wd, bos*
10. Hiawatha's wooing – A. – *1900, wd, bos*
10. Hiawatha's wooing – B. – *1907, s, wd, bos*
11. Hiawatha's wedding feast – A. – *1900, s, wd, bos*
11. Hiawatha's wedding feast – B. – *1907, wd, bos*
12. Son of Evening Star. – *UN, 1907, s, wd, bos*
13. Blessing the cornfields. – *1907, s, wd, bos*
14. Picture writing. – *1907, s, wd, bos*
15. Hiawatha's lamentation. – *1907, s, wd, bos*
16. Pau-Puk-Keewis. – *1907, wd, bos*
17. Hunting Pau-Puk-Keewis. – *1907, s, wd, bos*
18. Death of Kwasind. – *1907, wd, bos*
19. Ghosts. – *1907, s, wd, bos*
20. Famine. (Death of Minnehaha) – *1900, s, wd, bos*
21. White Man's Foot. – *UN,1907, s, wd, bos*
22. Hiawatha's Departure. – *1900, s, wd, bos*

5. Lady of the Lake
Scott, 24/24, S, f, BC, 1904

1. "He sorrowed o'er the expiring horse." – *wd*
2. "In listening mood, she seems to stand." – *wd, bos*
3. "'Tis thus our charmed rhymes we sing." – *s, wd, bos*
4. "'Wake, Allan-Bane,' aloud she cried." – *s, wd, bos*
5. "The hounds, the hawk, her cares divide." – *s, wd, bos*
6. "Grant me this maid to wife." – *s, wd, bos*
7. "Chieftains, forego!" – *s, wd, bos*

5

6

8. "The cross thus formed, he held on high." – *s, wd, bos*
9. "'Alas,' she sobbed, – 'and yet be gone.'" – *wd, bos*
10. "The messenger of fear and fate." – *s, wd, bos*
11. "With Alpine's Lord, the Hermit Monk." – *wd, bos*
12. "Ellen beheld as in a dream." – *s, wd, bos*
13. "He placed the golden circlet on." – *s, wd, bos*
14. "The fierce avenger is behind!" – *s, wd, bos*
15. "By Him whose word is truth!" – *s, wd, bos*
16. "Thy name and purpose! Saxon, stand!" – *s, wd, bos,* ^
17. "These are Clan-Alpine's warriors true." – *s, wd, bos*
18. "And locked his arms his foeman round." – *s, wd, bos*
19. "And ever James was bending low." – *s, wd, bos*
20. "Back, on your lives, ye menial pack!" – *s, wd, bos*
21. "Hear ye, my mates!" – *s, wd, bos*
22. "Hark! Minstrel! I have heard thee play." – *wd, bos*
23. "No word her choking voice commands." – *wd, bos*
24. "Then gently draw the glittering band." – *wd, bos*

Literature – Novels & Long Stories

6. Marley's Ghost[27] (A Christmas Carol)
Dickens, 24/25, S, f, UN, 1908

1. Scrooge's office. – *s, wd, bos*
2. Doorway of Scrooge's house. – *wd, bos*
3. *Effect.* Marley's face. – *wd, bos*
4. Scrooge's sitting-room. – *s, wd, bos*
5. *Effect.* Marley's ghost. – *s, wd, bos*
6. Scrooge's bedroom. – *E 6 #18, s, wd, bos*
7. *Effect.* Christmas Past. – *s, wd, bos*
8. The school room. – *s, wd, bos*
9. *Effect.* Ali Baba. – *wd, bos*
10. *Effect.* Robinson Crusoe. – *wd, bos*
11. Fezziwig's ball. – *s, wd, bos*
12. Scrooge's first love. – *s, wd, bos*
13. Husband, wife and daughter. – *s, wd, bos*
14. Christmas present. – *s, wd, bos,* ^
15. Bob Cratchit's home. – *s, wd, bos*
16. Miner's Cottage. – *s, wd, bos*
17. Nephew's house. – *wd, bos*
18. Same as 6 – Scrooge's bedroom. – *F 6, s, wd, bos*

19. *Effect.* Christmas Future. – *s, wd, bos*
20. On 'Change. – *s, wd, bos*
21. Marine store dealer's. – *s, wd, bos*
22. Interior of Cratchit's house. – *s, wd, bos*
23. The churchyard. – *s, wd, bos*
24. Buying turkey at door. – *s, wd, bos*
25. Interior of nephew's house. – *s, wd, bos*

7. Robinson Crusoe[28]
Defoe, 12/12, S, c, f, BC, 1894

1. His father entreats him to stay home. – *wd, bos*
2. He holds fast to a piece of wreck. – *wd, bos*
3. He loads his raft. – *wd, bos*
4. He begins to be ill. – *wd, bos*
5. He sails around his island. – *wd, bos*
6. He starts to explore the interior of the island. – *wd, bos*
7. He discovers human bones. – *wd, bos*
8. He gets a view of the wreck. – *wd, bos*

7

9. He delivers Friday from the savages. – *wd, bos*
10. Crusoe and Friday in cave. – *wd, bos*, ^
11. Fierce fight between the Spaniard & a savage. – *wd, bos*
12. Crusoe is overcome by...deliverance. – *wd, bos*

8. Uncle Tom's Cabin[29]
Stowe, 13/12, S, c, f, m, RBC, 1882

1. George Harris taking leave of his wife. – *wd, bos*
2. An evening in Uncle Tom's Cabin. – *wd, bos*
3. Eliza and Child on the Ice. – *wd, bos* ^
4. Uncle Tom sold to Haley. – *wd, bos*
5. Eva makes a friend of Uncle Tom. – *wd, bos*
6. Uncle Tom saves Eva from drowning. – *wd, bos*
7. George Harris resists the Slave Hunters. – *wd, bos*
8. Eva and Topsy. – *wd, bos*
9. Eva Reading to Uncle Tom. – *wd, bos*
10. Death of Eva. – *UN, 1882, as*
10v. Eva's Dying Farewell. – *1894+, wd, bos*
11. Legree's cruelty to Uncle Tom. – *wd, bos*
12. Death of Uncle Tom. – *wd, bos*

Literature – Plays, Opera

9. Carmen
Bizet, 12/12, S, f, BC, 1910

1. Act 1 – Carmen throwing rose to Don José. – *s, wd, bos*
2. Act 1 – Michaela's interview with Don José. – *s, wd, bos*
3. Act 1 – Carmen entreats Don José. – *s, wd, bos*
4. Act 1 – The escape of Carmen. – *s, wd, bos*
5. Act II – Carmen dances for Don José. – *s, wd, bos*
6. Act II – The Toreador's song. – *s, wd, bos*
7. Act III – Carmen reads death in the cards. – *UN, s, wd, bos*
8. Act III – Carmen interrupts the duelists. – *UN, s, wd, bos*, ^
9. Act III – The Toreador's invitation. – *s, wd, bos*
10. Act IV – Entrance of the Toreador and Carmen. – *s, wd, bos*
11. Act IV – Don José attacks Carmen. – *s, wd, bos*
12. Act IV – Death of Carmen. – *s, wd, bos*

10. Hamlet[30]
Shakespeare, 14/15, S, f, GEH, 1910

1. Act I, Sc. I – Hamlet and the Ghost. – *wd, bos*
2. Act I, Sc. 5 – Hamlet's Interview with Ghost. – *wd, bos*
3. Act I, Sc. 5 – Hamlet swearing Horatio to silence. – *wd, bos*
4. Act III, Sc. 1 – Hamlet's soliloquy. – *wd, bos*, ^
5. Act III, Sc. 2 – Hamlet's advice to the players. – *wd, bos*
7. Act III, Sc. 2 – Hamlet asking Gildenstern. – *wd, bos*
8. Act III, Sc. 3 – Hamlet surprises the King. – *wd, bos*
9. Act III, Sc. 4 – Hamlet kills Polonius. – *wd, bos*
10. Act III, Sc. 4 – Hamlet interviews his mother. – *wd, bos*
11. Act IV, Sc. 5 – Ophelia scattering flowers. – *wd*
12. Act V, Sc. 1 – Hamlet with skull of Yorick. – *wd*
13. Act V, Sc. 1 – Hamlet leaps into grave. – *wd, bos*
14. Act V, Sc. 2 – Duel between Hamlet and Laertes. – *wd*
15. Act V, Sc. 2 – Hamlet kills the king. – *wd*

11. Macbeth[31]

Shakespeare, 12/12, S, f, 1904

1. Act I, Sc. 3 – Macbeth, Banquo, witches. – *UN, n, as*
2. Act I, Sc. 4 – Macbeth and Banquo. – *UN, n, as*
3. Act I, Sc. 6 – Lady Macbeth welcoming Duncan. – *GEH, s, wd*
4. Act I, Sc. 7 – Lady Macbeth urging husband. – *GEH, s, d, wd*
5. Act II, Sc. 1 – "Is this a dagger which I see before me?" – *UN, n, as*
6. Act II, Sc. 1 – The murder of Duncan. – *UN, n, as*
7. Act III, Sc. 3 – The murder of Banquo. – *GEH, wd*
8. Act III, Sc. 4 – Banquo's ghost at the banquet. – *UN, n, as*
9. Act IV, Sc. 1 – Macbeth and the three witches. – *UN, n, as*
10. Act V, Sc. 1 – Lady Macbeth washing her hands. – *UN, wd*
11. Act V, Sc. 5 – "Fear not, till Burnham woods..." – *GEH, wd*
12. Act V, Sc. 7 – Killing of Macbeth by Macduff. – *GEH, wd, ^*

12. Merchant of Venice

Shakespeare, 11/12, S, f, UN, 1902–03

1. Act I. Sc. III. Antonio … and Shylock. – *n, as*
2. Act II. Sc. II. Old Gobbo and his son, Launcelot. – *s, wd*
3. Act II. Sc. V. Jessica throwing down a casket. – *s, wd*
4. Act III. Sc. I. Shylock bewailing loss. – *s, wd, ^*
6. Act III. Sc. II. Portia giving ring to Bassanio. – *n, as*
7. Act III. Sc. II. Bassanio reading letter from Antonio. – *n, as*
8. Act IV. Sc. I. Portia…speaking in court. – *s, wd*
9. Act IV. Sc. I. Shylock…to take the pound of flesh. – *n, as*
10. Act IV. Sc. I. Shylock hearing his sentence. – *s, wd*
11. Act IV. Sc. I. Portia…asking Bassanio for ring. – *s, wd*
12. Act V. Sc. I. Portia reproaching Bassanio. – *n, as*

13. Merry Wives of Windsor[32]

Shakespeare, 12/12, S, f, UN, 1913

1. Act I, Sc. 1 – Falstaff kissing Mrs. Page. – *n, bos*
2. Act I, Sc. 3 – Falstaff sending letters by Robin. – *n, bos*
3. Act II, Sc. 1 – Mrs. Ford & Mrs. Page. – *n, bos*
4. Act II, Sc. 2 – Falstaff giving message to Quickly. – *n, bos*
5. Act III, Sc. 3 – Falstaff getting into the basket. – *n, bos*
6. Act III, Sc. 4 – Fenton and Ann Page. – *n, bos*
7. Act IV, Sc. 2 – Falstaff disguised as an old woman. – *n, bos*
8. Act V, Sc. 3 – Fairies going to Herne woods. – *n, bos, ^*
9. Act V, Sc. 4 – Falstaff in disguise, the Fairies appear. – *n, bos*
10. Act V, Sc. 4 – Falstaff punished by the Fairies. – *n, bos*
11. Act V, Sc. 4 – Falstaff and the dames. – *n, bos*
12. Act V, Sc. 4 – Reconciliation of Page and Fenton. – *n, bos*

14. Othello[33]

Shakespeare, 12/12, S, f, GEH, 1909

1. Act I, Sc. 1 – "Here is her father's house." – *s, d, wd*
2. Act 1, Sc. 3 – "I am hitherto your daughter." – *UN, n, as*
3. Act I, Sc. 1 – "My dear Othello!" – *UN, n, as*
4. Act II, Sc. 3 – "What is the matter here?" – *UN, n, as*
5. Act III, Sc. 3 – "Why stay and hear me speak." – *UN, n, as*
6. Act III, Sc. 3 – "O! beware my lord of jealousy." – *UN, n, as*
7. Act IV, Sc. 1 – "I have not deserved this." – *wd*
8. Act IV, Sc. 2 – "Why do you weep?" – *s, wd*
9. Act V, Sc. 1 – "I am maimed forever." – *wd*

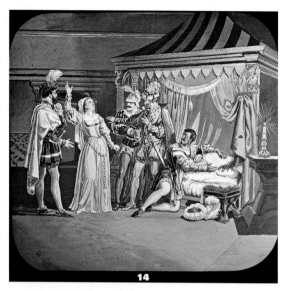

14

10. Act V, Sc. 2 – "I would not have thee linger in pain." – *wd*
11. Act V, Sc. 2 – "There lies your niece." – *wd*, ^
12. Act V, Sc. 2 – "Look on the tragic ending of this bed." – *wd*

15. Pygmalion and Galatea[34]
Gilbert, 6/6, S, f, BC, 1890

15

1. The Sculptor's Prayer. – *wd, bos*
2. The Statue comes to Life. – *wd, bos*
3. The Statue Advancing. – *wd, bos*, ^
4. The Indignant Wife. – *wd, bos*
5. Galatea returns to Pedestal. – *wd, bos*
6. Galatea Marble Again. – *wd, bos*

16. Romeo and Juliet[35]
Shakespeare, 15/15, S, f, GEH, 1910

1. Act I, Sc. 1 – The quarrel in Street. – *wd, bos*
2. Act I, Sc. 4 – Romeo and others in mask. – *wd, bos*

16

3. Act I, Sc. 5 – Romeo making love to Juliet. – *wd, bos*
4. Act II, Sc. 2 – Juliet at the Balcony. – *wd, bos*, ^
5. Act II, Sc. 6 – Romeo and Juliet at the Friar's. – *wd, bos*
6. Act III, Sc. 1 – Romeo's duel with Tybalt. – *wd, bos*
7. Act III, Sc. 5 – Romeo and Juliet at window. – *wd, bos*
8. Act III, Sc. 5 – Juliet beseeching her father. – *wd, bos*
9. Act IV, Sc. 3 – Juliet drinking sleeping draught. – *wd, bos*
10. Act IV, Sc. 5 – Capulet and family weeping. – *wd, bos*
11. Act V, Sc. 1 – Romeo and the Apothecary. – *wd, bos*
12. Act V, Sc. 3 – Duel between Paris and Romeo. – *wd, bos*
13. Act V, Sc. 3 – Romeo drinking the poison. – *wd, bos*
14. Act V, Sc. 3 – Death of Juliet. – *wd, bos*
15. Act V, Sc. 3 – Reconciliation. – *wd, bos*

Literature – Parlor Poetry

17. Annie and Willie's Prayer[36]
Snow, 6/6, S, RLM, 1902–03

17

1. Annie and Willie sent to bed early. – *s, wd, bos*
2. Annie and Willie praying at bedside. – *s, wd, bos*
3. Father going in storm to buy toys. – *d, wd, bos,* ^
4. Father and Aunt Mary arranging presents. – *s, wd, bos*
5. Children discovering their gifts. – *s, wd, box*
6. Father and his happy children. – *s, wd, bos*

18. Barbara Freitchie
(Barbara Frietchie)
Whittier, 1/1, S, m, MLCM, 1886

Barbara Freitchie. – *F 162, ca, wd, bos,* ^

18

19. Blue and The Gray, The★
Finch, 1/1, S, m, AN, 1894

The Blue and The Gray. (Let Us Have Peace) – *F 162, wd,* ^

19

20. Bridge, The
Longfellow, 4/4, S, f, AN, 1900

20

1. "I stood on the bridge at midnight." – *wd, bos*
2. "How often ... in the days that had gone by." – *wd, bos*
3. "And only the sorrow of others Throws its shadow." – *wd, bos,* ^
4. "I see the long procession Still passing." – *wd, bos*

21. Brook, The
Tennyson, 10/10, S, f, BRMA, 1902–03

21

1. "I come from haunts of coot and hern." – *wd*
2. "By thirty hills I hurry down." – *wd, bos*
3. "Till last by Philip's farm I flow." – *wd, bos*
4. "I chatter over stony ways." – *wd, bos*
5. "With many a curve my banks I fret." – *wd, bos*
6. "I wind about and in and out." – *wd, bos,* ^

7. "And here and there a foamy flake." – *wd, bos*
8. "I steal by lawns and grassy plots." – *wd, bos*
9. "I slip, I slide, I gloom, I glance." – *wd, bos*
10. "I murmur under moon and stars." – *wd, bos*

22. Casabianca
Hemans, 6/6, S, f, BC, 1907

1. The boy stood on the burning deck. – *s, wd, bos*
2. That father faint in death below. – *s, wd, bos*
3. Upon his brow he felt their breath. – *s, wd, bos*
4. They wrapt the ships in splendor wild. – *wd, bos*
5. There came a burst of thunder sound. – *wd, bos*
6. Ask of the winds that far around with fragments. – *wd, bos,* ^

23. Courtin', The
Lowell, 6/6, S, f, BC, 1894

1. "Zekle crep' up quite unbeknown." – *UN, wd, bos,* ^
2. "An' there sot Huldy all alone." – *wd*
3. "She thought no v'ice had such a swing." – *s, wd, bos*
4. "He stood a spell on one foot first." – *wd, bos*
5. "That last word pricked him like a pin." – *wd, bos*
6. "Tell Mother see how matters stood." – *wd, bos*

24. Curfew Shall Not Ring To-Night[37]
Thorpe. 10/10, S, f, BC, 1894

1. He with bowed head, sad and thoughtful. – *wd, bos*
2. "I've a lover in that prison." – *wd, bos*
3. "Bessie," calmly spoke the sexton. – *wd, bos*
4. She had listened while the Judges read. – *wd, bos*
5. She with quick steps bounded forward. – *wd, bos,* ^
6. She had reached the topmost ladder. – *wd, bos*
7. Out she swung, far out. – *wd, bos*
8. Firmly on the dark old ladder. – *wd, bos*
9. At his feet she tells her story. – *wd, bos*
10. Kneeling on the turf beside him. – *wd, bos*

25. Darius Green and His Flying Machine
Trowbridge, 8/8, S, f, RLM, 1902–03

1. Darius Considering the Idea of Flying. – *s, wd, bos*
2. Darius in Loft Making Wings, etc. – *wd, bos*
3. His Brothers Peeking at Him. – *wd, bos*
4. Darius Stays at Home with Toothache. – *s, wd, bos*
5. His brothers Sneaking into the Barn. – *s, wd, bos*
6. Darius Putting on his Flying Gear. – *wd, bos*
7. Darius Springs into the Air. – *wd, bos,* ^
8. And lands in a Heap in Cowyard. – *wd, bos*

26. Drake's Ode to The American Flag[38]
Drake, 6/5, S, f, 1881–1893

1. "When freedom … her mountain." (Columbia with Capitol) – *E 104, UN, 1881–93, ca, bos*
2. "Majestic Monarch of cloud." – *MLCM, 1894–1920, wd*
3. "Flag of the Brave." (Battle Princeton) – *E 166, UN, 1891, d,* ^
6. "Flag of the free heart's hope and home." (42 stars) – *E 162, E 220, E 222, E 223, GEH, 1881–93, wd*

6 v 1. "Flag of the free heart's hope and home." (45 stars) – *E 162, E 220, E 222, E 223, GEH, 1891–1911, wd*
6 v 2. "Flag of the free heart's hope and home." (48 stars) – *E 162, E 220, E 222, E 223, GEH, 1912–20, wd, bos*

27. How Persimmon's Took Cah ob der Baby[39]
Champney, 4/4, S, BC, 1881–1920

4. "'Ring,' he shouts, 'Ring! Grandpa.'" – *s, wd, ^*
5. "How they shouted! what rejoicing!" – *s, wd*
5 v. "How they shouted! what rejoicing." (close-up of bell tower) – *E 45, 1896–1920, s, wd*
6. "That old State-house bell is silent now." (bell alone) – *E 230, AN, wd*

29. John Gilpin's Ride[41]
Cowper, 20/20, S, f, BC, 1909

1. John Gilpin's spouse said to her dear. – *s, wd, bos*
2. John Gilpin kissed his loving wife. – *s, wd, bos*
3. Where they did all get in. – *PR, n, as*
4 . He saw three customers come in. – *s, wd, bos*
5. "The wine is left behind!" – *s, wd, bos*
6. And hung a bottle on each side. – *s, wd, bos*
7. Now see him mounted once again. – *s, wd, bos*
8. Away went hat and wig. – *s, wd, bos*
9. The wind did blow, the cloak did fly. – *wd, bos, ^*
10. Their gates wide open threw. – *s, wd, bos*

1. Persimmons and der Baby. – *wd*
2. Persimmons' Granny. – *wd*
3. Persimmons on Raft. – *wd, ^*
4. The Mother Finds her Baby. – *wd*

28. Independence Bell[40]
Unknown, 6/6, S, f, AN, 1896–97

1. "There was tumult in the city." (Indep. Hall) – *s, wd*
3. "Far aloft in that high steeple." – *s, wd*

29

6. Three hundred souls, the steamer's freight. – *s, d, wd, bos*
7. "Stand by the wheel five minutes yet." – *d, wd, bos*
8. The flames approach with giant strides. – *s, d, wd, bos, ^*
9. The pebbles grate beneath the keel. – *s, d, wd, bos*
10. His nerveless hands released their task. – *s, d, wd, bos*

31. Leap For Life, A
Colton, 6/6, S, f, AN, 1885~

31

1. "Old Ironsides at anchor lay." – *E 75, E 222, 1891, wd, bos*
2. "There stood the boy with dizzy brain." – *1885, wd, bos, ^*
3. "A rifle grasped And aimed it at his son." – *1885, s, wd, bos*
4. "That only chance your life can save, Jump boy!" *1885, wd, bos*
5. "He sank – he rose – he lived – he moved." – *1885, wd, bos*
6. "His father drew in silent joy Those wet arms." – *1887, wd, bos*

32. Little Breeches
Hay, 8/8, S, f, RLM, 1906

1. I Don't Go Much on Religion. – *s, wd, bos*
2. I come into Town – *wd, bos*
3. I went in for a Jug of Molasses. – *UN, d, wd, bos*
4. Hell to Split – *s, wd, bos*
5. At last We Struck Hosses and Wagon. – *wd, bos*
6. I Jest Flopped Down on My Marrow Bones. – *s, wd, bos, ^*
7. And Thar Sot Little Breeches, and Chirped. – *wd, bos*
8. They Just Scooped down and Toted Him. – *wd, bos*

33. Maud Muller
Whittier, 6/6, S, f, BC, 1894

1. Maud Muller on a Summer's day. – *wd, bos*
2. And blushed as she gave it, looking down. – *UN, wd, bos, ^*
3. The judge looked back. – *wd, bos*
4. Oft when the wine in his glass was red. – *wd, bos*
5. She wedded a man unlearned and poor. – *wd, bos*
6. Alas for the maiden, alas for the Judge. – *UN, wd, bos*

11. Down ran the wine into the road. – *s, wd, bos*
12. "Stop, Stop, John Gilpin! Here's the house!" – *s, wd, bos*
13. His horse at last stood still. – *s, wd, bos*
14. Whence straight he came with hat and wig. – *s, wd, bos*
15. Whereat his horse did snort. – *s, wd, bos*
16. And away went Gilpin's hat and wig. – *s, wd, bos*
17. She pulled out half a crown. – *s, wd, bos*
18. By catching at his rein. – *s, wd, bos*
19. "Stop thief, stop thief, a highwayman!" – *s, wd, bos*
20. Nor stopped till where he had got up. – *s, wd, bos*

30. John Maynard[42]
Alger, 10/10, S, f, BC, 1905

30

1. The Gallant Steamer "Ocean Queen." – *AN, d, wd, bos*
2. Ah! who beneath that cloudless sky. – *d, wd, bos*
3. A seaman sought the captain's side. – *d, wd, bos*
4. "Is there no hope – no chance of life?" – *s, d, wd, bos*
5. By name, John Maynard, eastern born. – *s, d, wd, bos*

32

33

34

35

34. Nellie's Prayer[43]
Sims, 12/12, S, UN, 1891

1. "Stooped down, with her eyelids streaming." – *d, bos*
2. "I knew that my Nell was an orphan." – *d, bos*
3. "It was there in the evening paper." – *d, bos*
4. "I had thought of him night and morning." – *d, bos*
5. "We walked by his side that morning." – *d, bos, ^*
6. "He held her up at the station." – *d, bos*
7. "Though now and again I fretted." – *d, bos*
8. "And she counted the days till daddy." – *d, bos*
9. "She prayed for her absent father." – *d, bos*
10. "She prayed in her childish fashion." – *d, bos*
11. "And my darling rushed towards me." – *d, bos*
12. "When the shock of surprise was over." – *d, bos*

35. Paul Revere's Ride[44]
Longfellow, 8/8, S, c, f, PR, 1896–97~

1. "He said to his friend, 'If the British march.'" – *s, wd, bos*
2. "Then he climbed the tower of the church." – *s, wd, ^*
3. "And lo! as he looks on the belfry's height." – *wd*
4. "And beneath from the pebbles in passing, a spark." – *1881–93, wd, bos*
5. "It was twelve by the village clock." – *s, wd*
6. "It was one by the village clock." – *s, wd*
7. "And one was safe and asleep in his bed." – *F 166, UN, d, wd*
8. "How the farmers gave them ball for ball." – *E 224, UN, 1881–93, wd, bos*

36. Pied Piper of Hamelin, The[45]
Browning, 8/8, S, f, BC, 1899

1. "Rats! They fought the dogs, they killed the cats." – *s, wd, bos*
2. "Rouse up sirs! Give your brains a racking." – *s, wd, bos*
3. "His queer long coat from heel to head." – *s, wd, bos*
4. "And out of the houses the rats came tumbling." – *s, wd, bos*

36

5. "Until they came to the river Weser." – *s, wd, bos,* ^
6. "And folks who find me in a passion." – *s, wd, bos*
7. "Tripping and skipping ran merrily after." – *s, wd, bos*
8. "And lo! As they reached the mountain side." – *s, wd, bos*

37. Raven, The[46]
Poe, 12/12, S, f, UN, 1894

37

1. "While I nodded, nearly napping." – *wd, bos*
2. "Here I opened wide the door." – *wd, bos*
3. "In there stepped a stately Raven." – *wd, bos*
4. "Tell me what thy lordly name is." – *wd, bos*
5. "Straight I wheeled a cushioned seat." – *s, wd, bos*
6. "But whose velvet violet lining." – *wd, bos*
7. "Then methought the air grew denser." – *wd, bos,* ^
8. "On this home by horror haunted." – *s, wd, bos*
9. "Prophet!" said I, " thing of evil." – *wd, bos*
10. "It shall clasp a sainted maiden." – *s, wd, bos*

11. "Be that word our sign of parting." – *wd, bos*
12. "And my soul from out that shadow." – *wd, bos*

38. Shakespeare's Seven Ages (of Man)
Shakespeare, 7/7, S, f, BC, 1896–97

38

1. The Infant. – *wd, bos*
2. The School Boy. – *wd*
3. The Lover. – *wd*
4. The Soldier. – *wd,* ^
5. The Justice. – *wd*
6. The Lean and Slippered Pantaloon. – *wd, bos*
7. The Last scene. – *wd*

39. Sheridan's Ride
Read, 6/6, S, f, AN, 1902–03~

1. "Telling the battle was on once more." – *wd, bos,* ^
2. "Hills rose and fell, but his heart was gay." – *wd, bos*
3. "Every nerve of the charger was strained." – *s, wd, bos*

39

4. "He is snuffing the smoke of the roaring fray." – *s, wd, bos*
5. "I have brought you Sheridan." – *F 169, 1888–89, s, wd, bos*
6. "And when their statues are placed on high." – *s, wd, bos*

40. Spectre Pig, The
Holmes, 8/8, S, f, AN, 1902–03

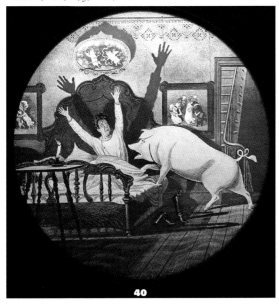

1. "It was the stalwart butcher man." – *wd, bos*
2. "And like a mighty pendulum." – *wd, bos*
3. "It was the butcher's youngest son." – *s, wd, bos*
4. "It was the butcher's daughter then." – *wd, bos*
5. "And hooting owl, and hovering bat." – *wd, bos*
6. "Now wake, now wake, thou butcher man!" – *wd, bos,* ^
7. "The shadowy spectre swept before." – *wd, bos*
8. "A ghastly shape was swinging there." – *wd, bos*

41. Thanatopsis
Bryant, 12/12, S, f, AN, 1904

1. "For his gayer hours, she has a voice of gladness." – *wd, bos*
2. "And she glides into his darker musings." – *wd, bos*
3. "When thoughts of the last bitter hour came." – *wd, bos*
4. "Not yet in the cold ground." – *wd, bos*
5. "And to the sluggish clod. – *wd, bos*
6. "Thou shalt lie down with patriarchs." – *s, wd*
7. "The venerable woods, rivers that move in majesty." – *wd, bos*
8. "And pour'd round all, old Ocean's gray." – *wd, bos*
9. "The planets, all the infinite host of heaven." – *E 214, wd, bos*
10. "Or lose thyself in the continuous woods. – *wd, bos,* ^
11. "Matron and maid, the speechless babe." – *s, wd, bos*
12. "Like one who wraps the drapery." – *wd, bos*

42. Village Blacksmith, The[47]
Longfellow, 6/6, S, f, MLCM, 1896–97

1. "Under a spreading chestnut tree." – *s, wd, bos*
2. "You can hear him swing his heavy sledge." – *s, wd, bos,* ^
3. "And children coming home from school." – *s, wd, bos*
4. "He goes on Sunday to the church." – *s, wd, bos*
5. "And with his hard, rough hand he wipes." – *s, wd, bos*
6. "Each morning sees some task begin." – *wd, bos*

43. Visit of Saint Nicholas[48]
(The Night Before Christmas)
Moore?, 7/6, S, c, f, m, RLM, 1885~

1. The Children were Nestled all Snug. – *1883–84, wd, bos*
2. Away to the Window I Flew Like a Flash. – *1900, wd, bos*
2 v. Away to the Window I Flew. – *UN, 1900?, bos*
3. A Miniature Sleigh and Eight Tiny Reindeer. – *E 253, 1883–84, wd, bos*
4. Down the Chimney St. Nicholas Came. – *E 253, 1900, s, wd, bos,* ^
5. And He Looked Like a Peddler. – *1883–84, wd, bos*
6. Merry Christmas to All. – *1883–84, wd, bos*

44. Wreck of the Hesperus, The[49]
Longfellow, 9/10, S, f, AN, 1894

1. It was the schooner Hesperus. – *wd*
2. Blue were her eyes as the fairy flax. – *wd*

43

44

3. The skipper, he stood beside the helm. – *wd*
4. Then up and spake and old sailor. – *wd*
5. Last night the moon had a golden ring. – *wd*
6. The snow fell hissing in the brine. – *UN, as,* ^
8. And bound her to the mast. – *wd*
9. Like a sheeted ghost the vessel swept. – *wd*
10. A fisherman stood aghast. – *wd*

Literature – Popular Songs

45. America[50]
Smith, 2/3, S, f, m, AN, 1893 i

2. "I love thy rocks and rills." – *E 104, 1908, d, wd, bos,* ^
3. "Let music swell the breeze." – *E 104, 1893, wd*
<u>Alternate Version</u>
3/12, S, AN, 1917–20 i
Slides 2 and 3, above, used?

45

6. (?) "My hand with rapture thrills – *F 162, 1899, wd*
7. "Let music swell the breeze." (bell) – *F 28, 1896–1920, s, wd*

46. Auld Lang Syne
Burns, 4/4, S, f, BC, 1906

46

1. Should Auld acquaintance be forgot. – *wd, bos*
2. We tak' a cup o' kindness yet. – *s, wd, bos*
3. We twa ha'e run about the braes. – *s, wd, bos*
4. And there's a hand my trusty feire. – *wd, bos,* ^

47. Comic Songs★[51]
Various, 3/?, G, 1894

Babies on Our Block. – *UN, wd, bos*
I Want to Be An Angel. – *BC, wd, bos,* ^
Listen to the Mockingbird. – *AN, wd, bos*

47

48. Dixie's Land (Dixie)[52]
Emmett?, 8/8, S, f, UN, 1902–03

48

1. Darkies Picking Cotton in the Fields. – *AN, s, wd, bos*
2. Planter's Home in South – Before the War. – *wd, bos*
3. Darkies Dancing by Light of Moon. – *s, wd, bos*
4. River Steamboat – Loading Cotton by Night. – *AN, wd, bos*
5. Camp-meeting in South by Torchlight. – *AN, s, wd, bos*
6. Confederate Officer leaving home for the War. – *s, wd, bos, ^*
7. Coming Home to Die – Return from the War. – *s, wd, bos*
8. Deserted Southern Home – After the War. – *wd, bos*

49. Home, Sweet Home[53]
Payne, 12/12, S, m, BC, 1887, 1904

1. "Mid pleasures & palaces." – *UN, 1904, s, wd*
2. "A charm from the skies. – *1904, s, wd*

49

4. "An exile from home." – *1887, s, wd*
5. "The birds singing gaily." – *1904, s, wd*
6. "2nd Chorus. Home, home … sweet home." – *1904, s, wd*
7. "How sweet 'tis to sit 'neath a … father's smile." – *1887, wd, ^*
8. "Let others delight 'mid new pleasures." – *1881–93, wd*
9. "3rd Chorus – Home, home…sweet home." – *UN, 1887, n, as*
10. "To thee I'll return, overburdened with care." – *UN, 1904, s, wd*
11. "No more from that cottage…will I roam." – *1887, wd*
11 v. "No more …will I roam." – *UN, 1894–20, as*
12. "Chorus – Home, home, sweet, sweet home." – *1904, wd*

50. Killarney[54]
Balfe (?), 2/10, S, BAC, 1899

9. "Tinge the cloud wreaths in that sky." – E 90, *wd, bos*
10. "Wings of Angels so might shine." (effect) – E 90, *wd, bos, ^*

50

51. Marching Thro' Georgia[55]
Work, 7/6, S, c, BC, 1891

1. "Bring the good old bugle," etc. – *s, d, wd*
2. "How the darkies shouted." – *d, wd*
3. "There were Union men." – *d, wd*
4. "Sherman's Yankee boys." – *d, wd*
5. "We made a thoroughfare." – *d, wd*
6. "Hurrah! Hurrah!" – *d, wd,* ^

Sherman's March. ("Marching Thro' Georgia") – *1885, d, wd*

52. Maryland, My Maryland[56]
Randall, 1/1, S, BC, 1917–20

Maryland, My Maryland. – *s, wd, bos,* ^

53. Old Black Joe[57]
Foster, 6/6, S, CAM, 1905

1. Gone are my Friends from the Cotton Fields. – *s, d, wd, bos*
2. 1st chorus. I'm Coming. – *s, d, wd, bos*
3. Grieving for Forms Now Departed . – *d, wd, bos*
4. 2nd chorus. I'm Coming. – *d, wd, bos*
5. The Children ... that I Held Upon My Knee. – *s, d, wd, bos*
6. 3rd chorus. I'm Coming. – *s, d, wd, bos,* ^

54. Old Kentucky Home
Foster, 6/6, S, f, CAM, 1896–97

1. "The sun shines bright in the old Kentucky home." – *s, wd, bos*
2. Chorus – "Weep no more my lady." – *s, wd, bos*
3. "They sing no more by the glimmer of the moon." – *s, wd, bos*
4. "The times have come when darkies have to part." – *s, wd, bos*

5. "A few more days and the trouble all will end." –
s, wd, bos, ^
6. "A few more days till we todder on the road." – s, wd, bos

55. Old Oaken Bucket
Woodworth, 3/3, S, AN, 1900~

1. The cot of my father, the dairy house nigh it. – *1900, wd*
2. How ardent I seized it, with hands. – *F 243, 1900, s, wd*
3. How sweet from the green mossy brim. – *1881–93, wd, ^*

56. Rally Round the Flag
Auner, 2/5, S, AN, 1917–20 i

1. Yes, we'll rally round the flag, boys. –
F 162, 1899, s, wd, bos, ^
2. Chorus: The Union forever! (American flag) – *F 171, 1912–20, wd*

57. Red, White and Blue[58]
Shaw, 4/4, S, f, AN, 1899

1. "O Columbia, the gem of the ocean." – *s, d, wd, bos, ^*
2. "When borne by the Red, White & Blue." – *s, d, wd, bos*
3. "When war waged its wide desolation." – *d, wd, bos*
4. "The wine cup, the wine cup bring hither." – *s, d, wd, bos*

58. Star Spangled Banner[59]
Key, 6/6, S, f, MLCM, 1896–97

1. "Oh, say can you see by the dawn's early light." –
E 104, s, wd
2. "And the rocket's red glare, the bombs bursting in air." –
s, wd, ^
3. "On the shore dimly seen thro' the mists of the deep." –
s, wd
4. "And where is that band who so vauntingly swore." – *s, wd*

5. "Oh, thus be it ever when freemen shall stand." – *s, wd, bos*
6. "And this be our motto, 'In God is our trust.'" – *s, wd*

59. Swanee Ribber (Swanee River)[60]
Foster, 8/8, S, m, CAM, 1893

1. Way down upon de Swanee Ribber. – *wd, bos*
2. Dere's where my heart is turning ebber. – *wd, bos*
3. All up and down the whole creation. – *wd, bos*
4. Chorus – All de world am sad and dreary. – *wd, bos*
5. All round de little farm I wandered. – *wd, bos*
6. When I was playing wid my brudder. – *wd, bos,* ^
7. One little hut among de bushes. – *wd, bos*
8. When will I see de bees a-humming. – *wd, bos*

60. Tenting on The Old Camp Ground
Kittredge, 5/5, S, BC, 1899

1. "Give us a song to cheer Our weary hearts." – *MLCM, s, wd, bos*
2. Chorus – " Many are the hearts looking." – *s, wd, bos,* ^
3. "Of the loved ones at home." – *s, wd, bos*
4. "Many are dead and gone of the brave." – *s, wd, bos*
5. "Many are lying near – Some are dead." – *s, wd, bos*

61. Tramp, Tramp, Tramp[61]
Root, 2/2, S, AN, 1885

1. The Prison. – *wd, bos*
2. The Liberation. – *wd, bos,* ^

62. United States Soldier's Dream (of Home)[62]
Campbell, 2/2, S, BC, 1906

1. Soldier Sleeping. – *AN, s, wd, bos,* ^
2. Vision of Home. – *wd*

63. Yankee Doodle
Shuckburgh?, 6/6, S, c, f, AN, 1902–03

63

1. "Father and I went down to camp." – *E 162, s, wd, bos*
2. "And there was General Washington." – *s, wd, bos*
3. "And there I see a little keg." – *s, wd, bos*
4. "The troopers, too, would gallop up." – *s, wd, bos*, ^
5. "And there they had a swamping gun." – *s, wd, bos*
6. "It scared me so, I streaked it off." – *s, wd, bos*

Literature – Religious

64. Ben Hur[63]
(Judah, Son of Hur)
Wallace, 34/24, S, c, f, BAC, 1894–95~

64

1. Balthazar in the desert awaiting Wise Men. – *E 158, 1895, s, wd, bos*
2. Wise Men Relating Histories. – *E 158, E 235, 1894, s, wd, bos*
3. Joppa Gate. – *E 158, 1895, s, wd, bos*
4. Wise Men conferring with Herod. – *E 135, E 156, E 158, E 160, 1895, s, wd, bos*
5. Adoration of the Wise Men. – *F 135, E 158, BU, 1896–97, ca, wd*
6. Ben Hur and Messala. – *E 158, 1894, s, wd, bos*
7. Ben Hur and his Mother. – *E 158, 1894, s, wd, bos*
8. The Tile Falling from the Roof. – *E 158, 1894, wd, bos*
9. Jesus gives Ben Hur to drink. – *E 158, 1895, wd, bos*
10. Ben Hur before Arrius on the Galley. – *E 158, 1894, s, wd, bos*
11. Ben Hur saves Arrius in the Sea Fight. – *E 158, 1895, s, wd, bos*
12. Ben Hur's First Visit to Simonides. – *E 158, 1894, s, wd, bos*
13. Ben Hur checks Messala's Steeds. – *E 158, 1895, s, d, wd, bos*
14. The Gambling Party. A Roman Orgie. – *E 158, 1895, wd, bos*
15. Ben Hur and Isis on the Lake. – *E 158, 1895, s, wd, bos*
16. Ben Hur training the Arabs. – *E 158, E 235, 1895, s, wd, bos*
17. Chariot race – Overthrow. – *E 158, E 235, BC, 1895, s, d, wd, bos*
18. The Wrestling Scene in the Palace – *E 158, 1894, s, wd, bos*
19. Tirzah and her Mother in the Dungeon. – *E 158, 1894, s, d, wd, bos*
20. Ben Hur Views Jerusalem. – *E 158, 1895, wd, bos*
21. Ben Hur Discovered by his Mother. – *E 158, 1895, s, wd, bos*
22. Amrah giving Food to her Mistress. – *E 158, 1894, wd, bos*
23. Ben Hur Finds his Mother. – *E 158, 1895, s, wd, bos*
24. Ben Hur and Esther. – *E 158, 1894, wd, bos*

Ben Hur at the Oar. – *E 158, E 235, BC, 1906, s, wd, bos*
Circus Maximus. – *E 68, 1899, ca, wd, bos*
The Winning Chariot. – *E 235, UN, 1894, bos* ^
St John and his disciples see Jesus. – *1909, s, wd, bos*
"Ecce Homo!" (Behold the Man!) – *E 156, E 206, E 211, UN, 1895, bos*
Arrius Going to Sea. (Regulus Leaving Rome for Carthage) – *F 180, BC, 1894, ca, d, wd, bos*
Three magi on camels. – *F 135, BU, 1896–97, s, wd, bos*

65

The Magi arrives at Jerusalem. – *F 69, 1909, ca ,d, wd*
v. (5?) River Jordan, Christmas Night. – *F 98, 1901, bos*
v. The New Born King. (angels) – *F 98, 1901, ca, d, wd, bos*

65. Game of Life, The
Unknown, 3/3, S, BC, 1900

1. The Game in Progress. – *d, wd*
2. The Game Lost. – *wd, ^*
3. The Game Won. – *wd*

66. Healing of the Daughter of Jairus, The
Willis, 6/6, S, f, BU, 1910

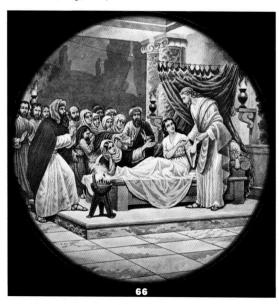

66

1. "The old man sunk upon his knees." – *s, wd, bos*
2. "He stood and taught the people." – *s, wd, bos*
3. "And murmured low, Master, my daughter!" – *wd, bos*
4. "She is not dead, but sleepeth." – *s, wd, bos*

67

5. "He moved the silken curtains silently apart." – *wd*
6. "And fixing her dark eyes full." – *wd, bos, ^*

67. Pilgrim's Progress[64]
Bunyan, 12/24, S, c, f, BC, 1896–97

2. Pilgrim Parting from his Family. – *s, wd, bos*
4. Pliable and Obstinate. – *s, wd, bos*
6. Worldly Wiseman. – *s, wd, bos*
8. Passion and Patience. – *s, wd, bos*
10. Christian Climbing the Hill of Difficulty. – *s, wd, bos*
14. The Valley of the Shadow of Death. – *wd, bos, ^*
15. Faithful Lifts Christian. – *s, wd, bos*
17. Death of Faithful. – *s, wd, bos*
18. River of Water of Life. – *wd, bos*
20. The Escape from Dungeon. – *s, wd, bos*
22. View of the Celestial City. – *s, wd, bos*
24. Ignorance Thrust into Hell. – *s, wd, bos*

68. Quo Vadis[65]
Sienkiewicz, 8/30, G, BC, f, 1898–99~

68

Roman Triumphal Procession. – *E 180, 1898, ca, wd*
Roman Forum under Nero. – *E 180, 1898, s, ca, wd, bos*
Vinicius embraces Lygia at Nero's Banquet. – *1899, s, ca, wd*
Ursus rescues Lygia. – *1899, s, ca, wd, bos*
Nero playing Lute while Rome burns. –
    E 180, 1898, s, ca, wd, bos, ^
Circus Maximus. – *F 64, BAC, 1899, ca, wd, bos*
Christian Martyrs awaiting death. – *BC, 1899, ca, d, bos*
"Quo Vadis, Domine?" – *BAC, 1899, s, ca, wd, bos*

69. Story of Other Wise Man[66]
(Fourth Wise Man, The)
Van Dyke, 36/40, S, f, BAC, 1908, 1911–12

1. Introduction. Drop Curtain – *UN, 1911–12, as*
2. Artaban welcomes his guests, the Magi. – *1911–12, wd*
3. Artaban and the Magi around Altar. – *1911–12, s, wd*
4. Artaban reading the Prophecy. – *1911–12, s, wd, bos*
5. Artaban shows three jewels to his friends. – *1908, s, wd, bos*
6. Three Magi in temple watching for star. – *1908, d, wd*

69

7. Artaban on his roof, beholds the star. – *1908, s, d, wd*
8. Artaban on horse speeding to place of tryst. – *1908, d, wd*
9. Artaban passing the sculptured rock. – *1911–12, wd*
10. Artaban dismounts to assist dying Jew. – *1908, s, wd, bos*
11. Artaban ministers to Jew and saves his life. – *1908, wd, bos*
12. The Jew tells Artaban where the Messiah. – *1911–12, wd, bos*
13. Artaban arrives at tryst and finds Magi gone. – *1908, wd*
14. Three Magi on camels guided by star. – *F 135, 1896–97, s, wd, bos*
15. Artaban sells his sapphire to buy camels. – *1908, s, wd*
16. Artaban journeys across dessert. – *1908, s, d ,wd*
17. The Magi arrives at Jerusalem. – *E 135, E 160, E 206, E 235, 1909, ca, d, wd*
18. Bethlehem. (by Night) – *F 135, 1911–12, ca, wd, bos*
19. Mary and Joseph arrive at Bethlehem. – *F 135, BU, 1908, s, ca, wd*
20. Woman in Bethlehem tells Artaban of Christ. – *1908, s, wd*
21. Adoration of the Magi. – *F 135, BU, 1895–97, ca, wd*
24. Artaban with ruby, bribes soldiers to spare child. – *1908, s, wd*
25. The Prayer of Artaban. – *1908, wd*
26. Artaban gazing at the Sphinx. – *1911–12, s, wd*
27. Artaban taking counsel with Rabbi. – *1911–12, s, wd*
28. Artaban feeding the hungry during famine. – *1911–12, s, wd*
29. Artaban assisting plague stricken victims. – *1908, wd*
30. Artaban visiting the captives in dungeon. – *1911–12, s, wd*
31. Artaban gazing at his pearl. – *1911–12, s, wd*
33. Artaban following multitude to Golgotha. – *1911–12, s, wd*
34. Artaban meets maiden about to be sold. – *1908, wd*
35. Artaban gives last jewel to ransom the maiden. – *1908, wd, bos*
37. Earthquake after the Crucifixion. – *1908, s, wd, ^*
38. Artaban fatally stricken supported by maiden. – *1908, s, wd*
39. The message from Heaven. – *1911–12, wd*
40. Artaban beholds the face of the King. – *1908, s, wd, bos*

70. Tabernacle in the Wilderness, The[67]
Dilworth, 2/10, S, UN, 1881–1920

1. Tabernacle – from model. – *1914–16, E 156, E 159, E 209, E 232, UN, ca, d*
3. High Priest in Linen Robes. – *BAC, wd*

Literature – Short Stories

71. Beauty and the Beast
Unknown, 1/8, S, GEH, 1914–16

8. The Beast Transformed into the Prince. – *wd, ^*

71

72. Bluebeard
Unknown, 1/8, S, GEH, 1914–16

3. Bluebeard Gives his wife Fatima the keys. – *wd*

73. Legend of Sleepy Hollow, The[68]
Irving, 6/6, S, f, GEH, 1910

1. Ichabod Crane, the Village Schoolmaster. – *wd*
2. Crane Relating Tales of Witchcraft. – *wd*
3. Crane Making Love to Katrina Van Tassel. – *wd*
4. Crane Dancing with Katrina. – *wd*

73

5. Crane Meeting the Headless Horseman. – *wd,* ^
6. Crane Pursued by the Headless Horseman. – *wd*

74. Little Match Girl
Anderson, 8/8, S, f, HRC, 1905

1. She tries in vain to sell her matches. – *s, wd, bos*
2. She strikes a match – Vision of warm stove. – *wd, bos*
3. She strikes another match – Vision of goose. – *wd, bos*
4. She strikes a third match – Vision of tree. – *wd, bos,* ^
5. She sees a vision of stars falling. – *UN, wd, bos*
6. Vision of Grandmother – She strikes the matches. – *wd, bos*
7. The Grandmother and child in sky. – *wd, bos*
8. The little match girl found frozen in the snow. – *wd, bos*

75. Man Without A Country, The[69]
Hale, 15/18, S, f, HRC, 1917

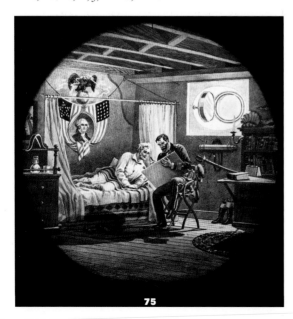

3. Aaron Burr captivates Nolan. – *wd, bos*
4. Nolan writing to Burr. – *s, wd, bos*
5. "I wish I may never hear of the United States." – *s, wd, bos*
7. Almost never allowed shore leave. (Old Ironsides) – *AN, F 31, 1891, wd, bos*
8. Nolan reading aloud. – *s, wd, bos*
9. He threw the book into the sea. – *s, wd, bos*
10. Mrs. Groff dances with Nolan. – *s, wd, bos*
11. Nolan takes charge of the gun. – *s, wd, bos*
12. The captain gives his sword to Nolan. – *s, wd, bos*
13. Nolan reading prayers. – *wd, bos*
14. Nolan interprets for the slaves. – *s, wd, bos*
15. "Pray God to bless that flag." – *wd, bos*
16. The shrine in Nolan's stateroom. – *UN, bos*
17. Nolan's death. – *s, wd, bos,* ^
18. Nolan's grave as he wished it to be. – *GEH, s, wd, bos*

76. Rip Van Winkle[70]
Irving, 6/6, S, c, f, RLM, 1881–93

1. Rip Playing with Children. – *wd, bos*
2. Rip at the Village Inn. – *wd, bos*
3. His Scolding Wife. – *wd, bos*
4. Rip on the Mountains. – *wd, bos*
5. Rip Returns Home. – *wd, bos,* ^
6. Rip Relating his Story. – *wd, bos*

Literature – Comic Sketches

77. Bridget's Dream[71]
No Author, 12/12, S, UN, 1910

1. Bridget falls asleep. – *s, wd, bos*
2. The clothes become animated. – *wd, bos*
3. Mr. Schurtz and Miss Robe dance. – *wd, bos*
4. Mr. Schurtz makes love to Miss Robe. – *wd, bos*
5. Mr. Schurtz asks Miss Robe's papa for her hand. – *wd, bos*
6. Miss Robe's papa kicks Mr. Schurtz out. – *wd, bos,* ^
7. Mr. Schurtz elopes with Miss Robe. – *wd, bos*
8. Miss Robe's papa runs after the lovers. – *wd, bos*
9. Mr. Schurtz and Miss Robe are married. – *wd, bos*
10. Miss Robe's papa forgives them. – *wd, bos*

77

78

11. They live happily ever after. – *wd, bos*
12. Bridget awakes from her dream. – *s, wd, bos*

78. How Jones Became A Mason[72]
No Author, 12/12, S, m, PR, 1891, 1905

1. Starting for the Lodge. – *1891, wd, bos*
2. At the Lodge Entrance. – *1905, s, wd, bos*
3. Preparing to Take Degree. – *1905, s, wd, bos*
4. The Oath of Secrecy. – *1891, wd, bos*
5. Riding the Goat. – *1891, wd, bos*
6. Climbing the Greased Pole. – *1905, s, wd, bos*
7. Tossed in a Blanket. – *1905, s, wd, bos, ^*
8. Running the Gauntlet. – *1905, s, wd, bos*
9. The Plunge into Water. – *1905, wd, bos*
10. Sitting on a hot Gridiron. – *1905, s, wd, bos*
11. Lowered into his Grave. – *1905, s, wd, bos*
12. Jones has Become a Mason. – *1891, wd, bos*

79. Mr. Spurt and His Auto[73]
No Author, 8/8, S, HFM, 1906

1. Mr. Spurt Buys an Automobile. – *s, wd*
2. He Gets Ready for a Ride. – *s, wd*
3. And Makes a fine Start. – *s, wd, ^*
4. Overtakes a Farmer in Market Wagon. – *wd*
5. And Passes Him in Great Style. – *wd*
6. Breaks Down in a Rain Storm. – *s, wd*
7. Farmer Comes up with Him. – *wd*
8. He Hires Farmer to Tow Him Home. – *s, wd*

80. Mr. Timorous and His Bull-Dog[74]
No Author, 12/12, S, AN, 1909

80

79

1. Mr. Timorous and wife are awakened. – *d, wd, bos*
2. They decide they must have a watch-dog. – *s, wd, bos*
3. A man brings a bull-dog. – *wd, bos*
4. Mr. Timorous buys dog. – *s, wd, bos*
5. The dog left outside house, howls all night. – *wd, bos*
6. The dog kept in house, howls all night. – *s, wd, bos*

7. Mrs. Timorous starts to go out. – *s, wd, bos*
8. Mr. Timorous comes home late at night. – *wd, bos*
9. He runs for his life to escape the dog. – *wd, bos*
10. He climbs into tree with dog after him. – *wd, bos,* ^
11. His cries attract neighbors. – *wd, bos*
12. Former owner of dog takes him away. – *s, wd*

81. Mrs. Casey and the Billy Goat
No Author, 12/12, S, AN, 1907

1. Mrs. Casey starts for church. – *s, wd, bos*
2. The goat makes a charge for her. – *s, wd, bos*
3. She holds the parasol in front. – *s, wd, bos*
4. She drops parasol and runs. – *s, wd, bos,* ^
5. Goat butts her in rear, she falls. – *s, wd, bos*
6. Officer O'Grady comes to her rescue. – *wd, bos*
7. He takes the goat by the horns. – *wd, bos*
8. The goat pushes him against watering trough. – *wd, bos*
9. Over he goes into the water. – *wd, bos*
10. He flounders in the trough. – *s, wd, bos*
11. And gets out on the other side. – *s, wd, bos*
12. The goat "holds the fort." – *s, wd, bos*

82. Paddy and His Pig[75]
No Author, 13/12, S, BC, 1905

1. Paddy buys a pig and starts for home. – *s, wd, bos*
1 v. Paddy and the Pig. – *UN, d, as*
2. Paddy takes a drop at the tavern. – *wd, bos*
3. Pig makes a bolt and Paddy falls. – *wd, bos*
4. Pig rushes into the kitchen. – *wd, bos*
5. Pig upsets the dinner table. – *wd, bos*
6. And frightens the housemaid. – *s, wd, bos*
7. As he comes out, Paddy stands in doorway. – *wd, bos*
8. Paddy is upset and has a ride on pig's back. – *s, wd, bos,* ^
9. Pig tumbles Paddy into a pond. – *s, wd, bos*
10. Pig gets into dog kennel. – *s, wd, bos*
11. Dog gets pig by the ear. – *s, wd, bos*
12. Paddy and his pig arrested. – *s, wd, bos*

83. Uncle Rastus and His Mule
No Author, 12/12, S, BC, 1906

1. Getting Ready to Plow. – *wd, bos*
2. Very Slow on the Start. – *wd, bos*
3. Mule Resents a Licking. – *wd, bos*
4. Mule Makes a Spurt. – *wd, bos*
5. Mule Sits Down Discouraged. – *wd, bos*
6. Uncle Rastus Coaxes Him with Switch. – *wd, bos*
7. Tries Putting Grass in His Ear. – *wd, bos*
8. Starts Again and Strikes a Stump. – *wd, bos,* ^
9. Mule Breaks Harness and Runs Away. – *wd, bos*
10. Uncle Rastus Throws Stone at Mule. – *wd, bos*
11. Mule Caught with Ear of corn. – *wd, bos*
12. Dinner horn blows – Mule Happy. – *wd, bos*

Religion – Hymns

84. Abide With Me[76]
Lyte, 12/10, S, c, f, m, BAC, 1894

1. Abide with me, fast falls the eventide. – *E 104, wd,* ^
2. When other helpers fail, and comforts flee. – *wd*
3. Swift to it's close ebbs out life's little day. (old man) –
   AN, wd
3 v. Swift to it's close ebbs out life's little day. (Last Supper) –
   wd
4. Change and decay in all around I see. –
   AN, 1891, ca, wd, bos
5. I need Thy presence every passing hour. – *wd*
6. Who like Thyself, my guide…can be? (Jesus) –
   E 256, E 257, wd
6 v. Who like Thyself, my guide. (Jesus with sheep) – *s, wd*
7. I fear no foe with Thee at hand to bless. – *BC, wd*

8. Where is death's sting? – *wd*
9. Hold Thou Thy cross before my closing eyes. – *wd*
10. Heaven's morning breaks. – *E 258, wd*

85. Calvary
Unknown, 3/12, S, BU, 1911–12

1. "The pilgrims throng thro' the city gates." – *wd, bos*
10. "The faithful shall hear His voice." – *wd, bos,* ^
11. (Refrain) "Come unto Me." (Peace, Peace) – *UN, d, bos*

86. Christmas Hymn, A
Dornett, 4/6, S, 1887~

1. "Had Rome been growing." – *UN, as*
2. "The Senator of haughty Rome." – *BC, wd,* ^
4. "How calm a moment may proceed." –
   E 104, E 135, BU, wd, bos
6. "For in that stable lay." – *UN, n, as*

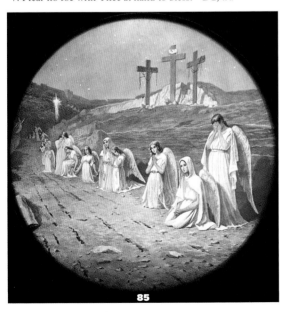

87. From Greenland's Icy Mountains[77]
(Missionary Hymn)
Heber, 12/12, S, f, m, BC, 1893

1. From Greenland's Icy Mountains. – *wd, bos,* ^
2. From India's coral strand. – *wd*
3. From many a… river. – *wd*
4. From many a palmy plain. – *wd, bos*
5. What though the spicy breezes Blow. – *wd, bos*
6. The Heathen in his blindness. – *wd*
7. Shall we, whose souls are lighted. – *wd*
8. Salvation, oh Salvation, The joyful sound. – *BAC, wd, bos*
9. Till each remotest nation has learned. – *BU, wd*
10. Waft, waft, ye winds his story. – *wd*
11. Till o'er our ransomed nature. – *BU, wd*
12. Redeemer, King, Creator. – *BAC, wd, bos*

88. God Be With You Till We Meet Again
Rankin, 5/5, S, BAC, 1899

1. "With his sheep securely fold you." – *BU, wd, bos*
2. Chorus – "Till we meet at Jesus' feet." – *s, wd, bos*
3. "Neath his wings securely hide you." – *s, wd*
4. "When life's perils which confound you." – *s, wd, bos,* ^
5. "Keep life's banner floating o'er you." – *s, wd*

89. Hold the Fort[78]
Bliss, 2/2, S, BC, 1902–03

First Verse and chorus. The Signal of Jesus. – *E 104, ca, wd, bos*
Second and third verses – The Victory. – *E 104, ca, wd,* ^

90. Holy City[79]
Adams, 14/12, S, BAC, f, 1899, 1902–03

2. "I stood in Old Jerusalem, beside the Temple." – *1899, wd*
3. "I heard the children singing." – *1899, s, wd, bos*
4. "Methought the voice of angels." (effect) – *E 91, 1899, wd, bos*
5. 1st chorus – "Jerusalem! Jerusalem!" – *E 91,1899, wd*
6. "Methought my dream was changed." – *1902–03, wd, bos*

7. "The sun grew dark with mystery." – *BU, 1899, wd*
8. 2nd Chorus–"Jerusalem!" (angels) – *E 252, 1902–03, wd, bos*
9. "I saw the Holy City beside the tideless sea." – *1899, wd*
10. "The light of God was in its streets." – *1899, s, wd*
11. "It was the new Jerusalem." – *1902–03, s, wd, bos*
12. 3rd Chorus – "Jerusalem! …" – *1902–03, wd, bos,* ^
12 v. 3rd Chorus. (angels playing trumpets) – *F 101, 1881–93, wd, bos*
v 1. "Tinge the cloud wreaths." – *F 50, 1899, wd, bos*
v 2. "Wings of Angles so might shine." (effect) – *F 50, 1899, wd, bos*

91. Jerusalem The Golden[80]
Neale, 4/4, S, f, BAC, 1891–1920

Angels Singing. (The Voice of Angels) – *F 90, BAC, 1899, wd, bos*

Angels playing harp. (Holy City – 1st Chorus) – *F 90, 1899, wd*
Angels kneeling before God. – *F 101, 1891, wd, bos*
Angels playing trumpets. *F 101, 1891–93, wd, bos, ^*

92. Jesus Lover of My Soul[81]

Wesley, 8/8, S, f, BU, 1902–03

1. "While the nearer waters roll." – *wd, bos, ^*
2. "Safe into the heaven guide." – *s, wd, bos*
3. "Leave, O leave me not alone." – *s, wd, bos*
4. "Cover my defenseless head." – *s, wd*
5. "Raise the fallen, cheer the faint." – *s, wd*
6. "False and full of sin I am." – *s, wd, bos*
7. "Let the healing streams abound." – *wd, bos*
8. "Freely let me take of thee." – *wd, bos*

93. Lead, Kindly Light[82]
Newman, 4/4, S, f

First Edition, BC, 1896–97?
1. "The night is dark and I am far from home." – *s, d, wd*
2. "I love to choose and see my path." – *d*
3. "O'er moor and fen, o'er crag and torrent." – *s, d, wd*
4. "And with the morn those angel faces smile." – *d*

Variant of First Edition, UN, 1896–97?
Slides: 1 – *s, bos*; 2 – *s, bos*; 3 – *s, bos, ^*, 4 – *s, bos*

"Second Edition", UN, 1897–1920
Slides: 1 – *wd*; 2 – *wd*; 3 – *wd*; 4 – *wd*

94. Let The Lower Lights Be Burning
Bliss, 4/4, S, UN, 1899

1. "Brightly beams our Father's mercy." – *s, wd, bos*
2. *Chorus* – "Let the lower lights be burning." – *s, wd, bos*

3. "Dark the night of sin has settled." – *s, wd, bos*
4. "Trim your feeble lamp, my brother." – *bos,* ^

95. My Mother's Bible[83]
Morris?/Williams?, M. B., 4/4, S, f, m, 1902–03

95

1. "When I stood at mother's knee." – *BC, s, wd, bos,* ^
2. *Chorus* – "Blessed book, precious book." – *AN, s, wd, bos*
3. "There she read of Jesus' love." – *BC, wd, bos*
4. "And I seek to do His will." – *WMAA, s, wd, bos*

96. Near The Cross[84]
Crosby, 4/4, S, UN, 1896–97

96

1. "Jesus keep me near the Cross." – *s, d, wd, bos*
2. "Near the Cross a trembling soul." – *s, d, wd, bos*
3. "There the bright and morning star." (effect) – *d*
4. "Bring its scenes before me." – *s, d, wd, bos*
5. "Till I reach the golden strand." – *s, d,* ^

97. Nearer My God To Thee[85]
Adams, 6/6, S, c, m, UN, 1895

97

1." E'en though it be a cross," – *wd, bos*
2. "My rest a stone." – *bos*
3. "Steps unto Heaven." – *bos,* ^
4. "Angels to beckon me." – *bos*
5. "Cleaving the sky." – *BAC, wd, bos*
6. "Nearer to Thee." – *BAC, wd, bos*

98. New Born King, The
Unknown, 5/10, S, f, 1901

3. "Lo! in a manger sleeping." – *F 135, BU, s, wd, bos*
4. "While o're his sleep a vigil keeping." – *F 104, UN, s, n,* ^
5. *First Refrain.*– "Glory to God, Hosanna sing!" – *BAC, wd*
6. "Jordan hushed her waters still." – *E 64, BU, ca, wd, bos*
10. "Glory to God, Hosanna sing." – *E 64, E 160, BAC, ca, d, wd, bos*

98

99. "Ninety and Nine"

Clephane, 10/10, S, f, BU, 1896–97

1. "There were ninety and nine." – *wd, bos*
2. "Away on the mountains wild and bare." – *wd, bos,* ^
3. "But the shepherd made answer." – *E 227, s, wd, bos*

4. "And altho' the road be rough and steep." – *wd, bos*
5. "How deep were the waters crossed." – *s, wd, bos*
6. "Ere he found his sheep that was lost." – *E 104, s, wd*
7. "Lord, whence are those blood drops?" – *s, wd, bos*
8. "Lord, whence are Thy hands so rent and torn?" – *s, wd, bos*
9. "There arose a glad cry to the gates of Heaven." – *s, wd, bos*
10. "Rejoice for the Lord brings back His own." – *s, wd, bos*

100. Onward Christian Soldiers

Barring-Gould, 4/4, S, f, BAC, 1899

1. "Onward Christian Soldiers, Marching as to war." – *E 228, s, wd*

2. "Like a might Army." – *E 228, wd, bos,* ^
3. "But the Church of Jesus Constant will remain." – *wd, bos*
4. "Blend with ours your voices In the triumph song." – *s, wd*

101. Rock of Ages[86]

Toplady, 14/18, S, m, 1887, 1891, 1906

Introduction. The Storm. – *UN, 1906, bos*

A. The Shipwreck. – *AN, 1891, wd, bos*
B. The Angry Sea. – *E 211, E 212, AN, 1887, wd, bos*
E. The Rock of Ages. – *E 211, E 212, UN, 1887, bos*
F. Simply to Thy Cross I cling. – *E 104, E 211, E 212, UN, 1887, bos*
G. Helping Hand. – *UN, 1887, bos*
H. Saved. – *UN, 1906, wd, bos,* ^
J. Angels Beckoning. – *UN, 1891, bos*
K. Angel Crowning Faith. – *UN, 1891, bos*
M. Ascension to Heaven. – *E 104, E 211, UN, 1891, bos*
N. The Golden Stairs and Pearly Gates. – *BAC, 1891, wd, bos*
O. Heaven. – *E 90, E 104, 1881–93, BAC, wd*
P. Safe in the Arms of Jesus. – *E 91, E 255, BAC, 1891, wd, bos*
Q. "All Hail the power of Jesus' Name." – *E 104, BU, 1906, wd, bos*

102. Tell Me The Old, Old Story

Hankey, 5/5, S, BAC, 1899

1. "Tell me the old, old story." – *s, wd*
2. *Chorus* – "Tell me the…story of Jesus." – *s, wd*
3. "That wonderful redemption, God's remedy." – *wd, bos*
4. "Remember! I'm the sinner." – *s, wd,* ^
5. "That the world's empty glory." – *UN, wd*

103. Throw Out The Life-Line

Ufford, 5/5, S, UN, 1899

1. "Throw out the life-line across the dark wave." – *s, wd, bos*
2. *Chorus* – "Throw out the life-line!" – *s, wd, bos*
3. "See! he is sinking! oh hasten to-day." – *E 104, s, wd, bos*
4. "Winds of temptation and billows of woe." – *s, wd, bos,* ^
5. "Haste then, my brother, no time for delay." – *s, wd, bos*

102

103

104. Illuminated Hymns[87]
Various Authors, 23/?, G, m, 1899 i

It came upon the midnight clear,
That glorious song of old,
From Angels bending near the earth,
To touch their harps of gold;
"Peace on the earth, good-will to men,
From heaven's all-gracious King:"
The world in solemn stillness lay
To hear the Angels sing.

Still through the cloven skies they come,
With peaceful wings unfurl'd;
And still their heavenly music floats
O'er all the weary world:
Above its sad and lowly plains
They bend on hovering wing,
And ever o'er its Babel sounds
The blessed Angels sing.

O ye beneath life's crushing load,
Whose forms are bending low,
Who toil along the climbing way,
With painful steps and slow!
Look now, for glad and golden hours
Come swiftly on the wing;
O rest beside the weary road,
And hear the Angels sing.

104

Abide with Me. – *F 84, BAC, 1894, wd*
America. – Goddess of Liberty. – *F 26, AN, 1894, ca, bos*

America (3 of 4 Verses)
America. 2[nd.] Rocks and rills. – *F 45, AN, 1908, d, wd, bos*
America. 3rd verse – Children singing. – *F 45, AN, 1893, wd*
America. 4th verse – Goddess of Liberty. –
    F 26, AN, 1894 ca, bos

Bringing in the Sheaves. – *F 151, BAC, 1895, wd*
Coronation: "All Hail the Power". – *F 101, BU, 1906, wd, bos*
From Greenland's Icy Mountains. – *F 115, MLCM, 1893, wd*
Hold the Fort. The Signal. – *F 89, BC, 1902–03, ca, wd, bos*
Hold the Fort. The Victory. – *F 89, BC, 1902–03, ca, wd, bos*
"In the Sweet Bye & Bye." – *F 101, UN, 1891, bos*
It came upon the midnight clear." – *F 86, BU, 1887, wd, bos, ^*
Jerusalem the Golden. – *F 90?, BAC, wd*
My Jesus as Thou Wilt. – *F 84, BAC, 1894, wd*
Ninety and Nine, The Lost Sheep. – *F 99, BU, 1896–97, s, wd*
O little Town of Bethlehem. – *F 135, BU, 1899, ca, wd, bos*
"Once in Royal David's City." – *F 98, UN, 1901, s, wd*
Rock of Ages. – *F 101, UN, 1891, bos*

Ring the Bells of Heaven. Jerusalem the Golden.
    – *F 101, BAC, 1881–93, wd, bos*
"Safe in Arms of Jesus." (on throne) – *F 101, BAC, 1891,*
    wd, bos
"Star Spangled Banner." – *F 58, AN, 1896–97, s, wd*
"Throw Out the Life-Line." – *F 103, UN, 1899, s, wd, bos*
Where is My Boy Tonight? – *F 201, AN, 1895, wd, bos*

Religion – Biography

105. Life of Luther
Unknown, 2/26, S, BAC, 1894 i

12. The death of Luther, 1546. – *BAC, 1894, wd, bos*
Luther in sight of Rome. – *BAC, 1910, wd, bos, ^*

106. Life of St. Paul[88]
Unknown, 25/36, S, f, BAC, 1899–1908~

105

106

1. Tarsus. – *wd*
2. Jerusalem.(?) – *BC, wd*
4. Conversion of Saul. – *E 156, 1899, ca, wd*
5. Damascus. – *E 204, GEH, wd, bos*
6. Saul's Escape from Damascus. – *1896–97, s, wd, bos*
8. Antioch. – *wd*
9. Elymas struck with Blindness. – *1905, s, d, wd*
10. Antioch in Pisidia. – *wd*
11. Paul and Barnabas at Lystra. – *1906, s, ca, d, wd*
13. Troas. – *wd*
14. Philippi. – *wd*
15. The Philippian Jailer. – *d, wd, bos*
17. Athens – Mars Hill. – *wd*
19. Corinth. – *wd*
20. Paul Making Tents at Corinth. – *1908, wd, bos*
22. Ephesus. – *wd*
26. Miletus. – *wd*
27. Rhodes. – *BC, wd*
29. Paul before Felix. – *E 159, 1899, s, ca, wd*
30. Paul before Agrippa. – *1908, wd, bos*
31. Paul Landing at Malta. – *1899, ca, d, wd, bos, ^*
34. Nero at Burning of Rome. – *F 68, BC, 1898, s, ca, wd*
35. Paul in Prison. – *E 156, 1906, ca, d, wd*
Paul Denouncing Paganism in Rome. – *UN, 1913, ca, d*
(Paul at Unknown Classical City.) – *wd*

107. Life of John Wesley
Unknown, 8/12, S, UN, 1905

2. Charter House School. – *n, bos*
3. Wesley and Club at Oxford. – *n, bos*
4. Wesley and the Moravians. – *n, bos*
6. The First Class Meeting. – *s, wd, bos*
8. Wesley and the Mob. – *n, bos*
9. Wesley at Gwennap Pit. – *n, bos*
10. Wesley Preaching in Double-decked Cottage. – *wd, bos*
11. Wesley on Horseback. – *s, wd, bos*

Religion – Bible Texts

108. Beatitudes, The
Bible, 10/10, S, f, BAC, 1899

108

1. Blessed are the poor in spirit. – *s, wd, bos*
2. Blessed are they that mourn. – *s, wd, bos*
3. Blessed are the meek. – *s, wd*
4. Blessed are they which do hunger and thirst. – *s, wd, bos, ^*
5. Blessed are the merciful. – *wd, bos*
6. Blessed are the pure in heart. – *s, wd*
7. Blessed are the peace makers. – *s, wd*
8. Blessed are they which are persecuted. – *s, wd*
9. Blessed are ye when men shall revile…you. – *s, wd, bos*
10. Rejoice and be exceeding glad. – *s, wd, bos*

109. Ecclesiastes[89]
Bible, 10/10, S, GEH, 1913

IN THE DAY WHEN THE KEEPERS OF THE HOUSE SHALL TREMBLE, AND THE STRONG MEN SHALL BOW THEMSELVES.

109

1. Remember Thy Creator. – *F 111, BAC, 1902–03, s, wd, bos*
2. While the evil days come not, etc. – *E 210, s, wd*
3. While the sun or the light, etc. – *E 210, wd*
4. In the days when the keepers, etc. – *E 210, s, wd,* ^
5. And the grinders cease, etc. – *E 210, wd*
6. And He shall rise up, etc. – *E 210, s, wd*
7. Also when they shall be afraid, etc. – *E 210, s, wd*
8. Because man goeth to his long home, etc. – *E 210, s, wd*
9. Or ever the silver chord be loosed, etc. – *E 210, wd*
10. Then shall the dust return, etc. – *E 210, s, wd*

110. First Psalm, The
Bible, 6/6, S, m, UN, 1905

1. "Blessed is the man that walketh not in the counsel of the ungodly." – *wd (?), n, as*
2. "But his delight is in the law of the Lord." – *E 156, s, wd*
3. "And he shall be like a tree planted by the rivers of water." – *bos*
4. "The ungodly are not so: but are like the chaff." – *E 156, s, wd,* ^
5. "Therefore the ungodly shall not stand in the judgment." – *BC, wd, bos*
6. "For the Lord knoweth the way of the righteous." – *s, wd*

111. Golden Bible Texts[90]
Bible, 13/12, S, BAC, 1902–03

A soft answer turneth away wrath. – *ca, wd*
Be thou faithful unto death. – *ca, wd, bos*
Cast thy burden upon the Lord. – *ca, wd, bos,* ^
Come unto me all ye that labor and are heavy laden. – *BU, s, ca, wd, bos*
Enter not into the path of the wicked. – *ca, wd*
Ho, everyone that thirsteth, come ye to the waters. – *ca, wd*
If thine enemy be hungry, give him bread to eat. – *ca, wd*
Lead me to the Rock that is higher than I. – *s, ca, wd*
Remember now Thy Creator. – *E 109, E 210, s, ca, wd, bos*
The Lord is thy keeper. – *s, ca, wd*
When thou passeth through the waters. – *s, ca, wd, bos*
Ye shall know them by their fruits. – *s, ca, wd*
Needle's Eye Gate. – *F 137, 1899, ca, wd*

111

112. Lord's Prayer, The
Bible, 7/7, S, BU, 1896–97

112

1. Our Father Who art in Heaven. – *d, wd*
2. Thy will be done. – *s, d, wd*
3. Give us this day our daily bread. – *d, wd*
4. Forgive us our debts. – *d, wd*
5. Lead us not into temptation. – *d, wd*
6. Deliver us from evil. – *wd*
7. Thine is the kingdom. – *s, wd,* ^

113. Palms, The
Bible, 5/6, S, f, BU, 1902–03

1. Around our way the Palm trees. – *wd, bos*
2. Jesus appears, He comes to dry our tears. – *wd,* ^
3. His voice is heard … – *as*
4. For light to all the world is given again. – *wd*

5. The children now sing the Redeemer's name. – *wd*
6. Hosanna! Glory to God! – *wd*

114. Psalm XXIII
(Twenty-third Psalm) *Bible, 6/6, S, f, BU, 1898*

1. "The Lord is my Shepherd, I shall not want." – *s, wd*
2. "He maketh me to lie down in green pastures." – *s, wd, bos*
3. "He restoreth my soul." – *s, wd, bos*
4. "Yea, 'though I walk through the valley . ..shadow of death." – *wd*
5. "Thou preparest a table before me." – *BAC, s, wd, bos*
6. "Surely goodness and mercy." – *E 156, BAC, wd, bos,* ^

115. Ten Commandments, The
Bible, 10/10, S, AN, 1896–97

1. "Thou shalt have no other Gods before Me." – *wd*
2. "Thou shalt not make … graven image." – *E 104, MLCM, s, wd*

3. "Thou shalt not take the name of the Lord." – *wd*
4. "Remember the Sabbath." – *wd*
5. "Honor thy father and thy mother." – *E 230, E 234, s, wd*
6. "Thou shalt not kill." – *F 118, BAC, ca, wd*
7. "Thou shalt not commit adultery." – *E 234, BU, wd*
8. "Thou shalt not steal." – *E 234, wd,* ^
9. "Thou shalt not bear false witness." – *E 234, wd*
10. "Thou shall not covet." – *E 234, s, wd*

Religion – Old Testament[91]

116. Creation of Earth[92]
Bible, 8/8, S, f?, BAC, 1907

Creation of Earth. Clouds and Darkness. – *E 210, ca, wd, bos*
Disturbance Indicating Formation. – *E 210, ca, wd, bos*

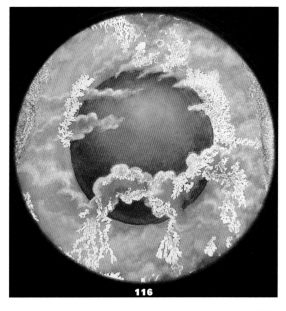

Clouds Take a Circular Form. – *E 210, ca, wd, bos*
Globe of Lava Appears. – *E 210, ca, wd, bos,* ^
Globe of Lava Gradually Cools. – *E 210, ca, wd, bos*
Appearance of Water. – *E 210, ca, wd, bos*
Indications of Land. – *E 210, ca, wd, bos*
The Continents Appear. – *E 210, ca, wd, bos*

117. Creation (of Life)★[93]
Bible, 11/16, G, f?, 1899~

Earth without Form. – *UN, ca*
Creation of Dry Land. – *E 210, UN, ca*
Creation of Grass and Trees. – *E 210, UN, ca*
Creation of Sun, Moon and Stars. – *E 156, E 159, E 210, BAC, 1901, ca, wd, bos,* ^
Creation of Fowls and Fishes. – *E 159, E 210, BAC, ca, d, wd*
Creation of Creeping Things and Beasts. – *E 156, E 159, E 210, UN, ca*
Creation of Adam. – *E 159, BAC, ca, d, wd*
Temptation of Eve. – *E 226, UN, 1900, ca*
Expulsion of Adam and Eve from Paradise. – *E 156, E 159, E 226, BAC, 1896–97, d, wd, bos*

Adam and Eve driven out of Eden. – *GEH, 1881–1920, wd, bos*
First Human Family. – *E 159, BAC, 1900, ca, d, wd*

118. Cain★
Bible, 4/9, G, f, BAC, 1900~

Cain Kills Abel. – *E 115, E 156, E 234, 1895–97, ca, wd,* ^
The Curse of Cain. – *1900, ca, wd, bos*
Cain Builds the First City. – *1900, ca, wd*
Three Tribes Descended From Cain. – *1900, ca, wd*

119. Noah★
Bible, 8/14, G, f, m, BAC, 1899–1900~

Wickedness of Man Before the Flood. – *E 156, E 204, 1900, ca, wd, bos*
Noah Building the Ark. – *E 226, 1899, ca, wd, bos*
Noah Entering the Ark. – *E 159, E 226, 1900, ca, d, wd, bos,* ^
Flood Destroying Man and Beast. – *E 156, E 159, 1895–97, ca, d, wd, bos*
The Ark on the Waters. – *E 214, E 226, 1900, ca, d, wd*
Interior of Ark. – *E 226, 1899, ca, d, wd*
Return of the Dove. – *E 226, 1895–97, ca, d, wd, bos*
Noah coming out of Ark. – *E 204, 1895–97, s, ca, d, wd*

120. Abraham and Sarah★
Bible, 9/14, G, c, f, m, 1895–1903~

Separation of Abraham and Lot. – *UN, 1902–03, ca*
Abraham's Journey to Canaan. – *E 156, BAC, 1910, ca, d, wd, bos*
Abraham and the Three Angels. – *E 156, BAC, 1895–97, ca, wd, bos*
Abraham, Sarah and 3 Angels. – *UN, 1895–97, ca, bos*
Sarah and the Angels. – *UN, 1900, ca, d*
Lot's Flight from Sodom. – *E 156, BAC, 1895–97, ca, d, wd*
Abraham Preparing for the Sacrifice. – *E 214, E 227, BAC, 1907, ca, d, wd, bos*
Abraham's Sacrifice. (Abraham offering Isaac) – *E 156, E 214, E 227, BAC, 1899, s, ca, d, wd, bos*
Abraham's Sacrifice. (Obedience) (without angels & ram) – *F 214, BAC, 1907, d, wd*

121. Jacob★

Bible, 5/9, G, c, f?, BAC, 1899–1903~

Esau sells his birthright. – *1917–20, s, d, wd, bos*
Isaac Blesses Jacob. – *E 156, 1899, ca, wd, bos*
Jacob Blesses his Twelve Sons. – *1902–03, ca, d, wd, bos*
Jacob Wrestling with Angel. – *E 204, 1895–97, ca, d, wd, bos,* ^
Jacob Going to Egypt. – *UN, 1902–03, ca*

122. Joseph★[94]

Bible, 12/23, G, c, f, BAC, 1895–1909~

The Chastity of Joseph. – *UN, 1909, ca*
Joseph Tending His Father's Flock. – *UN, 1899, s, ca, d*
Dreams of Joseph. – *E 156, 1895–97, ca, d, wd, bos,* ^
Joseph Thrown in a Well. – *1900, ca, wd, bos*
Joseph Interprets Dreams of … Baker. – *1899, s, ca, d, wd, bos*
Dreams of Pharaoh. (cattle) – *1881–1920, d, wd, bos*

Dreams of Pharaoh. (ears of corn) – *1881–1920, d, wd, bos*
Joseph Makes … Known. – *E 156, E 159, 1899, s, ca, d, wd, bos*
Cup Found in Benjamin's Sack. – *1895–97, ca, d, wd*
Joseph Denounces his Brothers as Spies. – *1914–16, ca, d, wd, bos*
Joseph Orders Simon Detained. – *1899, s, ca, wd, bos*
Joseph Selling Corn During Famine. – *1914–16, ca, d, wd, bos*

123. Moses★[95]

Bible, 32/37, G, c, f, BAC, 1895–1900, 1906–09, 1917–20~

Moses and Angel in Flaming Bush. – *E 156, E 204, GEH, 1895–97, ca, d, wd*
Burning Bush. (without Moses) – *F 204, GEH, 1896–97, d, wd*
Israelites in Egypt. – *E 156, E 159, UN, 1900, ca*
Moses and Reptile. – *1917–20, wd*
Reptile Disappears. – *1917–20, wd*
Moses' Rod Changes into a Serpent. – *E 204, UN, 1917–20, ca, d*
Moses' Hands Becomes Leprous. – *E 204, UN, 1917–20, ca, d*
Moses Slaying the Egyptians. – *1908, d, wd, bos*
Moses Hears Voice of God. (God Appears) – *E 204, 1917–20, ca, d, wd*
Plague of Murrain. – *1907, ca, d, wd, bos*
Plague of Darkness. – *1907, ca, d, wd, bos*
Angel of Passover. – *E 156, E 159, 1899, ca, d, wd, bos*
Moses and Aaron in Egypt. – *1908, s, d, wd, bos*
Moses and Aaron before Pharaoh. – *E 156, E 159, 1907, d, wd, bos*
Israelites Guided by Pillars of Fire. – *E 204, 1906, ca, d, wd*
Destruction of Pharaoh's Host. – *E 156, 1909, ca, d, wd, bos*
Song of Miriam. – *E 215, 1895–97, ca, d, wd, bos*
Israelites Receiving Manna. – *UN, 1899, ca*
Moses Receives Tables. – *E 156, E 214, 1902–03, ca, d, wd, bos,* ^
Moses Delivering Tables of Law. – *UN, 1895–97, ca, d*
The Golden Calf. – *F 124, 1894, s, ca, d, wd, bos*
Moses' hands held up by Aaron. – *E 156, 1914–16, ca, wd, bos*
Nadab and Abihu. – *F 124, 1894, s, ca, d, wd, bos*
Journeying to Canaan. – *F 124, 1894, s, ca, d, wd, bos*
Report of the Spies. – *F 124, 1894, s, ca, d, wd*
Moses Viewing the Promised Land. – *1908, s, ca, d, wd, bos*

Moses and The Brazen Serpent. – *F 124, 1894, s, ca, d, wd*
Balaam Stopped by Angel. – *1895–97, ca, d, wd, bos*
Death of Moses. – *1906, s, ca, wd, bos*
Joshua Commands the Sun. – *E 159, 1894, ca, d, wd, bos*
Joshua Sets Up a Great Stone. – *1914–16, ca, d, wd, bos*
Plague of Frogs. – *UN, 1917–20, ca, d, bos*

124. International Sunday School Lessons for 1895[96]
Bible, 22/26, G, f, BAC, 1894

124

The Golden Calf. – *E 123, E 156, s, ca, d, wd, bos*
Nadab and Abihu. – *E 123, s, ca, d, wd, bos*
Journeying to Canaan. – *E 123, E 156, E 159, s, ca, d, wd, bos*
Report of the Spies. – *E 123, E 156, E 204, s, ca, d, wd*
Moses and The Brazen Serpent. – *E 123, E 156, E 204, s, ca, d, wd*
New Home in Canaan. (Judah) – *E 204, s, ca, d, wd, bos*
Israelites Crossing the Jordan. – *E 232, s, ca, d, wd*
Fall of Jericho. – *E 156, s, ca, d, wd, bos*
Caleb's Reward. – *ca, d, wd, bos*
Cities of Refuge. – *s, ca, d, wd, bos*
Joshua Renewing the Covenant. – *E 156, s, ca, d, wd, bos*
Time of the Judges. – *E 156, s, ca, d, wd, bos*
Triumph of Gideon. – *E 156, s, ca, d, wd, ^*
Ruth's Choice. – *E 128, E 215, s, ca, d, wd, bos*
Child Samuel. – *E 130, s, ca, d, wd, bos*
Samuel The Judge. – *E 130, E 156, s, ca, d, wd, bos*
Saul Chosen King. – *E 130, E 156, s, ca, d, wd, bos*
Saul Rejected. – *E 130, s, ca, d, wd, bos*
Woes of Intemperance. – *s, ca, d, wd, bos*
David Anointed King. – *E 131, E 159, E 214, s, ca, d, wd, bos*
Goliath's Challenge to David. – *E 131, E 214, s, ca, d, wd, bos*
David and Jonathan. – *E 131, s, ca, d, wd, bos*

125. Story of Esther
Bible, 12/12, S, c, f, BAC, 1904~

1. King Ahasuerus Makes a Feast. – *wd, bos*
2. Queen Vashti Refusing to Obey. – *wd, bos*
3. Esther Espoused by Ahasuerus. – *E 212, wd, bos*
4. Mordecai Overhears Conspiracy. – *s, wd, bos*
5. The King Issues a Commandment. – *wd, bos*
6. Mourning of the Jews. – *wd, bos, ^*

125

8. The King Hearing the Records. – *wd, bos*
9. Triumph of Mordecai. – *E 156, wd, bos*
10. Esther accuses Haman. – *1883–84, wd, bos*
11. Haman Seized to be Hanged. – *wd, bos*
12. Jews Slaying their Enemies. – *s, wd, bos*
Esther Gleaning in the Fields of Boaz. – *wd*

126. Story of Daniel
Bible, 12/12, S, c, f, BAC, 1904~

1. Daniel and Companions. – *wd, bos*
2. Nebuchadnezzar Worships Daniel. – *wd, bos*
3. Dedication of Golden Image. – *s, wd, bos*
4. The Three Youths in Fiery Furnace. – *E 156, E 204, 1895–97, ca, d, wd, bos*
4 v. Children in Fiery Furnace. – *?, wd, bos, ^*
5. Nebuchadnezzar's Dream. – *wd, bos*
6. Daniel Interprets Dream of Nebuchadnezzar. – *E 156, E 159, wd, bos*

126

7. Feast of Belshazzar. – *E 156, E 204, UN, d, bos*
8. Daniel Made Governor. – *wd, bos*
9. Daniel at Prayer. – *wd, bos*
10. Conspiring Princes with Decree. – *s, wd, bos*
11. Darius Troubled About Daniel. – *wd, bos*

127. Story of Job
Bible, 8/8, S, BAC, 1914–16~

127

1. Messengers bring evil tidings to Job. – *s, wd, bos*
2. Job overcome by his grief. – *wd, bos*
3. Job and his friends. – *E 159, 1895–97, s, ca, wd, bos*
4. Eliphaz reproveth Job. – *s, wd, bos*
5. Elihu charges Job with presumption. – *s, wd, bos*
6. God out of whirlwind challenges Job. – *wd, bos, ^*
7. Job humbleth himself before God. – *s, wd, bos*
8. Job's friends are restored to him. – *s, wd, bos*

128. Story of Ruth
Bible, 8/8, S, c, f, BAC, 1914–16

1. Ruth and Naomi. (Ruth's Choice) – *F 124, 1894, s, ca, d, wd, bos*
2. Ruth in the fields of Boaz. – *E 212, E 215, GEH, s, wd, bos, ^*
3. Ruth favored by Boaz. – *E 212, 1883–84, wd, bos*
4. Ruth returns with her gleanings. – *s, d, wd, bos*
5. Ruth lying at the feet of Boaz. – *s, d, wd, bos*
6. Boaz gives Ruth six measures of barley. – *s, d, wd, bos*
7. Boaz redeems Naomi's land. – *d, wd, bos*
8. Ruth gives her son to Naomi to nurse. – *s, ca, d, wd, bos*

129. Samson★
Bible, 7/11, G, c, f, 1894–1906~

Mother of Samson. – *E 215, BAC, 1894, ca, d, wd, bos*
Samson and the Lion. – *UN, 1899, s, ca, d, bos*
Samson with Gates of Gaza. – *BAC, 1906, ca wd, bos*
Samson Slaying the Philistines. – *UN, 1891, ca, d, bos*
Samson and the Foxes. – *BAC, 1906, ca, d, wd, bos*
Samson in Prison. – *E 213, BAC, 1900, ca, d, wd*
Death of Samson. (Destroying Temple) – *E 156, E 159, UN, 1895–97, ca, d, bos, ^*

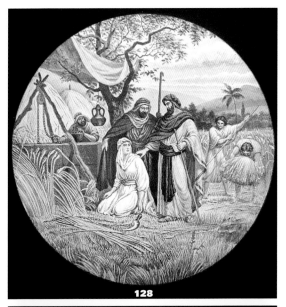

128

129

130. Samuel & Saul★[97]
Bible, 5/6, G, f, BAC, ?

Child Samuel. – *F 124, 1894, s, ca, d, wd, bos*
Hannah and Samuel. – *1900, s, ca, d, wd, bos*
Samuel The Judge. – *F 124, 1894, s, ca, d, wd, bos, ^*
Saul Chosen King. – *F 124, 1894, s, ca, d, wd, bos*
Saul Rejected. – *F 124, 1894, s, ca, d, wd, bos*

131. David★[98]
Bible, 16/19, G, c, f, m, BAC, 1906–16~

David the Shepherd Boy. – *E 214, 1908, ca, d, wd*
David Anointed King. – *F 124, 1895, s, ca, d, wd, bos*
Friendship of David and Jonathan. – *E 214, 1906, ca, wd, bos*
David and Jonathan. – *F 124, 1895, s, ca, d, wd, bos*
David Refusing Armor of Saul. – *E 214, 1911, s, ca, d, wd*
Goliath's Challenge to David. – *1911, s, ca, d, wd, bos*

David Chooses Stones from the Brook. – *E 214, 1914–16, s, ca, d, wd, bos*

David and Goliath. (throws stone) – *F 124, 1895, s, ca, d, wd, bos*

David slaying Goliath. – *E 156, E 214, 1909, ca, d, wd, bos, ^*

David with Head of Goliath. – *E 159, E 214, E 226, 1909, ca, d, wd, bos*

Saul Throws Javelin at David. – *E 214, 1914–16, ca, wd, bos*

Nathan Reproving David. – *1904, s, ca, d, wd*

Absalom entangled in the Oak (Death). – *E 157, 1900, ca, wd, bos*

King David Playing Harp. – *1917–20, ca, d, wd, bos*

David Fetched the Ark from Kirjath. – *E 156, 1900, s, ca, d, wd*

Hannah's Visit to Eli, the High Priest. – *1881–1920, wd, bos*

132. Captives in Babylon★[99]
Bible, 10/10, G, f, 1907–09~

Division of Tribes (Kingdoms) of Israel. – *F 156, BAC, 1914, s, ca, d, wd, bos, ^*

Three Tribes of Israel Led Captive. – *E 156, E 204, GEH, 1907, ca, d, wd*

Manassah Carried Captive to Babylon. – *F 156, BAC, 1914, s, ca, d, wd, bos*

Jerusalem as Destroyed by Nebuchadnezzar. – *E 156, UN, 1909, ca*

The Captives in Babylon. – *GEH, 1900, ca, d, wd*

Capture of Babylon. (Cyrus) – *F 204, GEH, 1895–97, ca, d, wd, bos*

Return of Captives of Babylon. – *F 204, GEH, 1913, ca, wd*

King Tiglath-Pileser sent tribes. – *F 156, BAC, 1914, wd, bos*

Isaiah sees Babylon Destroyed. – *E 156, E 204, BAC, 1910, ca, wd, bos*

Day of Judgment. Great Trumpet Shall Be Blown. – *BAC, 1914, ca, d, wd, bos*

133. Elijah★

Bible, 6/12, G, f, BAC, 1895–99~

Elijah Fed by Ravens. – *1899, ca, d, wd, bos,* ^
Elijah's Altar. – *1906, s, ca, d, wd, bos*
Elijah ascending to Heaven. – *E 156, 1895–97, ca, wd, bos*
Elisha and Widow's cruise. – *1911–12, ca, d, wd*
Naaman Healed of His Leprosy. – *1899, s, ca, d, wd*
Rebuilding the Temple. – *E 156, UN, 1895–97, ca, bos*

134. Jonah★[100]

Bible, 2/2, G, c, 1895–97(?)~

Jonah cast into the Sea. – *E 159, BAC, s, ca (?), d, wd*
Jonah cast forth by the whale. – *E 159, WAMA, ca (?), d, wd, bos,* ^

Religion – New Testament

135. Christmas★

Bible, 12/56, G, c, f, m, 1895–1908~

Zacharias and the Angel. – *E 160, BAC, 1899, s, ca, wd, bos*
Naming of John the Baptist. – *E 160, BAC, 1895–97, s, ca, wd*
Arrival of Mary and Joseph at Bethlehem. – *E 69, E 160, BU, 1908, s, ca, wd*
Birth of Christ No 1. Mary and Joseph. – *E 98, UN, 1895–97, s, ca, wd, bos*
Birth of Christ No 2. (angels appear) – *E 69, UN, 1895–97 (?), bos*
Bethlehem. (by Night) – *E 69, E 104, E 160, E 211, E 212, BU, 1899, ca, wd, bos*
Gloria in Excelsis. (How Calm) – *F 86, BU, 1886–87, wd, bos,* ^
Arrival of shepherds. – *E 206, E 228, BU, 1881–1920, wd*
Wise Men arriving … Jerusalem. – *F 69, BAC, 1909, ca, d, wd*
Wise Men Consulting Herod. – *F 64, BAC, 1895, s, wd, bos*
Magi Guided by Star. – *E 64, E 69, E 156, E 160, BU, 1896–97, s, d, wd, bos*
Adoration of Magi. – *E 69, E 206, E 235, BU, 1895–97, ca, wd*

136. Christ's Youth★[101]

Bible, 5/15, G, c, f, m, BU, ?

Jesus in Workshop. – *E 160, 1895–97, s, ca, d, wd, bos,* ^
On the way to Passover. – *F 160, 1915, s, d, wd*
On the way to Jerusalem. – *F 160, BU, 1915, s, ca, wd*
Jesus and Parents Going to Jerusalem. – *F160, BU, 1915, ca, d, wd, bos*
Jesus at the Temple Sacrifice. – *F 160, 1915, d, wd*

137. Christ's Ministry★[102]

Bible, 44/130, G, c, f, m, BU, 1895–99, 1909~

River Jordan. – *F 214, GEH, 1907, ca, wd*
Satan Asking Jesus to Make Bread of Stones. – *1906, s, ca, d, wd, bos*
Christ Tempted by Devil on Mountain Top. – *1910, ca, wd, bos*
Temptation of Christ on … Temple. – *1899, s, ca, d, wd, bos*
Angels Ministering to Christ. – *1910, ca, d, wd, bos*
John and Disciples See Jesus from Afar. – *UN, 1909, ca*

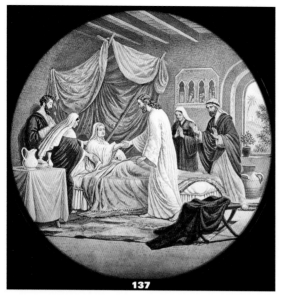

137

138

138. Calling the Disciples★[103]
Bible, 5/10, G, f, BU, 1906–09~

John the Baptist Before Herod. – *UN, 1909, ca*
Wedding at Cana. (water/wine) – *E 156, 1899, s, ca, d, wd, bos*
Christ and Nicodemus. – *E 156, 1895–97, s, ca, wd*
Jesus Preaching First Sermon. – *E 156, 1899, s, ca, d, wd*
Healing of Peter's Wife's Mother. – *1898, s, ca, d, wd, bos,* ^
Healing the Paralytic. – *E 156, 1899, s, ca, wd, bos*
Miraculous Draught of Fishes. – *1895–97, ca, d, wd*
Behold! the Lamb of God. – *E 211, 1895–97, ca, d, wd*
"Henceforth Thou Shalt Catch Men." – *1914–16, ca, d, wd*
Nathaniel under the fig tree. – *1906, s, ca, d, wd, bos*
Apostles collecting grain on Sunday. – *UN, 1895–97, ca, d, wd*
Healing the Centurion's Servant. – *1895–97, ca, d, wd, bos*
Calling the Disciples (See Set 138, below.)
The Raising of the Widow's Son of Nain. – *UN, 1881–1920, d, bos*
(Christ Healing.) – *1881–1920, s, wd*
(Christ Teaching by the Shore.) – *1881–1920, s, wd*
Christ and Fishermen. – *1914–16, ca, d, wd*
Christ Stilling the Storm. (Calming Waters) – *1895–97, ca, d, wd*
Demoniac of Gadara. – *UN, 1899, ca, d*
Jesus Curseth the Fig Tree. – *UN, 1900, ca, d*
Christ Sending Out…Disciples. – *E 156, 1895–97, ca, d, wd, bos*
Daughter of Herodias. – *UN, 1899, ca*
Christ, The Bread of Life. – *F 142, 1894, ca, d, wd, bos*
Christ taking disciples to high place – *GEH, 1881–1920, wd*
Transfiguration. – *F 142, 1894, ca, d*
They saw No Man…Save Jesus Only. – *1899, ca, wd, bos*
The Great Confession. – *F 142, 1899, s, ca, wd, bos*
Christ Healing the Lepers. – *E 156, 1895–97, s, ca, d, wd, bos*
The Good Samaritan. – *E 139, E 145, E 157, E 206, E 211, E 221, BAC, 1892, s, ca, wd*
Jesus Heals the Blind. (Sick) – *E 206, 1881–1920, s, ca, d, wd*
Christ and the Man Born Blind. – *F 142, 1894, ca, d, wd*
In the Needle's Eye Gate – *E 111, E 159, 1899, ca, wd*
Jesus in House of Mary and Martha. – *E 212, 1914–16, s, ca, wd*
Blind Bartimaeus. – *UN, 1899, ca, d*
Jesus eating with … Publicans. – *E 156, 1895–97, s, ca, d, wd, bos*
"Between us and you is a … gulf." – *E 143, 1895–97, ca, d, wd, bos*
Lazarus Sick at Bethany. – *BAC, 1899, s, ca, d, wd*
Zaccheus the Publican. – *F 142, 1894, s, ca, d, wd, bos*
(Christ in Cornfield.) – *1881–1920, wd*

Calling of Peter and Andrew. – *1906, ca, d, wd, bos*
Calling of Philip. – *1909, ca, d, wd, bos*
Calling of James & John. – *E 156, 1906, s, ca, d, wd, bos,* ^
Calling of Andrew and John. – *E 156, UN, 1909, ca, d*
Calling of Matthew. – *1895–97, ca, wd, bos*

139. Easter★
Bible, 25/144, G, c, f, BU, 1895–1909~

Christ and Tribute Money. – *1914–16, s, ca, d, wd, bos*
Christ Washing Apostles' Feet. – *1895–97, s, ca, d, wd, bos*
Garden of Gethsemane. – *E 206, 1891, ca, d, wd*
Christ's Prayer in the Garden. – *E 228, UN, 1909, ca, d*
Kiss of Judas. – *E 156, E 206, UN, 1892, ca, d, bos*
Peter's Denial of Christ. – *E 206, UN, 1891, ca, d, wd, bos*
Judas and the High Priests. (Selleth) – *1906, ca, wd, bos*

139

Judas Throwing Down the Blood Money. – *1902–03, s, ca, d, wd*

Judas Hangs Himself. – *1902–03, ca, d, wd, bos*

(Christ Blessing Disciples.*) – 1881–1920, wd*

Prayer after The Last Supper. – *E 156, E 206, 1917–20, d, wd, bos*

Simon the Cyrenean Helps Bear the Cross. – *E 206, 1906, s, ca, wd*

Jesus Nailed to the Cross. (Calvary) – *UN, 1906, ca, d*

Peter and John Running to Sepulcher. – *1906, ca, d, wd*

Three Marys at the Tomb. – *E 211, E 212, 1892, ca, wd, bos,* ^

Resurrection. – *F 142, 1894, ca, wd, bos*

Joseph of Arimathea Begs Body of Christ. – *1909, s, ca, d, wd*

Return from Calvary. – *1881–1920, s, d, wd, bos*

Resurrection. (dissolve/angels?) – *1895–97, ca, d*

Ascension of Christ. – *E 205, E 206, E 212, 1900, ca, d, wd*

"He Is Risen." – *UN, 1899, ca, d*

"And a Little Child Shall Lead Them." – *UN, 1906, ca*

Via Dolorosa. – *UN, 1909, ca, d*

Pilate Washing His Hands. – *E 206, 1906, ca, d, wd*

Incredulity of Thomas. (Doubting) – *E 206, 1895–97, ca, d, wd, bos*

140. Acts of the Apostles[104]
Bible, 8/15, S, f, BAC, 1899 i

140

Pentecost. – *E 156, 1895–97, ca, wd, bos*

Peter and John at the Beautiful Gate. – *E 156, 1906, s, ca, d, wd*

Death of Ananias. – *1906, s, ca, d, wd, bos*

Peter's Vision. – *E 156, 1899, ca, d, wd, bos,* ^

Phillip and the Eunuch. – *E 157, BAC, 1899, s, ca, d, wd*

Phillip Baptizes the Eunuch. – *UN, 1899, as*

Healing of Tabitha. – *1914–16, s, d, wd*

Angel Showing Jerusalem to John. – *E 156, 1895–97, ca, d, wd, bos*

141. Peter and Philip
Bible, 8/15, G, f, 1906–1920~

Peter and Risen Lord. – *F 142, BU, 1894, s, ca, d, wd, bos*

Christ's Charge to Peter. – *BU, 1906, s, ca, d, wd*

Peter's Healing of the Sick. – *BAC, 1914–16, d, wd, bos*

141

Peter Dictating Epistles. – *BAC, 1914–16, ca, d, wd*

Peter's Contrition for his Sin. – *GEH, 1881–1920, wd*

Peter and Malchus. – *UN, 1917–20, ca, d,* ^

Peter Meets High Priest. – *BAC, 1881–1920, wd*

Savior's Parting Words. – *F 142, BU, 1894, s, ca, d wd, bos*

142. International Sunday School Lessons for 1895 – First and Second Quarters[105]
(New Testament) *Bible, 12/28, S, BU, 1894*

John the Baptist Beheaded. – *BAC, ca, wd, bos*

Christ, The Bread of Life. – *E 137, ca, d, wd, bos*

The Great Confession. – *E 137, E 156, s, ca, wd, bos*

Transfiguration. – *E 137, E 156, ca, d, wd*

The Good Samaritan. – *F 137, BAC, 1892, s, ca, wd*

Christ and the Man Born Blind. – *E 137, E 144, E 156, ca, d, wd*

Zaccheus the Publican. – *E 137, E 156, s, ca, d, wd, bos,* ^

The Wicked Husbandmen. – *E 143, E 154, BAC, d, wd*

Watchfulness. – *E 143, E 228, BAC, s, ca, wd*

142

Resurrection. – *E 139, E 206, E 211, s, ca, d, wd, bos*
Peter and the Risen Lord. – *E 141, s, ca, d, wd, bos*
The Savior's Parting Words. – *E 141, E 156, s, ca, d wd, bos*

143. Parables of Christ[106]
Bible, 41/44, S, c, f, BAC, 1899~

143

1. The Wheat and the Tares. – *E 156, s, ca, wd, bos*
2. The Hidden Treasure. – *ca, d, wd, bos*
3. The Pearl of Great Price. – *E 159, 1895–97, s, ca, d, wd, bos*
4. The Net Cast into the Sea. – *UN, ca, d*
5. The Unmerciful Servant. – *E 153, ca, d, wd*
6. The Laborers in Vineyard. – *ca, d, wd*
7. The Two Sons. – *UN, ca*
8. Marriage of King's Son. (Garment) – *E 149, E 159, ca, wd, bos*
9. a. "The door was shut." (Wise & Foolish) – *E 155, ca, wd, bos*
10. The Talents. – *s, ca, wd*
11. The Sheep and the Goats. – *E 159, ca, wd, bos*
12. The Seed Growing Secretly. (Sower) – *UN, ca*
13. The Householder – Watchfulness. – *F 142, 1894, s, ca, wd*
14. The Two Debtors. – *s, ca, wd*
16. The Importunate Friend. – *ca, d, wd, bos*
17. The Rich Fool. – *E 156, 1895–97, s, ca, d, wd*
17. a. Death of Rich Fool. – *1895–97, s, ca, wd, bos*
18. Servants Watching – Return from Wedding. – *s, ca, wd*
19. The Wise Steward. – *s, ca, wd*
20. The Barren Fig Tree. (Unfruitful) – *ca, d, wd*
21. The Great Supper. "Come...things are now ready." – *ca, wd*
21. a. "The poor and maimed and blind and lame." – *UN, ca*
22. Tower – King Going to War. – *ca, d, wd*
23. The Lost Piece of Money. – *s, ca, d, wd*
24. The Prodigal Son. – *s, ca, wd, bos*
25. The Unjust Steward. (Unrighteous) – *ca, d, wd*
26. The Rich Man and Lazarus. (Beggar) – *E 156, ca, wd*
26. a. "Between us and you is a...gulf." – *F 137, 1895–97, ca, d, wd, bos*
27. Unprofitable Servants. – *ca, wd, bos*
28. The Unjust Judge. – *s, ca, wd*
29. The Pharisee and Publican. – *BU, 1895–97, ca, wd, bos*
30. The Pounds. – *1896–97, ca, wd*

31. House on Rock and on Sand. (Foolish Man) – *1898, s, ca, d, wd, bos*
32. The Leaven. – *ca, d, wd, bos*
33. The Lost Sheep. (Dark the Night) – *BU, s, ca, wd*
34. Candle Under a Bushel. – *s, ca, d, wd, bos*
35. New Cloth on Old Garment. – *s, ca, wd, bos*
36. New Wine in Old Bottles. – *s, ca, wd, bos, ^*
38. The Mustard Seed. – *UN, ca*
39. The Wicked Husbandmen. – *F 142, 1894, ca, wd*
40. The Fig Tree and All Trees. – *BU, ca, wd*

144. Story of the Blind Man, The
Bible, 8/8, S, f, BU, 1907

144

1. The blind man sitting by wayside begging. – *wd, bos*
2. Jesus sees him and sends him to Pool of Siloam. – *F 142, 1894, wd, os*
3. The blind man groping his way to the pool. – *s, wd*
4. He washes and his sight is restored. – *wd, bos, ^*
5. He arrives home; family and neighbors amazed. – *wd*
6. He is brought before council and questioned. – *s, wd*
7. He is cast out from council. – *s, wd*
8. He meets Jesus and worships Him. – *wd, bos*

145. Good Samaritan, The[107]
Bible, 8/8, S, f, m, BAC, 1896–97~

0. Man Going from Jerusalem to Jericho. – *E 214, E 221, wd, bos*
1. He Falls Among Thieves. – *E 214, E 221, wd, bos*
1 v. Man Lying Wounded. – *E 214, E 221, s, wd*
2 . The Priest Passes By on Other Side. – *E 214, s, wd*
3. The Levite Looks and Passes By. – *E 214, s, wd*
4. The Samaritan Binds Up His Wounds. – *F 137, 1892, s, ca, wd, ^*
5. And Sets Him on His Own Beast. – *E 214, s, wd, bos*
6. And Brings Him to an Inn, etc. – *E 214, E 221, s, wd, bos*

146. Good Shepherd, The[108]
Bible, 10/10, S, f, BU, 1907

1. He that entereth not by the door is a robber. – *wd, bos*
2. He that entereth by the door is the shepherd. – *s, wd, bos*

145

146

3. He calleth his own sheep by name. – *s, wd, bos*
4. He goeth before them, and the sheep follow him. – *s, wd, bos*
5. A stranger will they not follow. – *s, wd, bos*
6. The thief cometh not, but to destroy. – *wd, bos,* ^
7. The hireling fleeth, because he careth not. – *s, wd, bos*
8. The good shepherd giveth his life for the sheep. – *s, wd, bos*
9. Other sheep I have, which are not of this fold. – *s, wd, bos*
10. And I will give unto them eternal life. – *BAC, wd, bos*

7. "Go out quickly into the streets and lanes of the city." – *wd*
8. "Go out into the highways and hedges." – *wd*
9. The supper room filled. – *wd,* ^
10. "None of those bidden shall taste of my supper." – *wd*

147. Great Supper, The
Bible, 10/10, S, f, BAC, 1907

1. A certain man made a great supper. – *wd*
2. And sent his servant to announce supper. – *wd*
3. "I have bought a piece of ground." – *wd*
4. "I have bought five yoke of oxen." – *wd*
5. "I have married a wife." – *wd*
6. "The servant came and showed his lord these things." – *wd*

148. Laborers in the Vineyard[109]
Bible, 6/6, S, BAC, 1917–20

148

147

1. Householder hires laborers for vineyard early. – *E 204, s, wd,* ^
2. Laborers … hired the third hour. – *E 204, s, wd, bos*
3. Laborers hired the sixth hour. – *s, wd, bos*
4. More laborers hired the eleventh hour. – *s, wd, bos*
5. Householder orders steward to call the laborers. – *s, wd*
6. Laborers each paid a penny. – *s, wd*

149. Marriage of the King's Son

(Wedding Feast)
Bible, 11/10, S, f, BAC, 1907

149

1. A King made a marriage for his son. – *F 143, ca, wd, bos*
2. They would not come. – *1898, wd*
3. Again he sent for other servants. – *wd*
4. And the king was wroth. – *wd*
5. He sent forth his armies. – *wd*
6. Go into the highways. – *1898 (?), wd*
7. The wedding was furnished with guests. – *wd*
8. Man without a wedding garment. – *wd*
8 v. Man Who Had No Wedding Garment. – *BAC, 1898, wd*
9. He was speechless. – *wd, bos, ^*
10. Cast him out. – *wd, bos*

150. Prodigal Son, The[110]

Bible, 10/10, S, c, f, BAC, 1893~

150

1. He journeys to a far country. – *wd*
2. And there wastes his substance. – *wd*
3. He lives riotously. – *E 157, wd*
4. Until he has spent all. – *wd, bos*
5. He is sent into the fields to feed swine. – *wd*
6. He would fain fill himself with swine husks. – *wd, ^*
7. He returns to his father's house. – *wd*
8. His father has compassion on him. – *E 156, wd*
9. His return celebrated with … merry making. – *1902–03, s, wd*
10. The elder brother remonstrates with his father. – *1902–03, wd*

151. Sower, The

Bible, 6/6, S, f, BAC, 1895

151

1. A sower went forth to sow. – *wd*
2. Some fell by the wayside. – *wd*
3. Some fell on stony places. – *wd*
4. Some fell among thorns. – *wd*
5. Others fell in good ground. – *E 104, 1895, wd*
6. And brought forth fruit, etc. – *s, wd, ^*

152. Talents, The

Bible, 8/8, S, f, BAC, 1907

1. The Talents Delivered to the Servants. – *s, wd, bos*
2. Trading with the Talents. – *s, wd, bos*
3. Hiding Talent in the Ground. – *s, wd*
4. The Return of the Master. – *wd, ^*
5. The Servants' Account Shown. – *wd, bos*
6. The Master's "Well done." – *wd*
7. The One Talent in Napkin. – *s, wd*
8. The Wrath of the Master. – *s, wd, bos*

152

153

153. Unmerciful Servant, The
Bible, 6/6, S, f, BAC, 1908

1. Have patience with me. – *F 143, 1899, ca, d, wd,* ^
2. Pay me that thou owest. – *s, d, wd*
3. And cast him into prison. – *s, d, wd*
4. And came and told their lord. – *d, wd*
5. I forgave thee all that debt. – *d, wd*
6. And delivered him to the tormentors. – *s, d, wd*

154. Wicked Husbandmen, The[111]
Bible, 8/8, S, f, BAC, 1906

154

1. A Certain Man Planted a Vineyard. – *s, d, wd*
2. Husbandmen Beating Servant. – *F 142, 1894, d, wd,* ^
3. Another Servant Wounded with Stones. – *s, d, wd, bos*
4. Another Servant Killed by Husbandmen. – *s, d, wd, bos*
5. Lord of the Vineyard Sends His Son. – *d, wd*
6. Husbandmen Plotting Against the Son. – *d, wd, bos*

7. Body of Son Cast out of Vineyard. – *s, d, wd, bos*
8. Wicked Husbandmen Destroyed. – *d, wd*

155. Wise and Foolish Virgins
Bible, 8/8, S, f, BAC, 1904

155

1. Ten virgins going to meet the bridegroom. – *s, wd*
2. While the bridegroom tarried they all slumbered. – *E 156, s, wd*
3. And at midnight there was a cry made. – *s, wd*
4. Then all the virgins arose, and trimmed their lamps. – *s, wd*
5. And the foolish said unto the wise, Give us your oil. – *wd, bos*
6. But the wise answered saying, Not so. – *UN, d*
7. And while they went to buy, the bridegroom came. – *s, wd*
8. Afterward came also other virgins. – *F 143, 1888–89, ca, wd, bos,* ^

Religion – Miscellaneous

156. Bible Story in Pictures, The[112]
Stebbins, 89/158, S, 1914 i

156

Creation of Sun, Moon and Stars. – *F 117, BAC, 1901, ca, wd, bos*
Creation of Creeping Things and Beasts. – *F 117, UN, 1899, ca*
Expulsion of Adam and Eve from Paradise. – *F 117, BAC, 1896–97, d, wd, bos*
Cain Slaying Abel. – *F 118, BAC, 1895–97, ca, wd*
Wickedness of Mankind Before the Flood. – *F 119, BAC, 1900, ca, wd, bos*
Flood Destroying Man and Beast. – *F 119, BAC, 1895–97, ca, d, wd, bos*
Abraham's Journeying to Canaan. – *F 120, BAC, 1910, ca, d, wd, bos*
Abraham and Three Angels. – *F 120, BAC, 1895–97, ca, wd, bos*
Lot's Flight from Sodom. – *F 120, BAC, 1895–97, ca, d, wd*
Abraham's Sacrifice. – *F 120, BAC, 1899, ca, d, wd, bos*
Isaac Bless Jacob. – *F 121, BAC, 1899, ca, wd, bos*
Dreams of Joseph. – *F 122, BAC, 1895–97, ca, d, wd, bos*
Joseph Makes Himself Known (Reveals Himself) to his Brethren. – *F 122, BAC, 1899, s, ca, d, wd, bos*
Israelites in Egypt. – *F 123, UN, 1900, ca*
Moses and the Burning Bush. – *F 123, GEH, 1895–97, ca, d, wd*
Moses and Aaron before Pharaoh. – *F 123, BAC, 1907, d, wd, bos*
Angel of Passover. – *F 123, BAC, 1899, ca, d, wd, bos*
Pharaoh's Host Drowning. – *F 123, BAC, 1909, ca, d, wd, bos*
Moses' hands held up by Aaron and Hur. – *F 123, BAC, 1914–16, ca, wd, bos*
Moses Receives Law Tables – *F 123, BAC, 1902–03, ca, d, wd, bos*
The Golden Calf. – *F 124, BAC, 1894, s, ca, d, wd, bos*
The Tabernacle in the Wilderness. – *F 70, UN, 1914–16, ca, d*
Report of the Spies. – *F 124, BAC, 1894, s, ca, d, wd*
Moses and Brazen Serpent. – *F 124, BAC, 1894, s, ca, d, wd*
Journeying to Canaan. – *F 124, BAC, 1894, s, ca, d, wd, bos*
Fall of Jericho. – *F 124, BAC, 1894, s, ca, d, wd, bos*

Joshua Renewing Covenant. – *F 124, BAC, 1894, s, ca, d, wd, bos*
Time of the Judges. – *F 124, BAC, 1894, s, ca, d, wd, bos*
Triumph of Gideon. – *F 124, BAC, 1894, s, ca, d, wd*
Samson Destroys the Temple. – *F 129, UN, 1895–97, ca, d, bos*
Samuel The Judge. – *F 124, BAC, 1894, s, ca, d, wd, bos*
Saul Chosen King. – *F 124, BAC, 1894, s, ca, d, wd, bos*
David Slaying Goliath. – *F 131, BAC, 1909, ca, d, wd, bos*
David Brings Ark to Jerusalem. – *F 131, BAC, 1900, s, ca, d, wd*
David the Psalmist. – *F 114, BAC, 1898, wd, bos*
Solomon's Temple. – *F 209, UN, ca*
Division of Tribes of Israel. – *E 132, BAC, s, ca, d, wd, bos*
Sacrifice to Moloch. – *E 159, BAC, ca, wd*
Asa Destroying the Idols. – *BAC, s, ca, d, wd, bos*
Jehosaphat Establishes Courts of Justice. – *UN, as*
Elijah Ascending to Heaven. – *F 133, BAC, 1895–97, ca, wd, bos*
Three Tribes Carried into Captivity. – *E 132, GEH, 1907, ca, d, wd*
Isaiah sees Babylon Destroyed. – *F 132, BAC, 1910, ca, wd, bos*
Manassah Carried Captive. – *E 132, BAC, s, ca, d, wd, bos*
The Samaritans. (The ungodly are like the chaff ...) – *F 110, UN, 1905, s, wd*
Jerusalem Destroyed and the Jews Carried Captive. – *F 132, UN, 1909, ca, wd*
Daniel interprets Nebuchadnezzar's Dream. – *F 126, BAC, 1904, wd, bos*
Three Hebrews in Fiery Furnace. – *F 126, BAC, 1904, wd, bos*
Feast of Belshazzar. – *F 126, UN, 1904, d, bos*
King Cyrus issues a Proclamation. – *E 159, E 204, BAC, ca, wd, bos*
Rebuilding the Temple. – *F 133, UN, 1895–97, ca, d, bos*
Triumph of Mordecai. – *F 125, BAC, 1904, wd, bos*
Dedication of the Walls of Jerusalem. – *BAC, s, d, wd, bos,* ^
Simon the Just Compiling the Old Testament. (But his delight is in the law) – *F 110, UN, 1905, s, wd*
Death of Eleazer Maccabaeus. – *E 233, GEH, d, wd*
Pompey Makes Judea a Roman Province. – *UN, as*
Magi Following the Star. – *F 135, BU, 1896–97, s, d, wd, bos*
The Magi Before Herod. – *F 64, BAC, 1895, s, d, wd, bos*
Jesus and parents going to Jerusalem. – *F 160, BU, 1915, ca, d, wd, bos*
Calling of John and Andrew. – *F 138, UN, 1909, ca, d*
Wedding at Cana. – *F 137, BU, 1899, s, ca, d, wd, bos*
Christ and Nicodemus. – *F 137, BU, 1895–97, s, ca, wd*
Jesus Preaching at Nazareth. – *F 137, BU, 1899, s, ca, d, wd*
Calling of James and John. – *F 138, BU, 1906, s, ca, d, wd, bos*
Healing the Paralytic. – *F 137, BU, 1899, s, ca, wd, bos*
Jesus eating with Publicans and Sinners. – *F 137, BU, 1895–97, s, ca, d, wd, bos*
Parable of the Tares. – *F 143, BAC, 1899, s, ca, wd, bos*
Sending Out The Apostles. – *F 137, BU, 1895–97, ca, d, wd, bos*
The Great Confession. – *F 142, BU, 1894, s, ca, wd, bos*
The Transfiguration. – *F 142, BU, 1894, ca, d*
The Good Samaritan. – *F 137, BAC, 1894, s, wd*
Parable of The Rich Fool. – *F 143, BAC, 1895–97, s, ca, d, wd*
The Prodigal Son. (Swineherd) – *F 150, BAC, 1892, wd*
The Prodigal Son – The Return. – *F 143, BAC, 1892, wd*
The Man Born Blind. – *F 142, BU, 1894, ca, d, wd*
The Rich Man. (Lazarus) – *F 137, BAC, 1895–97, ca, d, wd, bos*
Christ Healing...Lepers. – *F 137, BAC, 1895–97, s, ca, d, wd, bos*
Zaccheus the Publican. – *F 142, BU, 1894, ca, d, wd, bos*
The Ten Virgins. – *F 155, UN, 1904, d*
Prayer after The Last Supper. – *F 139, BU, 1917–20, d, wd, bos*
Kiss of Judas. – *F 139, UN, 1892, ca, d, bos*
"Ecce Homo!," "Behold the Man!" – *F 64, UN, 1895, bos*
Savior's Parting Words. – *F 142, BU, 1894, s, ca, d, wd, bos*
Pentecost. – *F 140, BAC, 1895–97, ca, wd, bos*
Healing the Man at the Gate. – *F 140, BAC, 1906, s, ca, d, wd*
Conversion of Saul. (Paul) – *F 106, BAC, 1899, ca, wd*

Vision of Peter. – *F 140, BAC, 1899, ca, d, wd, bos*
Paul in Prison. – *F 106, BAC, 1906, ca, d, wd*
An Angel Shows John the New Jerusalem. – *F 140, BAC, 1895–97, ca, d, wd, bos*

157. Catholic Catechism★[113]
Unknown, 4/148+, G, BAC, ?

2. Philip and Eunuch. – *F 140, BAC, 1899, s, ca, d, wd*
113. Absalom entangled in Oak – *F 131, 1900, ca, wd, bos,* ^
140. He lives riotously. – *F 150, 1892, wd*
148. The Samaritan Binds Up His Wounds. – *F 137, 1892, s, wd*

158. Jewish Life[114]
Unknown, 26/26, S, BAC, 1917–20 i

1. Balthazar in Desert. – *F 64, 1895, s, wd, bos*

2. Meeting of the Wise Men. – *F 64, 1894, s, wd, bos*
3. Joppa Gate, Time of Christ. – *F 64, 1895, s, wd, bos*
4. Wise Men conferring with Herod. – *F 64, 1895, s, wd, bos*
5. Adoration of the Wise Men. – *F 135, 1895–97, ca, wd*
6. Judean Garden Scene. – *F 64, 1894, s, wd, bos*
7. Interior of Judean Home – Balcony. – *F 64, 1894, s, wd, bos*
8. On the Housetops in Jerusalem. – *F 64, 1894, wd, bos*
9. Travelers at the Fountain. – *F 64, 1895, wd, bos*
10. Roman General…to War. – *F 180, BC, 1894, ca, d, wd, bos*
11. A Galley Slave Pleading For Mercy. – *F 64, 1894, s, wd, bos*
12. A Roman Galley Interior. – *F 64, 1906, s, wd, bos*
13. A Roman Sea Fight. – *F 64, 1895, s, wd, bos*
14. A Visit to a Roman Nabob. – *F 64, 1894, s, wd, bos*
15. Oriental Beauty Protected. – *F 64, 1895, s wd, bos*
16. A Roman Gambling Party. – *F 64, 1895, wd, bos*
17. An Egyptian Princess. – *F 64, 1895, s, wd, bos,* ^
18. Training Horses for Chariot Races. – *F 64, 1895, s, wd, bos*
19. Overthrow–Roman Chariot Race. – *F 64, 1895, d, wd, bos*
20. A Wrestling scene in Rome. – *F 64, 1894, s, wd, bos*
21. Discovery of Prisoners in Dungeon. – *F 64, 1894, s, wd, bos*
22. View of Jerusalem, Time of Christ. – *F 64, 1895, wd, bos*
23. The Sleeper Discovered on Door Steps. – *F 64, 1895, s, wd, bos*
24. Provisions Brought to Lepers. – *F 64, 1894, wd, bos*
25. Meeting of Old Friends. – *F 64, 1895, s, wd, bos*
26. Interior of Jewish Home in Jerusalem. – *F 64, 1894, wd, bos*

159. Photodrama of Creation, The[115]
International Bible Students' Assoc., 36/366, S, BAC, 1914 i

Creation of Sun, Moon and Stars. – *F 117, 1901, ca, wd, bos*
Creation of Fowls and Fishes. – *F 117, 1899, ca, d, wd*
Creation of Creeping Things and Beasts. – *F 117, UN, 1899, ca*
Creation of Adam. – *F 117, 1899, ca, d, wd*
Expulsion of Adam and Eve. – *F 117, 1896–97, d, wd, bos*
First Human Family. – *F 117, 1900, ca, d, wd*
Noah Entering the Ark. – *F 119, 1900, ca, d, wd, bos*
Hell. – *F 245, PR, 1895–97, ca, wd,* ^
Flood Destroying Man and Beast. – *F 119, 1895–97, ca, d, wd, bos*
Destruction of Sodom. (Flight) – *F 120, UN, 1895–97, ca, d, wd*

Job's Adversity and Restitution. (Job and his Friends) – *F 127, 1895–97, s, ca, d, wd, bos*

Joseph and His Brethren. (Known) – *F 122, 1899, s, ca, d, wd, bos*

Israelites in Bondage. – *F 123, UN, 1900, ca*

Moses and Aaron before Pharaoh. – *F 123, 1907, d, wd, bos*

Eating the Passover. – *F 123, 1899, ca, d, wd, bos*

The Typical Tabernacle. – *F 70, UN, 1914–16, ca, d*

Israelites Entering Canaan. – *F 124, 1894, s, ca, d, wd, bos*

Joshua's Long Day. (Joshua Commands Sun) – *F 123, 1895–97, ca, d, wd, bos*

David Anointed by Samuel. – *F 124, 1894, s, ca, d, wd, bos*

Goliath Beheaded by David. – *F 131, 1909, ca, d, wd, bos*

Hauling Temple Timbers. (Cedars) – *F 204, UN, 1914–16, s, bos*

The Temple of the Lord. – *F 209, UN, 1914–16, ca, wd*

King Solomon's Sacrifice. (Temple) – *F 204, 1914–16, ca, wd, bos*

The Temple Consecrated. (Glory) – *F 204, 1914–16, ca, d, wd, bos*

Jerusalem Desolated 70 Years. – *F 204, GEH, 1894, s, wd, bos*

Nebuchadnezzar's Dream Interpreted. – *F 126, 1904, wd, bos*

King Cyrus issues Proclamation. – *F 156, 1914–16, ca, wd, bos*

Enters "The Hell Belly." (Jonah) – *F 134, 1895–97, s, ca (?), d, wd*

Resurrection Prefigured – Matt.12:40. (Jonah cast forth) – *F 134, WAMA, 1895–97, ca (?), d, wd, bos*

The Pearl of Great Price. – *F 143, 1895–97, s, ca, d, wd, bos*

Marriage of the King's Son. – *F 143, 1899, ca, wd, bos*

Sheep and Goats Parable. – *F 143, 1899, ca, wd, bos*

Moloch Prototype of Torment Deity. (Sacrifice to Moloch) – *F 156, 1914–16, ca, wd*

The Needle's-Eye Gate. – *F 137, BU, 1899, ca, wd*

St. Paul before Felix. – *F 106, 1899, s, ca, wd*

Socialism Prefigured by Samson. (Death of Samson) – *F 129, UN, 1895–97, ca, d, bos*

160. Story of the Very First Christmas, The[116]
Wilder, 13/35, S, BU, 1915 i

Zacharias and the Angel. – *F 135, BAC, 1895–97, s, ca, wd, bos*

Naming John the Baptist. – *F 135, BAC, 1895–97, s, ca, wd*

Mary and Joseph arriving at Bethlehem. – *F 135, 1908, s, ca, wd*

The Angel Host. – *F 98, BAC, 1901, ca, d, wd, bos*

160

Wise Men Following the Star. – *F 135, 1896–97, s, d, wd, bos, ^*

Wise Men arriving in Jerusalem. – *F 69, BAC, 1909, ca, d, wd*

Wise Men Before Herod. – *F 64, BAC, 1895, s, wd, bos*

Star Stood Over … Young Child. (Bethlehem) – *F 135, 1899, ca, wd, bos*

Jesus in Workshop of Joseph. – *F 136, 1899, s, ca, d, wd, bos*

Who Led Caravan? (To Jerusalem) – *E 136, 1915, s, ca, wd*

Holy Family, Camped for Night. (On the way to Passover) – *E 136, 1915, s, d, wd*

Jesus and parents going to Jerusalem. – *E 135, E 156, 1915, ca, d, wd, bos*

Boy Jesus Watching Temple Sacrifice. – *E 136, 1915, d, wd*

161. Miscellaneous Religious Slides★
No Author, 9/?, G, BAC, 1881–1920

161

Paul's Sight Restored. – *d, wd, bos*

Just Judge. – *wd*

Musicians. – *wd*

Herod's Temple. – *wd, bos*

High Priest. – *wd*

Jerusalem Destroyed by Titus. – *UN, bos, ^*

Herod's Daughter with Head of John the Baptist. – *UN, d*

Death of St Joseph. – *UN, d*

Golden Age. (The wolf shall lie down) – *1909, s, ca, d, wd*

History – American[117]

162. Americana★ (Misc.)[118]
No Author, 20/27, G, c, f, AN, 1893–1903~

Allegorical Picture, "Let us have Peace." – *E 19, E 222, E 223, 1894, wd*

American Eagle on Shield. – *E 225, 1881–1920, d, wd*

American Flag. (6, 6 v 1, 6 v 2) – *F 26, GEH, 1893, wd*

American and British Flags. – *GEH, 1881–1920, wd, bos*

Barbara Freitchie. – *MLCM, E 18, E 223, E 243, 1886, ca, wd, bos*

Columbia Mourning for Loss of Maine. – *F 188, BC, 1898, s, wd, bos*

162

"Gloria Mundi" – Columbia and Britannia. – *1899, s, wd*
"Hail Columbia." – *E 243, 1894, ca, wd*
Naval Hero. (Columbia and Dewey) – *UN, 1899, bos*
Old Glory: Sailor with Flag. – *MLCM, E 243, 1895–97, ca, wd, ^*
Origin of the American Flag. (composite) – *1917–20, wd*
Our Banner in the Sky. – *E 45, 1899, wd*
Our Martyred Presidents. – *BC, 1902–03, wd, bos*
"Rally 'Round the Flag." – *E 56, 1899, s, wd, bos*
"Remember the Maine." (ship/slogan) (dissolve?) – *AMPAS, 1899, s, wd, bos*
Uncle Sam. – *1899, d, bos*
Volunteer's Departure. – *E 223, 1888–89, wd, bos*
Volunteer's Return. – *E 223, 1888–89, wd, bos*
White Man's Burden. – *PR, 1909, wd, bos*
Yankee Doodle. – *F 63, 1902–03, s, wd, bos*

163. Early Period, 1492–1542+
No Author, 5/13, G, f, AN, 1899–1903~

163

Landing of Norsemen in America, 1002. – *1917–20, d, wd, bos*
Discoveries of the Cabots, 1497. – *HRC, 1902–03, wd, bos, ^*
Ponce de Leon discovering Florida, 1512. – *PR, 1902–03, s, d, wd*
Balboa Discovering the Pacific, 1513. – *HRC, 1899, wd, bos*
Burial of DeSoto, 1542. – *HRC, 1894, wd, bos*

164. Colonial Period, 1607–1698+
No Author, 18/43, G, f, AN, 1899–1903~

164

Landing at Jamestown, 1607. – *1883–84, wd*
Smith Rescued by Pocahontas. – *E 173, E 224, MLCM, 1881–1920, wd, bos*
Landing of Hendrick Hudson, 1609. – *1885, wd, bos*
The Mayflower at Sea. – *E 222, E 223, 1891, wd, bos*
Purchase of Manhattan, 1626. – *PR, 1906, s, wd, bos*
The March of Miles Standish. – *E 1, GEH, 1885, d, wd, bos*
John Alden and Priscilla at Seaside. – *F 1, 1908, s, wd, bos*
First Thanksgiving, 1631. – *MLCM, 1902–03, wd, bos*
Settlement of New Hampshire, 1637. – *1902–03, s, wd*
Settlement of Delaware, 1637. – *HRC, 1902–03, wd*
Last Fight of the Pequods, 1637. – *BC, 1902–03, s, wd, bos, ^*
Marquette on the Mississippi, 1673. – *BC, 1899, s, wd*
Death of King Philip, 1676. – *NBMAA, 1902–03, wd, bos*
Discussion of Charter at Hartford, 1687. – *BC, 1902–03, s, wd, bos*
Destruction of Schenectady, 1690. – *BC, 1902–03, wd, bos*
Trial for Witchcraft, 1692. – *1899, s, wd, bos*
Execution of Bridget Bishop, 1692. – *1899, s, wd, bos*
Expedition Against St Augustine, 1702. – *1902–03, s, wd*

165. French and Indian War, 1754–1760+
No Author, 4/10, G, f, 1896–1901~

Franklin's Experiment with kite, 1752. – *E 175, UN, 1901, s, wd*
First tone of the Liberty Bell. – *AN, 1896–97, s, d, wd, bos*
General Wolfe Climbing the Heights of Abraham, 1759. – *E 181, HRC, 1899, s, wd, bos*
Boston Tea Party, 1773. – *MLCM, 1881–93, wd, ^*

165

166

167

166. Revolution, 1775–1783+

No Author, 27/48, G, c, f, m, AN, 1881–1920

Battle of Lexington, 1775. – *E 222, E 223, E 230, 1893, wd, bos*
Struggle on Concord Bridge. – *E 35, UN, 1881–1920, d, wd*
Putnam Leaving the Plow, 1775. – *1881–1920, s, wd, bos*
Capture of Ticonderoga, 1775. – *1881–1920, wd, bos*
The Spirit of 1776. – *E 230, MLCM, 1881–1920, wd, bos*
Betsey Ross showing Flag. – *E 171, 1899?, wd, bos*
v. Betsey Ross showing Flag. (elaborate house) – *UN, 1899?, as*
Evacuation of Boston, 1776. – *1885, s, wd, bos*
Sergeant Jasper at Fort Moultrie, 1776. – *E 171, 1899, d, wd, bos*
Daniel Boone Rescuing Daughter, 1776. – *HRC, 1899, s wd, bos*
Battle of Long Island, 1776. – *1881–1920, wd, bos*
Battle of Harlem Plains, 1776. – *1899, wd, bos*
Execution of Nathan Hale, 1776. – *1899, s, wd, bos,* ^
Battle of Trenton, 1776. – *1885, wd, bos*
Battle of Princeton, 1777. (Flag of Brave) – *F 26, UN, 1891, d*
Gen. Muhlenburg showing his uniform. 1776. – *1917–20, wd, bos*
Surrender of Burgoyne, 1777. – *1881–1920, wd, bos*
Moll Pitcher at Monmouth. – *E 222, E 223, 1881–1920, wd, bos*
Capture of Stony Point, 1779. – *E 222, 1881–1920, wd, bos*
Benj. Franklin in his garden. – *1906, bos*
British Evacuating New York, 1783. – *1902–03, s, wd, bos*
Arrival of Lewis & Clark, Columbia River, 1803. – *1906, BC, wd*
Transfer of Louisiana to United States, 1803. – *1906, s, wd*
Decatur's Conflict at Tripoli, 1804. – *HRC, 1885, wd, bos*
Duel Between Burr and Hamilton, 1804. – *RBC, 1899, s, wd, bos*
Celebration of Louisiana Purchase, 1804. – *UN, 1881–1920, s, wd*
First Steamboat, 1807. – *MLCM, 1894, wd*

167. War of 1812 +

No Author, 10/12, G, f, AN, 1902–07~

British impressment of American seamen, 1812. – *1907, s, wd, bos*
Commander Perry at Lake Erie, 1813. – *E 223, PR, 1891, s, wd*

Attack on Privateer General Armstrong, 1814. – *1902–03, wd, bos*
Destruction (Burning) of Washington by British, 1814. – *RBC, 1902–03, s, wd, bos,* ^
Attack on Fort McHenry, 1814. – *UN, 1902–03, wd, bos*
Treaty of Ghent, 1814. – *1881–1920, wd, bos*
Opening of the Erie Canal, 1825. – *1907, wd*
First Railroad Train, 1830. – *E 170, UN, 1894, s, wd*
Defense of the Alamo, 1836. – *MLCM, 1899, s, wd, bos*
Santa Anna a prisoner, 1835. – *MLCM, 1902–03, wd, bos*

168. Mexican War, 1846–1848+

No Author, 6/9, G, f, AN, 1902–08~

Fremont placing Flag on Mt. Peak. – *HRC, 1902–03, wd, bos,* ^
Battle of Buena Vista, 1847. – *HRC, 1891, d, wd, bos*
Scott Entering Mexico, 1848. – *1891, d, wd, bos*
Discovery of Gold in California. – *K-MOMI, 1902–03, s, wd*
Westward Ho. – *K-MOMI, E 245, 1902–03, ca, wd*
Old Pony Express. – *BC, 1908, s, wd*

168

169. Civil War, 1861–1865+
No Author, 16/54, G, c, f, m, BC, 1881–1903~

169

John Brown on way to Execution, 1859. – *PR, 1886, d, wd*
Bombardment of Fort Sumter, 1861. – *E 222, E 223, E 225, 1895, wd, ^*
Battle of Bull Run, 1861. – *1881–1920, d, wd*
Siege of Vicksburg, 1863. – *E 185, 1885, wd, bos*
Battle of Gettysburg, 1863. – *E 222, UN, 1891, d, bos*
v 1. Battle of Gettysburg, 1863. – *E 222, GEH, 1881–1920, wd, bos*
v 2. Battle of Gettysburg, 1863. – *AN, 1881–1920, wd*
Battle of Lookout Mountain, 1863. – *1881–93, wd*
Siege of Petersburg, 1864. – *1881–1920, wd, bos*
Farragut at Mobile Bay. – *UN, 1886, d, bos*
Sheridan's Ride, 1864. – *E 39, AN, 1888–89, wd, bos*
Capture of Jeff. Davis, 1865. – *1885, wd*
Soldier's Dream of Home. (effect dissolve) – *1881–1920, wd*

Last stand, U.S. Scouts attacked by Indians. – *AN, 1902–03, s, wd*
Assassination of Garfield, 1881. – *F 184, AN, 1882, wd, bos*

170. Transportation★
No Author, 4/4, G, f?, UN, 1881–1920

170

Old Canal Boat. – *UN, 1917–20, d, ^*
Highwaymen. – *PR, 1881–93, wd*
First Railroad Train, 1830. – *F 167, UN, 1894, s, wd*
Traveling in Olden Time. – *F 245, AN, 1895–97, ca, wd*

171. Origin of U. S. Flag
Unknown, 12/16, S, f, GEH, 1917–20 i

1. Liberty and union flag. – *wd*
2. Red pine tree flag. – *wd, ^*
3. Blue pine tree flag – *wd*
4. White pine tree flag. – *wd*
5. Yellow rattlesnake flag. – *wd*
6. Rattlesnake flag – red and white stripes. – *wd*

171

7. Blue flag with crescent. – *wd*

8. Sergeant Jasper at Fort Moultrie. – *F 166, AN 1899, d, wd, bos*

10. Grand union flag. – *wd*

12. Betsey Ross making flag. – *F 166, AN, 1899, wd, bos*

13. Flag with 13 stars and stripes. – *F 223, wd*

16. Flag today. – *GEH, 1917–20, wd*

172. U.S. Flags, Miscellaneous★
No Author, 7/7, G, GEH, 1881–1920

1777 American Flag. – *wd*
Bunker Hill Flag. – *wd*
Confederate Flag. – *wd*
Flag. (3 vertical stripes with boxed cross in center) – *wd*
Flag. (3 horizontal stripes, white on top) – *wd*
Flag. (Irish/Eng)? (2 quadrants of 3 lions each.) – *wd*
Texas Flag. (big star with stripes) – *wd*

173. Passing of the Indian, The[119]
Unknown, 1/70, G, 1902–03 i

173

Smith Rescued by Pocahontas, 1607. – *F 164, MLCM, 1881–1920, wd, bos,* ^

History – Biography

174. Life of Columbus
Unknown, 2/12, S, f, 1902–03

6. Columbus subdues mutiny of the crew. – *HRC, wd, bos*
11. Columbus explaining eclipse to natives. – *HRC, bos,* ^

175. Life of Benjamin Franklin[120]
Unknown, 9/13, S, f, UN, 1902–03~

1. Young Franklin learning the tallow chandler's trade. – *d, wd*
2. Franklin working in his brother's printing office. – *s, d, wd*
3. Franklin's first arrival in Philadelphia. – *s, d, wd*
4. Franklin in printing office in London. – *s, d, wd*

174

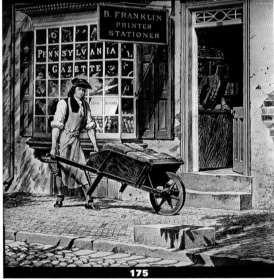

175

5. Franklin acting as his own porter. – *d, wd,* ^
6. Franklin and wife at their frugal breakfast. – *as*
7. Franklin's experiment with the kite. – *F 165, 1901, s, d. wd*
11. Franklin speaking in Constitutional Convention. – *s, d, wd*
12. Last moments of Benjamin Franklin. – *d, as*

176. Life of Lincoln[121]
Unknown, 12/24, S, f, m, RBC, 1898 i

1. Birthplace of Lincoln. – *s, wd*
2. Lincoln on Flat Boat. – *s, wd*
4. Lincoln's Debate with Douglas. – *s, wd*
5. Lincoln Raising Flag on Independence Hall. – *s, wd*
6. Lincoln's First Inauguration. – *s, wd*
7. Lincoln Visiting Hospital. – *s, wd*
9. Speech at Gettysburg. – *s, wd*
10. Lincoln's Visit To Richmond. – *s, wd*
11. Assassination, – *1881–1893, wd*
Lincoln Studying by fire light. – *1917–20, s, wd*

176

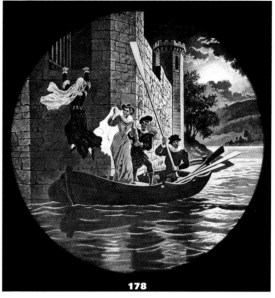

178

Lincoln Splitting Fence Rails. – *1917–20, s, wd,* ^
Lincoln at New Orleans Slave Market. – *1917–20, s, wd*

177. Life of Washington [122]
Unknown, 4/24, S, f, AN, 1888–91~

177

4. Washington at Fort Duquesne, 1758. – *RBC, 1891, d, wd, bos*
5. Washington Taking Command, 1775. – *1891, d, wd, bos*
Washington as Surveyor, 1748. – *NBMAA, 1888–89, s, wd,* ^
Washington as Laborer. (Farmer) – *UN, 1881–1920, bos*

178. Life of Mary, Queen of Scots [123]
Unknown, 12/12, S, f, UN, 1891 i

2. Interview with John Knox. – *E 181, bos*
3. Mary Stuart and her secretary. – *E 181, bos*
4. Death of Rizzio, 1556. – *F 181, 1888–89, d, bos*
5. Surrender of Mary Stuart. – *F 181, 1888–89, bos*
6. Signing her Abdication. – *E 181, bos*
7. Escape from Loch Leven. – *E 181, d, bos,* ^

8. Mary Stuart at the battle of Langside. – *E 181, bos*
9. Mary's interview with Elizabeth. – *F 181, GEH, 1888–89, wd, bos*
10. Elizabeth signing death warrant. – *F 181, 1888–89, bos*
Mary Stuart's first view of Rizzio, 1563. – *E 181, GEH, 1887, wd*
11?. Death Warrant read to Mary. – *E 181, GEH, 1891, wd, bos*
Mary Queen of Scots aboard ship. – *1881–1920, bos*

History – General

179. Seven Ancient Wonders of the World [124]
Unknown, 7/7, S, f, m, UN, 1894

The Pyramids of Egypt. – *E 218, d, wd*
Mausoleum of Artemisia. – *s, d, wd*
Temple of Diana. – *d, wd*

179

Wall and Hanging Gardens of Babylon. – *E 204, wd,* ^
The Colossus of Rhodes. – *s, wd*
Statue of Jupiter Olympus. – *wd*
The Pharos of Alexandria. – *d, wd*

180. Greek/Roman/European History★
No Author, 11/227, G, f, BC, 1898–1900~

180

Battle of Marathon. – *1899, s, ca, wd, bos*
Caesar Crossing the Rubicon. – *1895–97, s, ca, wd, bos,* ^
Nero at burning of Rome. – *F 68, 1898, s, ca, wd, bos*
Regulus Leaving Rome for Carthage. – *E 64, E 158, 1894, ca, d, wd, bos*
Roman Forum under Nero. – *F 68, 1898, s, ca, wd, bos*
Roman Emperor's Triumph. – *F 68, 1898, ca, wd*
Death of Frederick Barbarossa, 1190. – *1899, wd, bos*
Gutenberg showing first proof, 1450. – *UN, 1888–89, wd*
Era of the Reformation, 1510. – *UN, 1900, wd*
Execution of Protestants in Netherlands, 1573. – *UN, 1899, bos*
Death of Gustavus Adolphus at Lutzen, 1632. – *1898, wd, bos*

181. English/Irish History
No Author, 42/342, G, 1894–99, 1917–20~

Landing of Romans, 55 BC. – *K-MOMI, 1899, s, d, wd, bos*
Massacre of Druids, 61 AD. – *BC, 1917–20, d, wd, bos*
St. Augustine before Ethelbert, 597. – *UN, 1917–20, d, bos*
King Canute and his Courtiers, 1017. – *K-MOMI, 1899, wd, bos*
Death of William Rufus, 1100. – *K-MOMI, 1899, d, wd, bos*
Richard I pardons Robin Hood, 1194. – *E 233, BC, 1913, s, wd*
Battle of Stirling, 1297. – *PR, 1899, s, d, wd, bos,* ^
Battle of Bannockburn, 1314. – *PR, 1899, d, wd, bos*
Wat Tyler Killing the Tax Collector. – *BC, 1917–20, d, wd, bos*
Death of Wat Tyler, 1381. – *UN, 1892, wd*
Surrender of Margaret at Tewksbury, 1471. – *K-MOMI, 1899, s, d, wd, bos*
Battle of Flodden Field, 1513. – *PR, 1899, s, d, wd, bos*
The Field of the Cloth of Gold, 1520. – *E 182, BC, 1881–93, wd, bos*
Miracle Play in Coventry, 1525. – *BC, 1917–20, d, wd, bos*
Death of Rizzio, 1556. – *E 178, UN, 1888–89, d, bos*

181

Mary Stuart Leaving France, 1561. (aboard ship) – *F 178, UN, bos*
Knox's interview with Mary Stuart, 1561. – *F 178, UN, 1891, bos*
Mary Stuart and her Secretary, 1562. – *F 178, UN, 1891, bos*
Mary Stuart's first view of Rizzio, 1563. – *F 178, GEH, 1887, wd*
Surrender of Mary Stuart, 1567. – *E 178, UN, 1888–89, bos*
Mary Stuart signing her abdication, 1567. – *F 178, UN, 1891, bos*
Mary Stuart Escaping Loch Leven, 1568. – *F 178, UN, 1891, d, bos*
Mary Stuart at Battle of Langside, 1568. – *F 178, UN, 1891, bos*
Interview between Mary Stuart and Queen Bess, 1587. – *E 178, GEH, 1888–89, wd, bos*
Elizabeth signing death warrant of Mary. – *E 178, UN, 1888–89, bos*
Death warrant read to Mary, 1587. – *F 178, GEH, 1891, wd, bos*
Queen Bess knighting Drake, 1589. – *BC, 1917–20, d, wd, bos*
Harvey demonstrating circulation of blood. – *UN, 1917–20, d, wd*
Great fire in London, 1666. – *BC, 1899, s, wd, bos*
Siege of Limerick, 1691. – *E 234, BC, 1891, wd, bos*
Battle of Culloden, 1746. – *BC, 1894, s, wd, bos*
Wolfe climbing heights of Abraham, 1759. – *F 165, PR, 1899, s, wd, bos*
Trial of Robert Emmett, 1803. – *UN, 1891?, bos*
Execution of Roger Emmett, 1803. – *BC, 1891, d, wd, bos*
Duchess of Richmond's Ball, 1815. – *BC, 1902–03, s, wd, bos*
Trial of Daniel O'Connell, 1844. – *BC, 1894, wd, bos*
Massacre of English by Sepoys 1857. – *PR, 1899, d, wd, bos*
Boers Going to War, 1899. – *F 192, PR, 1902–03, s, wd, bos*
Boer horsemen going into battle. – *F 192, PR, 1900, s, wd, bos*
Boers under Gen. Kock resisting attack at Elandslaagle, 1899. – *F 192, PR, 1902–03, s, wd, bos*
British Lancers cutting off retreat of Boers at Elandslaagle, 1899. – *F 192, PR, 1900, s, wd, bos*
Coronation of Edward VII, 1902. – *BC, 1917–20, wd, bos*

182. French History
No Author, 16/187, G, BC, 1896–99~

Massacre of the Sicilian Vespers, 1282. – *1899, s, wd, bos*
Burning of Jacques de Molay, 1314. – *1899, s, wd*

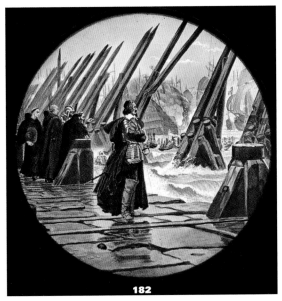

182

184

Death of Charles the Bold, 1477. – *1899, wd, bos*
The Field of the Cloth of Gold, 1520. – *F 181, 1881–93, wd, bos*
Queen Catherine urging Charles IX to sign decree for
    Massacre of St Bartholomew, 1572. – *1891, d, wd, bos*
Massacre of the Huguenots, the Morning After. – *UN,
    1906, bos*
Assassination of Henri III, 1589. – *1888–89, d, wd, bos*
Assassination of Henri IV, 1610. – *1899, wd, bos*
Richelieu at siege of Rochelle, 1628. – *1899, d, wd, bos,* ^
Mob returning from Versailles with King, 1789. – *1902–03,
    s, wd, bos*
Louis XVI and mob at Tuilleries, 1792. – *1885, wd, bos*
Death of Princess Lamballe, 1792. – *1917–20, wd, bos*
Fête of Reason, 1793. – *1899, wd, bos*
Dantonists on the way to Guillotine, 1794. – *1896–97, d,
    wd, bos*
"The Old Guard" at Waterloo, 1815. – *UN, 1906, d, wd, bos*
Execution of Maximilian, 1867. – *HRC, 1899, wd*
Louis VI Ball. – *PR, 1881–1920, s, wd*

183. Miscellaneous Flags ★
No Author, 1/27, G, GEH, 1906

Norway Flag. – *wd*

History – Current Events

184. Life of Garfield[125]
No Author, 1/12, S, AN, 1882 i

Assassination of Garfield, 1881. – *E 169, wd, bos,* ^

185. Life of U. S. Grant
Unknown, 11/12, S, f, BC, 1887 i

2. Lieutenant Grant Aiming a Canon. – *HRC, wd, bos*
3. Capture of Fort Donelson. – *1881–1920, wd*
4. Major-General Grant's Charge at Shiloh. – *wd*
5. Siege of Vicksburg. – *F 169, 1885, wd, bos*
6. Grant's Triumphal Entry into Vicksburg. – *PR, wd, bos*
7. Capture of Petersburg, Va. – *wd, bos*
8. Surrender of Lee. – *E 223, E 225, 1881–1920, wd, bos*

185

9. Taking the Oath; Second Inauguration. – *HRC, wd, bos*
11. Death-bed of Grant. – *HRC, wd, bos*
Allegory: "Let us have Peace." – *HRC, 1887, wd,* ^
Grant's Funeral Car. – *HRC, 1888, wd*

186. Life of McKinley
Unknown, 12/12, S, f, AN, 1902–03 i

1. Birthplace of McKinley, Niles, Ohio. – *wd, bos*
2. Young McKinley enlisting as private, 1861. – *wd*
3. Lieut. McKinley leading rescue of guns, 1863. – *s, wd, bos*
4. McKinley presenting his tariff bill, 1890. – *s, wd, bos*
5. McKinley speaking in campaign for Harrison, 1892. – *wd,
    bos,* ^
6. Inauguration of McKinley as President, 1896. – *wd, bos*
7. McKinley and Cabinet discussing War. – *F 189, 1899,
    wd, bos*
8. The signing of the Protocol, 1898. – *F 189, PR, 1899,
    wd, bos*
9. McKinley's Last Speech, Buffalo, Sept. 5, 1901. – *s, wd, bos*

186

188

10. The shooting of McKinley, Sept. 6, 1901. – s, wd, bos
11. Mrs. McKinley's last interview with her husband. – s, wd, bos
12. Body of McKinley lying in state at Washington. – wd, bos

187. Destruction of St. Pierre★ (Martinique Disaster)
No Author, 2/2, S, BC, 1902–03

187

Destruction of St. Pierre, Martinique by volcano, May 1902. – wd
Destruction of St. Pierre No 2, People Fleeing. – s, wd, bos, ^

188. Maine Disaster[126]
No Author, 4/4, G, f, m, 1898–99~

Maine in Havana Harbor. – E 223, 1898, UN, bos
Explosion of Maine at Havana. – E 222, 1898, UN, as, ^
Court Inquiry on Maine Disaster. – AMPAS, 1906, wd

Columbia Mourning Loss of Maine. – E 162, 1899, BC, s, wd, bos

189. Spanish-American War, 1898[127]
No Author, 49/46, G, c, f, m, AMPAS, 1899~

McKinley & Cabinet Discussing Spanish Question. (War) – E 186, wd, bos
Capture of First Naval Prize, April 22. – wd, bos
American Fleet Before Havana Harbor, April 22. – UN, s, wd, bos
Bombardment of Matanzas, April 27. – wd, bos
Firing the 13 inch Gun at Mantanzas. – s, wd, bos
Admiral Dewey's Victory at Manila, May 1. – s, wd, bos
Admiral Dewey Directing Movements of Fleet. – s, wd, bos
Destruction of Spanish Fleet at Manila. – E 222, UN, bos
Surrender of Spanish Fort at Cavite. (?) – s, wd
Death of Ensign Bagley on the Winslow, May 11. – s, wd, bos
Bombardment of San Juan, Puerto Rico, May 12. – wd, bos
Embarkation of U.S. Troops for Cuba. – 1900, s, wd, bos

189

Hobson on Bridge of Merrimac, June 3. – *s, wd, bos*
Merrimac Under Fire from the Spanish Guns. – *wd*
Sinking of the Merrimac. – *wd, bos*
v. Sinking of the Merrimac. – *UN, as*
Hobson's Rescue by Admiral Cevera. – *wd, bos*
Bombardment of Santiago, June 6. – *UN, s, bos*
Bombardment of Moro Castle, Santiago. – *s, wd, bos*
Landing of U.S. Marines, June 10. – *UN, s, wd, bos,* ^
Stand of Marines at Camp McCalla, June 11. – *wd, bos*
The Vesuvius in Action, June 14. – *wd, bos*
Landing of Shafter in Cuba. – *wd, bos*
Charge of the Rough Riders. (Death of Capt. Capron) – *s, wd, bos*
"Well done, boy!" (Capt. Capron Sr. viewing Son) – *s, wd, bos*
Spanish Method of Fighting. – *s, wd*
Battle of El Caney, July 1. – *s, wd, bos*
Battle of El Caney, Final Charge. – *1900, s, wd, bos*
Colored Infantry at El Caney, July 1. (Attack of) – *wd, bos*
Charge on San Juan Hill. (Roosevelt leading …) – *E 222, UN, bos*
Capture of Block-house at San Juan. – *s, wd, bos*
On the hill at El Poso, July 1. – *s, wd, bos*
Admiral Cevera's Dash from Santiago, July 3. – *s, wd, bos*
The Gloucester Sinking "Furor" and "Pluton." July 3. – *d, wd, bos*
Destruction of Cevera's Fleet, July 3. – *E 223, UN, d, bos*
"Don't cheer! The poor fellows are dying." – *s, wd, bos*
Capt Phillip's Prayer on the "Texas." – *s, wd, bos*
Admiral Cevera Received by Capt. Evans. – *s, wd, bos*
Commodore Schley on his Flagship, the Brooklyn. – *s, wd, bos*
Surrender of Santiago, July 14. – *UN, s, bos*
Raising U.S. Flag on City Hall, Santiago, July 14. – *wd, bos*
Night Attack at Manila. – *wd, bos*
Signing the Protocol, August 13. – *E 186, PR, wd, bos*
First Flag of Truce after Peace – Porto Rico. – *wd, bos*
Defeat of Spanish troops at Manila, August 13. – *wd, bos*
Peace Commission at Paris. – *s, wd, bos*
(U.S. Medical Camp.) (Red Cross) – *s, wd*
U.S. Gunboat. (dissolve base) – *1901, wd, bos*
Searchlight of US Battleship. (dissolve, lever) – *UN, 1901, bos*

190. War in Cuba, 1900
No Author, 12/14, G, f, AMPAS, 1900–01~

190

General Weyler and Staff in Field. – *1900, s, wd, bos*
Charge of Cavalry under Maceo. – *1900, wd, bos*
Spanish Soldiers Devastating Cuba. – *1900, s, wd, bos*
Spanish Soldiers Murdering Insurgents. – *1900, s, wd, bos*
Cuban Prisoners of War Executed by Spaniards. – *1900, s, wd, bos*
Starving Reconcentrados in Havana. – *E 223, 1900, s, wd, bos*
Expedition Landing Military Stores. – *1908, s, wd, bos*
Spanish Cavalry with Captured Pacificos. – *1900, s, wd, bos*
Death of Gen. Maceo. – *1901, s, wd, bos*
General Gomez's Victory at Saratoga. – *1902–03, s, wd, bos*
Soldier's Return. (Home From the War) – *1902–03, s, wd, bos,* ^
United States and Cuban Flags. – *GEH, 1898–1920 (?), wd, bos*

191. War with Filipinos, 1899
No Author, 4/4, G, f, AMPAS, 1899~

191

Defeat of Filipinos, February 5. – *s, wd, bos*
Privates of 20th Kansas Swimming River. – *wd, bos*
Col. Funston's Charge. (Feat) – *s, wd, bos,* ^
Capture of Aquinaldo, 1901. – *1902–03, s, wd*

192. Boer War, 1899[128]
No Author, 4/13, G, PR, 1900

Boers Going to War, 1899. – *E 181, 1902–03, s, wd, bos*
Boers under Gen. Kock resisting attack of British at Elandslaagle, 1899. – *E 181, s, wd, bos*
British Lancers cutting retreat of Boers at Elandslaagle, 1899. – *E 181, s, wd, bos*
Forward, Attacking Mafeking. (Boer horsemen) – *E 181, s, wd, bos,* ^

193. Russo–Japan War, 1905[129]
No Author, 4/38, G, UN, 1905

Admiral Togo's (Directing) Victory. – *UN, d, bos,* ^
Generals Nogi (and Stoessel), Surrender of Port Arthur. – *UN, s, d, wd, bos*
Russian Battle Ships Czaravitch and Pallada sunk Feb 8, 1904. (by Japanese Torpedo Boats) – *UN, d, bos*
Battle of Mukden. – *UN, d, bos*

192

193

Temperance

194. Drunkard's Daughter, The[130]

Stephenson, 6/6, S, c, AN, 1882

1. Her mother dying, she is left alone in the world. – *wd, bos*
2. She endeavors to support herself by sewing. – *wd, bos*
3. Payment for work is refused for alleged imperfections. – *wd, bos*
4. Unable to pay rent, turned into the street. – *wd, bos*
5. In a moment of despair she plunges into eternity. – *BC, wd, bos,* ^
6. "Take her up tenderly, lift her with care." – *BC, wd, bos*

195. Drunkard's Reform, The[131]

Unknown, 6/6, S, RBC, 1887

1. He squanders his hard earned money in drink. – *wd, bos,* ^
2. His child's clothes are ridiculed; his pride is touched. – *wd, bos*
3. He forms a resolution and leaves the tavern. – *wd, bos*
4. He informs his wife of his resolve. – *wd, bos*
5. His sobriety raises him to a position of foreman. – *wd, bos*
6. The Happy Home of the Reformed Man. – *E 229, wd, bos*

196. "Father, Dear Father, Come Home With Me Now"[132]

Work, 6/6, S, m, PR, 1887

1. "The clock in the steeple strikes one." – *s, wd*
2. "With poor brother Bernie so sick in her arms." – *UN, as*
3. "The clock in the steeple strikes two." – *s, wd,* ^
4. "The night has grown colder, and Bernie is worse." – *wd*
5. "The clock in the steeple strikes three." – *s, wd*
6. "We are alone, for poor Bernie is dead." – *wd, bos*

194

195

196

198

197. Intemperance Subjects
No Author, 5/6, G, AN, 1914–16 i

199. Ten Nights in a Bar Room[134]
Arthur, 12/12, S, c, m, AN, 1881–1893

197

199

The Drunkard's Home. (base picture) – *wd, bos*
Drunkard's Home. (drunk on floor) – *E 229, wd, bos*
Whiskey Demon. (mill & still)? – *BC, 1881–93, wd, bos*
Delirium Tremens. – *1909, s, d, wd, bos,* ^
Thrift and Sloth: What Money Can Buy. – *PR, wd, bos*

198. Raid of the Moonshiners[133]
No Author, 3/3, S, GEH, 1895

Raid of the Moonshiners No 1. – *PR, ca, wd, bos*
Raid of the Moonshiners No 2. – *wd, bos*
Raid of the Moonshiners No 3. – *wd, bos,* ^

1. The Arrival at the "Sickle and Sheaf." – *wd, bos*
2. Joe Morgan's little Mary begs him to come home. – *wd, bos*
3. Slade throws glass at Joe Morgan and hits Mary. – *wd, bos*
4. Joe Morgan suffering the Delirium Tremens. – *wd, bos*
5. Death of Joe Morgan's Little Mary. – *wd, bos*
6. Frank Slade and Tom Wilkins on a spree. – *wd, bos*
7. Willie Hammond induced to gamble. – *wd, bos*
8. Harvey Green stabs Willie Hammond to death. – *wd, bos,* ^
9. Quarrel between Slade and his son Frank. – *wd, bos*
10. Frank Slade kills his father with a bottle. – *wd, bos*
11. Meeting of the Citizens in the Bar Room. – *wd, bos*
12. The departure from the "Sickle and Sheaf." – *wd, bos*

200. Two Paths of Virtue and Vice, The[135]
Unknown, 4/4, S, RBC, 1881

1. Childhood. – *s, wd, bos*
2. Youth. – *s, wd, bos*
3. Manhood. – *s, wd, bos,* ^
4. Old Age. – *UN, wd, bos*

201. Where is My Boy To-Night? (Wandering)
Lowry, 6/6, S, m, AN, 1895

1. "The boy of my tenderest care." – *BC, s, wd, bos,* ^
2. "As he knelt at his Mother's knee." – *E 234, wd, bos*
3. "O could I see you now, my boy." – *wd, bos*
4. "But bring him to me with all his blight." – *E 104, wd, bos*
5. "O where is my boy tonight?" – *wd, bos*
6. "My heart o'er flows for I love him, he knows." – *wd, bos*

202. William Jackson's Treat[136]
(Champagne to the End) *Unknown, 4/4, S, AN, 1885*

1. More Champagne! remarked William Jackson. – *wd, bos*
2. Bourbon again – and oh, I say, I'm Will Jackson. – *wd, bos,* ^
3. Don't you go thinkin' I'm bust. I'm Bill Jackson, Guv. – *wd, bos*
4. Bill goes out, and the next you hear Of his last treat. – *wd, bos*

203. Temperance, Miscellaneous★
No Author, 1/?, G, AN, 1881–1920

Skeleton Ball – Minuet of Witches. – *s, wd, bos,* ^

Secret Society[137]

204. Royal Arch (Masonic)
Masons, 46/124, G, m, GEH, 1894–97~

204

a. Burning Bush with Moses. – *E 123, 1895–97, ca, d, wd*
b. Burning Bush without Moses. – *E 123, 1896–97, d, wd*
1. Map of the Country. – *1895, wd, bos*
2. Tower of Babel. – *1896–97, wd*
3. The City of Babylon. – *1896–97, wd, bos*
4. Hanging Gardens. – *F 179, PR, 1894, wd*
5. Feast of Belshazzar. – *F 126, UN, 1904, d, bos*
6. Babylon Taken by Cyrus. (Capture of Babylon) – *E 132, 1895–97, ca, d, wd, bos*
7. The River Euphrates. – *1896–97, wd, bos*
8. Plains of Anath. – *1896–97, wd, bos*
9. Ruins of Rabbath. – *1896–97, wd, bos*
10. Country of Mesopotamia. – *1896–97, wd, bos*
11. The Sandy Desert. – *1896–97, wd, bos*
12. The City of Palmyra. – *1902–03, s, d, wd, bos*
13. The Ruins of Palmyra. – *1896–97, wd, bos*
14. The City of Damascus. – *F 106, 1896–97, wd, bos*
15. The Ruins Near Damascus. – *1896–97, wd, bos*
16. The Forests of Lebanon. – *UN, 1896–97, bos*
17. The Quarries of Zeradatha. – *1896–97, wd, bos*
19. The Ruins of Jerusalem. – *E 159, 1894, s, wd, bos*
20. The Tabernacle of Zerubbabel. – *E 227, 1896–97, wd, bos*
21. Plains of Shinar. – *1907, wd, bos*
22. Mt. Ararat. – *E 232, 1907, wd, bos*
23. Capture of Babylon. (Jews Led Captive) – *F 132, 1907, ca, d, wd*
24. Return of Captives – unsafe bridge. – *E 132, 1913, ca, wd*
25. Underground Vault Below Ruins. – *1917–20, wd, ^*
31. Cyrus Issues Proclamation. – *F 156, BAC, 1914–16, ca, wd, bos*
Noah leaving Ark. (Mt. Ararat) – *F 119, BAC, 1895–97, s, ca, d, wd*
Clay Grounds. – *F 209, 1896–97, s, wd*
Territory of Judah. (Canaan) – *F 124, BAC, 1894, s, ca, d, wd, bos*
Brazen Serpent. (Moses and) – *F 124, BAC, 1894, s, ca, d, wd*
Return (Report) of the Spies. – *F 124, BAC, 1894, s, ca, d., wd*

Jacob Wrestling with Angel. – *F 121, BAC, 1895–97, ca, d, wd, bos*
King Solomon. – *F 209, 1907, wd*
Furnace of Fire. (Three Youths in the) – *F 126, UN, 1895–97, ca, d, wd, bos*
Dispute in the Vineyard. No 1. – *F 148, BAC, 1917–20, s, wd*
Dispute in the Vineyard. No 2. – *F 148, BAC, 1917–20, s, wd, bos*
Pillar of Fire. – *F 123, BAC, 1906, ca, d, wd*
Moses' Rod Becomes a Serpent. – *F 123, UN, 1917–20, ca, d*
Moses' Hands Becomes Leprous. – *F 123, UN, 1917–20, ca, d*
Moses Hears Voice of God. – *F 123, UN, 1917–20, ca, d*
Solomon Consecrates Temple. – *E 159, BAC, 1914–16, ca, d, wd, bos*
Glory at Consecration. – *E 159, BAC, 1914–16, ca, d, wd, bos*
(Cutting) Cedars of Lebanon. – *E 159, E 209, UN, 1914–16, s, bos*
Before the Flood. – *F 119, BAC, 1900, ca, wd, bos*
Isaiah sees Babylon Destroyed. – *F 132, BAC, 1910, ca, wd, bos*

205. Scottish Rite
(Masonic)
Masons, 3/27, G, 1913 i

205

Ascension. (single slide) – *F 139, BU, 1900, ca, d, wd*
Citadel of Joppa. – *BC, wd*
Nicosia. (Cyprus) – *GEH, 1917–20, wd, ^*

206. Commandery (Masonic)[138]
Masons, 21/80, G, f, m, 1892~

(Soldier Sleeping Before Tomb.) – *UN, 1892, n, as*
Angel at Sepulcher. – *UN, 1892, wd?, as*
Three Marys at the Tomb. – *E 211, E 228, BC, 1892, wd, bos, ^*
Ascension of Christ. (single slide) – *F 139, GEH, 1900, ca, d, wd*
Resurrection of Christ. – *BC, 1894, ca, wd*
Adoration of shepherds. – *F 135, BU, 1881–1920, wd*
Three Wise Men. (Arrive) – *F 69, BU, 1909, ca, d, wd, bos*
Visit of the Wise Men. – *F 135, BU, 1895–97, ca, wd*
Garden of Gethsemane. – *F 139, BU, 1891, ca, d, wd*
Betrayal Kiss. (of Judas) – *F 139, UN, 1892, ca, d, bos*
Pilate Washes His Hands. – *F 139, BU, 1906, ca, d, wd*

206

Peter's Denial. – *F 139, UN, 1891, ca, d, wd, bos*
King Solomon. – *F 209, GEH, 1907, wd*
King Hiram. – *F 209, GEH, 1907, wd*
Simon of Cyrene. (Cyrenean) – *F 139, BU, 1906, s, ca, wd*
"Ecce Homo!" – *F 64, UN, 1895, bos*
Easter Dawn. (Resurrection) – *F 142, BU, 1894, s, ca, d, wd, bos*
Ascension into Heaven. – *F 139, BU, 1900, ca, d, wd*
Healing the Blind. – *F 137, BAC, 1881–20, d, wd, bos*
Doubting Thomas. – *F 139, BU, 1895–97, ca, d, wd, bos*
Prayer after The Last Supper. – *F 139, BU, 1917–20, d, wd, bos*

207. Ascension (Knights Templar – Masonic)[139]
Masons (KT), 6/6, S, GEH, 1907

207

1. Christ Standing Among Disciples. – *wd, (1) wd, (2) n? ^*
2. Christ Just Above Disciples. – *wd, (1) wd, (2) n?*
3. Cloud with Opening. – *wd, (1) wd, (2) n?*
4. Christ Appears in Cloud. – *wd, (1) wd, (2) n?*
5. Christ Appears Afar Off. – *wd, (1) wd, (2) n?*
v. Christ Appears farther off & is Lost to View. – *wd, (1) wd, (2) n?*

208. Moveable Ascensions (Masonic)[140]
Masons, 1/1, S, GEH, 1881–1920

Lever Ascension. (Christ disappears into cloud.) – *E 226, n, wd*

209. Blue Lodge (Masonic)[141]
Masons, 21/92, S, m, GEH, 1896–1907~

209

Cutting down Cedars. – *F 204, UN, 1914–16, s, bos*
Floating Logs to Joppa. – *E 210, 1896–97, wd*
Workmen in the Quarries. – *E 210, 1907, s, wd, bos*
  5a. Group: Faith, Hope, Charity. – *E 231, PR, 1897, wd*
  5b Faith. *UN, 1897?, as*
  5c. Hope. – *F 232, BC, 1897, wd.*
  5d. Charity. – *F 232, BC, 1897, wd*
10. Tabernacle in Wilderness. – *F 70, UN, 1881–1920, ca, d*
Clay Grounds. – *E 204, 1896–97, s, wd*
13d. Justice. – *1907, wd*
16d. Corinthian. – *1907, wd*
16f. Origin of Architecture. – *1907, wd*
23. Building of King Solomon's Temple. – *UN, 1888–89, as*
23a. Temple Completed. – *E 156, E 159, UN, 1914–16, ca*
24. Ancient Three Grand Masters. – *1907, wd*
24a. King Solomon. – *E 206, 1907, wd*
24b. Hiram, King of Tyre. – *E 206, 1907, wd*
24c. Master Workman. – *1907, wd*
26. Fellowcraft's Lodge. – *1888–89, wd*
27. Master Mason's Lodge. – *1888–89, wd*
30. Bee Hive. – *E 215, E 220, AN, 1881–1920, wd*
36. The Scythe. – *E 214, E 220, 1881–20, wd, ^*
37a. Coffin and Open Grave. – *1907, wd*
37b. Sprig of Acacia. – *F 210, 1907, wd*
37d. Funeral of Master Builder. – *1881–1920, wd*

210. Blue Lodge Additional (Masonic)[142]
Masons, 37/46, G, GEH, 1913~

1. The Master Builder. – *1913, wd*
2. The Unfinished sanctum sanctorum. – *1913, wd*
3. At the South Gate. – *1913, wd*
4. At the West Gate. – *1913, wd*
5. At the East Gate. – *1913, wd*
6. Rubbish of Temple. – *1913, wd*
7. The Brow of Hill. – *1913, wd*

210

211

8. Passage to Ethiopia. – *1913, wd*
9. Twelve F.C. Before King Solomon. – *1913, n, as*
10. Parties of Three. – *1913, wd*
11. Finding Sprig of Acacia. – *E 209, 1907, wd*
12. The Clefts of the Rocks. – *1907, wd*
1. Clouds and Darkness. – *F 116, BAC, 1907, ca, wd, bos*
2. Disturbance Shows Formation. – *F 116, BAC, 1907, ca, wd, bos*
3. Clouds Take a Circular Form. – *F 116, BAC, 1907, ca, wd, bos*
4. Globe of Lava Appears. – *F 116, BAC, 1907, ca, wd, bos*
5. Globe of Lava Cools. – *F 116, BAC, 1907, ca, wd, bos*
6. Appearance of Water. – *F 116, BAC, 1907, ca, wd, bos*
7. Indications of Land. – *F 116, BAC, 1907, ca, wd, bos*
8. The Continents Appear. – *F 116, BAC, 1907, ca, wd, bos*
Creation of Sun, Moon and Stars. – *F 117, BAC, 1901, ca, wd, bos*
Creation of Dry Land. – *F 117, UN, 1899, ca*
Creation of Trees and Grass. – *F 117, UN, 1899, ca*
Creation of Birds and Fishes. – *F 117, BAC, 1899, ca, d, wd*
Creation of Beasts. – *F 117, UN, 1899, ca*
Workmen in the Quarries. – *F 209, 1907, s, wd, bos,* ^
Bringing Logs to Joppa. – *F 209, 1896–97, d, wd*
1. Remember Thy Creator. – *F 111, BAC, 1902–03, s, wd, bos*
2. While the evil days come not, etc. – *F 109, 1913, s, wd*
3. While the sun or the light, etc. – *F 109, 1913, wd*
4. In the days when the keepers, etc. – *F 109, 1913, s, wd*
5. And the grinders cease, etc. – *F 109, 1913, wd*
6. And He shall rise up, etc. – *F 109, 1913, s, wd*
7. Also when they shall be afraid, etc. – *F 109, 1913, wd*
8. Because man goeth to his long home. – *F 109, 1913, s, wd*
9. Or ever the silver chord be loosed, etc. – *F 109, 1913, wd*
10. Then shall the dust return, etc. – *F 109, 1913, s, wd*

211. White Shrine of Jerusalem (Masonic)
Masons, 11/12, G, 1913 i

2. Behold! the Lamb of God. – *F 137, BU, 1895–97, ca, d, wd*
3. Marys at the Tomb. – *F 139, BU, 1892, ca, wd, bos*
4. Easter Dawn. (Resurrection) – *F 142, BU, 1894, s, ca, d, wd, bos*
6. Angry Sea. – *F 101, AN, 1887, wd, bos*
7. Rock of Ages. – *F 101, UN, 1887, bos*

8. Simply to Thy Cross I Cling. – *F 101, UN, 1887, bos*
9. Ascension to Heaven. – *F 101, UN, 1891, bos*
10. Heaven. – *F 245, UN, 1895–97, ca*
Three Magi guided by star. – *F 69, BU, 1896–97, s, d, wd, bos*
Bethlehem by Night. – *F 135, BU, 1899, ca, wd, bos,* ^
"Ecce Homo!" – *F 64, UN, 1898, bos*

212. Order of the Eastern Star (Masonic)
Masons, 17/59, G, 1907

212

1. Emblazoned Altar. – *GEH, 1907, d, wd*
2. Jephthah Going to Battle. – *BAC, 1907, d, wd, bos*
6. Sacrifice of Adah. – *BAC, 1907, s, ca, d, wd, bos*
11. City of Bethlehem. – *F 135, BU, 1899, ca, wd, bos*
12. Boaz and Ruth. – *F 128, GEH, 1883, s, wd, bos*
13. Boaz favors Ruth. – *F 128, BAC, 1914–16, wd, bos*
16. Esther Espoused (Before Athaseurus). – *F 125, BAC, 1904~, wd, bos*

17. Esther Seeks Athaseurus (Passing Guards). – *F 125, BAC, 1904~, wd, bos*
21. Christ with Mary and Martha. – *F 137, BU, 1914–16, s, ca, wd*
22. Martha meeting Jesus. – *BU, 1907, wd*
24. Marys at the Tomb. – *F 139, BU, 1892, ca, wd, bos*
27. Benevolence. (with children) – *BAC, 1907, s, wd, bos*
28. Electra with Cross. – *GEH, 1907, wd, ^*
30. Ascension. – *F 139, BU, 1900, ca, d, wd*
31. Heaven. – *F 245, UN, 1895–97, ca*
34. The Angry Sea. – *F 101, AN, 1887, wd, bos*
35. Rock of Ages. – *F 101, UN, 1887, bos*
36. Simply to Thy Cross I Cling. – *F 101, UN, 1887, bos*

213. Knights Templar[143] (Masonic)
Masons, 1/?, G, ?

Samson in Prison. – *F 129, BAC, 1900, ca, d, wd, ^*

214. Oddfellows[144]
Oddfellows, 40/74, G, GEH–BAC, 1896–97, 1907~

1. Roses in Full Bloom. – *GEH, 1907, wd*
2. Roses Withered. – *GEH, 1907, wd*
3. Springtime With Flowers Blooming. – *GEH, 1907, wd*
4. Autumn with Leaves Falling. – *GEH, 1907, wd, ^*
5. Man in His Strength. – *GEH, 1907, wd, bos*
6. Man Lying Dead. – *GEH, 1907, s, wd*
7. Man Burnt at Stake. – *GEH, 1907, wd*
4. Scythe. – *F 209, GEH, 1881–1920, wd*
4b. Motto – From Darkness to Light. – *GEH, 1896–97, wd*
6b. Motto – In Friendship Forever. – *GEH, 1896–97, wd*
The Ark. – *BAC, F 119, 1900, ca, d, wd*
11b. Motto – Brotherly Love. – *GEH, 1896–97, wd*
Pines on Mountain Side. – *GEH, 1896–97, wd*
River Jordan. – *E 137, GEH, 1907, ca, wd*
Narrow Defile. – *GEH, 1896–97, wd*
15. The Coffin. – *E 220, GEH, 1881–1920, wd*
15b. Motto – Truth, the Imperil Virtue. – *GEH, 1896–97, wd*
  1. Abraham's Obedience. (Prep) – *F 120, BAC, 1907, ca, d, wd, bos*
  2. Abraham Offering Isaac. – *E 120, BAC, 1907, ca, d, wd, bos*
  3. Abraham's Sacrifice. – *F 120, BAC, 1899, s, ca, d, wd, bos*

2. Moses & 10 Commands. – *F 123, BAC, 1902–03, ca, d, wd, bos*
3. David a Shepherd Boy. – *F 131, BAC, 1908, ca, d, wd*
4. Samuel Anoints David. – *F 124, BAC, 1895–97, s, ca, d, wd, bos*
5. David Refuses Armor. – *F 131, BAC, 1911–12, s, ca, d, wd*
6. David Chooses Stones. – *F 131, BAC, 1914–16, s, ca, d, wd, bos*
7. Goliath's Challenge. – *F 124, BAC, 1894, s, ca, d, wd, bos*
8. David Casts Stone. (D&G) – *F 131, BAC, 1895, s, ca, d, wd, bos*
9. David Slays Goliath. – *F 124, BAC, 1909, ca, d, wd, bos*
10. David with Goliath's Head. – *F 131, BAC, 1909, ca, d, wd, bos*
13. Saul Casts His Javelin. – *F 131, BAC, 1914–16, ca, wd, bos*
14. Friendship of David, Jonathan. – *F 131, BAC, 1895, ca, wd, bos*
0. From Jerusalem to Jericho. – *F 145, BAC, 1898, wd, bos*
1. He Falls Among Thieves. – *F 145, BAC, 1898, wd, bos*
1a. Man Lying Wounded. – *F 145, BAC, 1898, s, wd*
2. The Priest Passes By. – *F 145, BAC, 1898, s, wd*
3. The Levite Looks and Passes By. – *F 145, BAC, 1898, s, wd*
4. The Samaritan Binds Up Wounds. – *F 137, BAC, 1892, s, ca, wd*
5. Sets Him on His Own Beast. – *F 145, BAC, 1898, s, wd, bos*
6. And Brings Him to an Inn. – *F 145, BAC, 1898, s, wd, bos*
Churchyard Scene. (Planets) – *F 41, AN, 1904, wd, bos*

215. Daughters of Rebecca (Oddfellows)
Oddfellows, 7/24, G, BAC, 1907 i

Sarah. – *1894, wd*
Bee Hive. – *F 209, AN, 1881–1920, wd*
Mother of Samson. – *F 129, 1894, ca, d, wd, bos, ^*
Ruth & Naomi. (Choice) – *F 128, 1895, s, ca, wd, bos*
Ruth in Field of Boaz. – *F 128, GEH, 1914–16, s, wd, bos*
Miriam. (Song of) – *F 123, 1895–97, ca, d, wd, bos*
Esther Espoused by the King. – *F 125, 1904, wd, bos*

216. Knights of Pythias, First Rank[145]
(Story of Damon and Pythias)
Knights of Pythias, 19/13+, S, m, GEH, 1891–94, 1896–97~

1. Friends Damon and Pythias. – *1896–97, wd*
2. Damon Condemned to Die. – *1896–97, wd*
Pythias intercedes for Damon. – *1893, wd, bos*
3. Pythias's Appeal to Dionysius. – *1896–97, wd?, bos*
3a. Pythias in Dungeon. – *1891, wd*
4. Damon's Homeward Flight. – *1891, wd*
v. Damon's Flight to Family. – *1896–97, wd*
5. Pythias in Dungeon, Calantha's Appeal. – *1896–97, wd,* ^
6. Damon's Farewell to His Family. – *1896–97, wd, bos*
6a. Attempt of Damon's Slave to Prevent his Return
    (Horse slain) – *1891, wd, bos*
7. Pythias at Headsman's Block. – *1896–97, s, wd*
7a. Damon Returning (running) to Save Pythias. – *1891,*
    wd, bos
7b. The People See Damon Approaching. – *1913(?), s, wd*
8. Pythias saved by Damon's Arrival. – *1896–97 (?), wd, bos*
9a. Heroes Honored By King. – *1896–97, wd, bos*
10. Beautiful Unknown Shore. – *1894, wd, bos*
Damon and Pythias. (arrival) – *1899 (?), s, wd, bos*
Damon and Pythias. Headsman's Block. – *1996–97 (?), s, wd*
Damon and Pythias. Registering a vow. – *1896–97, s, wd*

217. Knights of Pythias, Third Rank, Monitor
Knights of Pythias, 8/10, S, m, GEH, 1902–03

2. Sunshine and Shadow. – *wd*
3. Darkness and Death. – *wd*
4. Where We with Loved Ones Dwell. – *s, wd*
5. Budding Flowers and Sparkling Stream. – *wd, bos*
6. Majestic Mountains and Peaceful Homes. – *wd, bos*
7. Sunset Glows with Rubies. – *wd,* ^
9. Stars of Sympathy and Love. – *wd, bos*
10. Rays of Light from a Heaven of Peace. – *wd, bos*

218. Knights of Pythias, Third Rank, Pythagoras[146]
Knights of Pythias, 9/10, S, f, m, GEH, 1893–94, 1902–03~

1. Ancient Egyptian Arts (pyramids) – *F 179,1894, d, wd*
2. Science of Arabia (magician). – *1902–03, s, wd, bos*
(hobgoblins revolving dissolve) – *UN, 1902–03, d, bos*
3. The Philosopher. – *1902–03, wd, bos*

3a. Lore of Chaldean Sages. – *1913, wd*
4. The Flowery Plain. – *E 228, 1893, wd*
5. The Mountain's Side. (Winding Road) – *1893, wd*
9. Where Hideous Creatures Climb. (Dwell) – *1893,*
   wd, bos, ^
10. The Hero. – *1894, wd, bos*

219. Knights of Pythias, Sixth Senator
Knights of Pythias, 8/7, S, GEH, 1894, 1906~

1. The Battlefield. – *1896–97, wd*
1 v. The Battlefield. – *1906, s, wd*
2. Two Horsemen Meet in Deadly Conflict. – *1894, wd*
3. Unhorsed and Sorely Hurt. – *1906, s, wd*
4. An Esquire in Course of Duty. – *1894, wd*
5. Brings Water in His Helmet. – *1894, wd*
6. Champion and Defender. – *1902, wd,* ^
The Emblem. – *1906, wd*

218

219

220. Woodmen of the World

Woodmen of the World, 15/36, S, GEH, 1896–97, 1902–03~

220

221. Knights of the Mystic Chain

Knights of the Mystic Chain, 6/8, S, BAC, 1908 i

221

3. Sunrise on Forest. (Mt. Peak) – *1896–97, wd, bos, ^*
4. Emblems of Woodcraft. – *1902–03, wd*
5. Woodmen Chopping in Forest. – *1896–97, wd, bos*
9. Log House in Clearing. – *UN, 1896–97, n, as*
13. Deathbed Scene. – *E 236, UN, 1896–97, wd, as*
14. Unveiling Monument. – *1896–97, wd*
17. American Flag. – *F 26, 1881–1920, wd*
22. Purity. (Apocalypse) – *E 230, E 236, 1902–03, wd, bos*
23. Funeral at Grave. (Bury the Dead) – *E 226, E 236, 1902–03, wd*
24. Paying of Assessment by Sovereigns. – *1902–03, wd*
25. Paying of Certificate to Widow. – *E 231, 1902–03, s, wd*
29. Bee Hive. – *F 209, AN, 1881–1920, wd*
31. Coffin. – *F 214, 1881–1920, wd*
34. The Scythe. – *F 209, 1881–1920, wd*
35. Funeral Procession. – *1902–03, s, wd*

2. Interior of Widow's Hut. – *UN, 1908, s, n*
3. Going from Jerusalem to Jericho. (Stranger) – *F 145, 1898, wd, bos*
4. He Falls Among Thieves. – *F 145, 1898, wd, bos, ^*
5. A Man Lying Wounded. – *F 145, 1898, s, wd*
6. Good Samaritan with Stranger. (Binds His Wounds) – *F 137, 1892, s, wd*
7. Good Samaritan with Stranger at Inn. – *F 145, 1898, s, wd, bos*

222. Patriotic Order Sons of America

Patriotic Order Sons of America, 16/29, S, f, m, 1885–89~

2. The Mayflower. – *F 164, AN, 1891, wd, bos*
4. Battle of Lexington. – *F 166, AN, 1881–1920, wd, bos*

222

11. Battle of Monmouth. – *F 166, AN, 1881–1920, wd, bos*
12. Battle Stony Point. – *F 166, AN, 1881–1920, wd, bos*
16. Old Ironsides. – *F 31, AN, 1891, wd, bos*
19. Firing on Fort Sumter. – *F 169, AN, 1895, wd*
21. Battle of Gettysburg. – *F 169, AN, 1891, d, bos*
21 v. Battle of Gettysburg – *F 169, GEH, ?, wd, bos*
22. Blue and Gray. – *F 162, AN, 1896–97, wd*
23. Destruction of the Maine. – *F 188, UN, 1898, as*
24. Manila Bay. (Destruction) – *F 189, UN, 1899, bos*
25. San Juan Hill. – *F 189, UN, 1899, wd*
26. Scene of Peace. (Industrial) – *PHM, 1888–89, wd*
27. Public School House. – *E 223, GEH, 1885, wd, bos*
28. Goddess of Liberty. (rocks) – *E 223, AN, 1886–87, wd, bos,* ˄
29. "Stars & Stripes." (Am. Flag) – *F 26, GEH, 1888–1920, wd*

223. Patriotic Order of America
Patriotic Order of America, 17/29, S, m, AN, 1901 i

223

1. Goddess of Liberty. – *F 222, 1896–97, wd, bos*
2. The Mayflower. – *F 164, 1891, wd, bos,* ˄
5. Washington Bowing to Molly Pitcher. – *F 166, 1881–1920, wd, bos*
7. American Flag with Thirteen Stars. – *E 171, GEH, 1913, wd*
8. Battle of Lexington. – *F 166, 1881–1920, wd, bos*
13. Battle at Lake Erie. – *F 167, PR, 1891, s, wd*
15. Firing on Fort Sumpter. – *F 169, 1895, wd*
17. Mother of '69 Bidding Her Soldier Son Goodbye (Volunteer's Departure.) – *F 162, 1888–89, wd, bos*
18. Barbara Freitchie Waving the Flag. – *F 162, MLCM, 1886, ca, wd, bos*
20. Surrender of Lee. – *F 185, 1881–1920, wd, bos*
21. Scene of Peace – Soldier Returning. – *F 162, 1888–89, wd, bos*
23. School House. – *F 222, GEH, 1885, wd, bos*
24. Half-starved Cubans. – *F 190, 1900, s, wd, bos*
25. The Battleship Maine. – *F 188, UN, 1898, bos*
27. Destruction of Cervera's Fleet. – *F 189, UN, 1899, bos*
28. The Blue and the Gray. – *F 162, 1896–97, wd*
29. Stars and Stripes Unfurled. – *F 26, GEH, 1888–1920, wd*

224. Brotherhood of the Union[147]
Brotherhood of the Union, 3/50?, G, GEH, ?

Seventy Star Flag. – *1917–20, wd*
Pocahontas. – *F 164, 1881–1920, wd, bos*
(Concord Bridge Battle.) – *F 25, UN, 1881–1920, wd, bos*

225. Grand Army of the Republic
Grand Army of the Republic, 5/20, S, AN, 1881–1920

225

9. Widow and Orphan Soliciting Charity. – *E 226, E 236, GEH, 1885, wd*
13. Eagle on Shield. (Loyalty). – *F 162, 1881–1920, d, wd*
14. Bombardment of Fort Sumter. – *F 169, 1895, wd*
17. American Flag. – *GEH, 1881–1920, wd*
18. Surrender of Lee. – *F 185, 1881–1920, wd, bos,* ˄

226. Knights of Malta[148]
Knights of Malta, 17/41, G, f, m, 1896–1920~

227

4. Visit the Sick. – *GEH, 1896–97, s, wd*
5. Bury the Dead. (Funeral) – *GEH, F 220, 1902–03, wd*
7. Harbor the Harborless (Widow & Orphan … Charity) –
   F 225, GEH, 1885, wd
Burning Bush. (without fire) – *GEH, 1881–1920, wd*
Burning Bush. (with fire and angel) – *GEH, 1881–93, wd?, as*
David with Goliath's Head. – *F 131, BAC, 1909, ca, d, wd, bos*
Eve Tempted. – *F 117, UN, 1900, ca*
Angel with Flaming Sword. (Expulsion) – *F 117, BAC,
   1896–97, d, wd, bos*
Noah Builds the Ark. – *F 119, BAC, 1899, ca, wd, bos*
Noah Enters the Ark. – *F 119, BAC, 1900, ca, d, wd, bos*
Interior of Ark. – *F 119, BAC, 1899, ca, d, wd*
Return of the Dove. – *F 119, BAC, 1895–97, ca, d, wd, bos*
Ark on the Waters. – *F 119, BAC, 1900, ca, d, wd*
Ascension. (moveable). – *F 208, BU, 1907, ca, d, wd*
Hell, With Motto. – *F 244, PR, 1895–97, ca, wd, ^*
Hand Rising from Sea. (small) – *GEH, 1917–20, wd*
Hand Rising from Sea (large) – *UN, 1917–20, wd*

227. Sublime Order of the Great Cross
Sublime Order of the Great Cross, 4/6, S, ?

1. The Gate. – *F 99, BU, 1896–97, s, wd, bos*
2. Abraham and Isaac preparing the Sacrifice. – *F 120, BAC,
   1907, ca, d, wd, bos, ^*
3. Abraham's Sacrifice. – *F 120, BAC, 1899, ca, d, wd, bos*
The Tabernacle of Zerubbabel. – *F 204, GEH, 1896–97,
   wd, bos*

228. Knights of the Golden Eagle
Knights of the Golden Eagle, 11/34, S, 1902–03 i

4. Flowery Plain. – *F 218, GEH, 1893, wd, ^*
6. Watchfulness. – *F 142, BAC, 1895, s, ca, wd*
10. Hell. – *F 245, PR, 1895–97, ca, wd*
12. Three Marys at Tomb. – *F 206, BC, 1892, wd, bos*
15. Christ's Prayer in the Garden. – *F 139, UN, 1909, ca, d*
16. Shepherds at Nativity. – *F 135, BU, 1881–1920, wd*
20. Like a might Army. – *F 100, BAC, 1899, wd, bos*
28. Three Angels. – *GEH, 1881–1920, wd*

228

29. Onward, Christian Soldiers. – *F 100, BAC, 1899, s, wd*
30. Heaven. – *F 245, UN, 1895–97, ca*
Monks Kneeling. – *GEH, 1898, wd*

229. American Mechanics. (United)
American Mechanics, 2/7, S, AN, 1888–89 i

6. Temperate Home. (Family Happiness) – *F 195, AN, 1887,
   wd, bos*
Intemperate Home. (Drunkard's Home) – *F 197, 1914–16,
   wd, bos*

230. Jr. Order of American Mechanics
Jr. OUAM, 8/27, G, 1917–20 i

Public School. – *GEH, 1881–1920, wd, bos*
Vessel Landing Immigrants. – *MLCM, 1917–20, wd, ^*
Liberty Bell. – *F 28, AN, 1896–97, wd*
Battle of Lexington. – *F 166, AN, 1881–1920, wd, bos*

229

232

230

233

Flag Waving in the Breeze. – *F 26, GEH, 1888–1920, wd*
The Spirit of 1776. – *F 166, MLCM, 1881–1920, wd, bos*
Virtue. (Purity) – *F 220, GEH, 1902–03, wd, bos*
Home Fireside. – *F 115 (#5), AN, 1896–97, s, wd*

231. Brotherhood of Locomotive Firemen
BOLF, 6/14, S. PR, 1896–7

6. Payment of Certificate. – *F 220, wd*
7. Faith, Hope and Charity. – *F 209, wd*
10. Charity. – *F 232, wd*

232. Knights and Ladies of Honor
KLH, 2/11, S, PR, 1896–7

1. Charity. – *E 209, E 231, wd*
6. Hope. – *E 209, wd, ^*

233. Foresters of America
Foresters, 1/12, S, BC, 1913 i

10. The King pardons Robin Hood. – *F 181, BC, 1913, s, wd, ^*

234. Orangemen
Orangemen, 4/19, G, 1917–20 i

Siege of Limerick. – *F 181, BC, 1891, wd, bos, ^*
Crossing the Jordan. – *F 124, BAC, 1894, s, ca, d, wd*
Tabernacle. – *F 70, UN, 1917–20, ca, d*
Mount Ararat. – *F 204, GEH, 1907, wd, bos*

235. Order of Maccabees
Order of Maccabees, 1/12, S, GEH, 1917–20 i

Death of Eleazer the Maccabee. – *F 156, GEH, 1914–16, d, wd, ^*

234

235

236. Moose Lodge (Loyal Order of)[149]
Moose, 14/?, G, ?

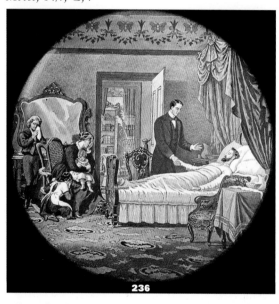

236

Village Church, Summer. – *F 246, AN, 1881–93, wd, bos*

Village Church, Christmas Eve. – *F 246, AN, 1881–93, wd, bos*

"Honor thy father and thy mother." – *F 115, AN, 1896–97, s, wd*

"Thou shall not kill." – *F 118, BAC, 1895–97, ca, wd*

"Thou shall not commit adultery." – *F 115, BU, 1896–97, wd*

"Thou shall not steal." – *F 115, AN, 1896–97, wd*

"Thou shall not bear false witness. – *F 115, AN, 1896–97, wd*

"Thou shall not covet thy neighbor's house." – *F 115, AN, 1896–97, s, wd*

Widow and Orphan Soliciting Charity. – *F 225, GEH, 1885, wd*

Deathbed Scene. – *F 220, UN, 1896–97, wd, as, ^*

Wandering Boy. 2. – *F 201, AN, 1895, wd, bos*

Funeral at Grave. (Bury the Dead) – *F 220, GEH, 1902–03, wd*

Purity. – *F 220, GEH, 1902–03, wd, bos*

Stars and Stripes Unfurled. (before sun). – *F 26, GEH, 1888–1920, wd*

237. Tribe of Ben Hur[150]
Association, 7/32, S, ?

237

2. The Wise Men Relating their Histories. – *F 64, BAC, 1894, s, wd, bos, ^*

21. Adoration of the Magi. – *F 135, BU, 1895–97, ca, wd*

17. The Magi arrive at Jerusalem. – *F 69, BAC, 1909, ca, d, wd*

Ben Hur at the Oar. – *F 64, BC, 1906, s, wd, bos*

16. Ben Hur training the Arabs. – *F 64, BAC, 1895, s, wd, bos*

17. The Chariot race – the Overthrow. – *F 64, BC, 1895, d, wd, bos*

The Winning Chariot. – *F 64, UN, 1894, bos*

238. American Insurance Union[151]
American Insurance Union, 2/?, G, ?

17. Conventional American Flag. (unfurled) – *GEH,?, wd,* ^
29. Conventional Am. Flag. – *F26, GEH, 1888–20, wd*

239. Secret Society, Miscellaneous
No Author, 5/?, G, GEH, 1881–1920

Middle-Aged Man Walking. – *s, wd, bos,* ^
Oak Tree. (Masonic?) – *GEH, wd, bos*
Our Public Schools and the Holy Bible Therein. – *wd*
Empty Room. – *wd*
Eagle Supporting Young Eagles in Flight. – *n, as*

Comic Singles And Dissolves[152]

240. Comic, Animals★
No Author, 8/8, G, AN, 1894~

Attack of the Monster – 1. The Wicked Flea. – *MLCM,*
1881–1920, wd, bos
Attack of the Monster – 2. Boarding-house Bedbug. –
1881–1920, wd, bos, ^
Every dog has his day. – *wd, bos*
Excuse haste and a bad pen. – *BC, wd, bos*
Peace. Boarding-house, No. 1. – *RBC, wd, bos*
War. Boarding-house, No 2. – *RBC, wd, bos*
She stoops to conquer. – *wd, bos*
Why did you sup on pork? – *BC, wd, bos*

241. Comic, Children★
No Author, 16/16, G, AN, 1894~

Crying Over Spilt Milk. – *wd*
Schoolboy's First Cigar. 1.
Very Manly. – *RBC, 1881–1920, wd, bos*
Schoolboy's First Cigar. 2. Very Sick. – *RBC, 1881–1920, wd, bos,* ^
Forbidden Fruit – School Boys Smoking. – *F 245, RBC, 1881–93, wd, bos*
Grab the ball, Johnny. I'll wait. – *wd, bos*
How doth the Little Busy Bee. – *wd*
Jack at Church. – *BC, F 245, 1883–84, ca, d, wd*
Mary had a little Lamb. – *wd*
Stolen Pleasures are sweet – No.1. – *wd, bos*
No pleasure without Pain – No. 2. – *wd, bos*
Thou art so near and yet so far. – *wd, bos*
Victor and Vanquished. – *wd, bos*
I wonder if it's loaded – No 1. – *wd, bos*
It was loaded – No. 2. – *wd, bos*
What are the wild waves saying? – No. 1. – *wd*
Scoot, brother, scoot – No. 2. – *wd, bos*

242. Comic, Ethnic★
No Author, 19/20, G, c, m, BC, 1894~

242

Bulldozed. – *1881–1920, wd, bos*
Coolness between Friends. – *BC, wd, bos*
Chinese Question Settled. 1. The Rivals. – *1881–1920, wd, bos*
Chinese Question Settled. 2. Resolved. – *UN, 1881–1920, wd*
Division of Labor. – *AN, wd, bos*
Excellent Hunting for the Indians. – *HRC, wd, bos*
Fop of Past and Present. 1. The Pre-historic Fop. – *1881–1920, wd, bos*
Fop of Past and Present. 2. 15th Amendment. – *1881–1920, s, wd*
Golly, no wonder Missis don't get up. – *AN, wd, bos*
Great Expectations. – *AN, wd, bos*
Masher – No. I. – *wd, bos*
Masher Crushed – No.2. – *wd, bos*
Moving Day. – *wd, bos*
Mr. Murphy is Rising with the World. – *NBMAA, wd, bos*
Summit of Happiness 1. Darkey Serenading. – *1881–1920, wd, bos*

Depth of Despair. 2. Falls in Rain barrel. – *1881–1920, wd, bos,* ^
Three Graces. – *wd, bos*
Triumph of Women's Rights, Woman expects. – *UN, wd, bos*
Triumph of Women's Rights, Man expects. – *UN, d, wd*

243. Comic, Love★
No Author, 5/5, G, c, AN, 1894

243

Bride and One Year After. – *wd, bos*
Girl I left behind me. – *wd*
Goodbye, Sweetheart, Goodbye. – *wd, bos*
They all do it. (Family Feud) – *RBC, wd, bos*
Venus Rising from the Sea. – *MLCM, wd, bos,* ^

244. Comic, Miscellaneous Singles★[153]
No Author, 9/9, G, AN, 1881–1920

244

Pleasure Party. – *1894, ca, wd, bos*
Something has got to come. No.1. (dentist pulls) –
    1881–1920, wd
Something did come. No. 2 (tooth flies) – *1881–1920, wd*
Too Late for the Train. – *K-MOMI, 1894, wd, bos,* ^
Two heads are better than one. – *1894, wd, bos*
In Happy Moments – Drunk. – *1901, s, wd, bos*
Unhappy Moments – Star of the Evening. – *1901, wd, bos*
What is Life (Home) without a Mother in Law? – *BC,*
    1881–1920, wd
Three Systems of Medicine. (Freezing or Puking.) (Allopathy,
    Hydropathy, Homeopathy) – *1881–1920, MLCM, s, wd, bos*

Miscellaneous

245. Artistic Gems[154]
No Author, 27/337, G, m, 1881–93~

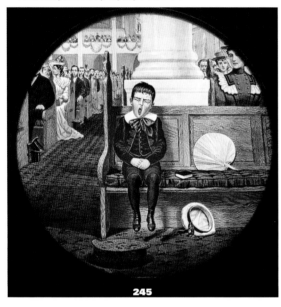

245

American Railway Restaurant. – *AN, 1885, ca, wd, bos*
Barbara Freitchie. – *F 162, AN, 1886, ca, wd, bos*
Bringing Home the Christmas Tree. – *UN, 1894, ca*
Bull Fight in Spain. – *BC, 1892, ca, wd, bos*
Erin. – *BC, 1881–93, ca, wd, bos*
Festival Night in Venice. – *PR, 1887, ca, wd*
Fondly Gazing – companion to Gone. – *UN, 1902–03, ca*
Forbidden Fruit. (boys smoking) – *E 241, RBC, 1881–83,*
    wd, bos
Good Night – Staircase. – *E 252, UN, 1891, ca, d*
Good Night – Cherubs. – *E 252, BC, 1888–89, ca, wd*
Good Night – Wreath of Flowers. – *E 252, UN, 1885, ca, bos*
Good Night – Owls & Bats. – *E 252, E 253, BC, 1900, ca,*
    wd, bos
Good Night – Witch/Broom. – *E 251, E 253, BC, 1900, ca,*
    wd, bos
Hail Columbia. – *F 162, AN, 1894, ca, wd*
Heaven. – *E 211, E 212, E 228, UN, 1896–97, ca*
Hell. – *E 159, E 226, E 228, PR, 1896–97, ca, wd, bos*
Jack at Church. – *E 241, BC, 1886, ca, d, wd, bos,* ^
Mammoth Cave. – *BC, 1881–93, ca, wd, bos*
Mermaid's Home. – *E 253, AN, 1881–93, wd, ca*
Mirage in the Desert. – *F 250, BAC, 1892, ca, wd, bos*
Old Glory – Sailor with Flag. – *F 162, MLCM, 1895–97, ca, wd*

Old Oaken Bucket. – *E 55, AN, 1881–93, ca, wd*
Rebel Skeddadle. – *BC, 1881–93, ca, wd, bos*
Scene at Fire. – *E 249, GEH, 1881–93, ca, d*
Tiger Hunting in India. – *UN, 1891, d, bos*
Traveling in Olden Time. – *E 170, AN, 1895–97, ca, wd*
Westward Ho. – *F 168, PR, 1902–03, ca, wd*

Dissolves [155]

246. Christmas Dissolves★[156]
No Author, 4/4, G, AN, 1881–93

246

Christmas Evening 1. The Happy Home. – *1881–93, MLCM,*
    ca, wd, bos, ^
Christmas Evening 2. Homeless. – *1881–93, ca, wd, bos*
Village Church. 1. Summer. – *E 236, 1881–93, wd, bos*
Village Church. 2. Christmas Eve. – *E 236, 1881–93, wd, bos*

247. Enchanted Grotto, The[157]
No Author, 4/4, S, BC, 1898

The Enchanted Grotto, No 1. – *s, wd, bos*
The Enchanted Grotto. Alligator. – *GEH, s, wd*
The Enchanted Grotto No 3. The Rival of the Goddess.
    (lever) – *s, wd, bos,* ^
Arrival of the Rival of the Goddess of the Lake. – *s, n*

248. Fire in New York[158]
No Author, 2/4, S, 1895–97

Fire in New York City. 2. Going to Fire. – *F 245, UN,*
    1896–97, s, bos, ^
Fire in New York City. 3. Engines at Work. – *GEH,*
    1895–97, ca

249. Steamboat Race in Mississippi[159]
No Author, 3/3, S, c, K-MOMI, 1881–1893

Steamboat Race in Mississippi. 1. Wooding up. – *wd, bos,* ^
Steamboat Race in Mississippi. 2. The Race. – *wd*
Steamboat Race in Mississippi. 3. The Explosion. – *wd?, as*

247

248

249

250

250. Dissolving Views – Miscellaneous[160]
No Author, 13/132, G, f, m, 1881–93~

American Landscape. 1. Summer. – *MLCM, 1881–93, wd*
American Landscape. 2. Winter. – *UN, 1881–93, wd, as*
Bay of Naples and Vesuvius. 1. Day. – *BC, 1885, wd?*
Bay of Naples and Vesuvius. 2. Night. – *BC, 1885, wd?*
Bay of Naples and Vesuvius. 3. Eruption. – *BC, 1885, wd, bos*
Faust and Marguerite. 1. Faust in his studio. – *BC, 1885, wd*
Faust and Marguerite. 2. Vision of Marguerite. – *BC, 1885, wd*
Mirage in the Desert. a. Dying of Thirst. – *BAC, 1891, ca, wd, bos*
Mirage in the Desert. b. Lake of Water. – *E 245, UN, 1891, ca, bos*
St Peters and Castle of St Angelo – Day. – *MOMI, 1881–1920, wd, bos*
St Peters and Castle of St Angelo – Night. – *MOMI, 1881–1920, wd, bos, ^*

Wood-nymph's Bath. 1. Lake in Forest. – *AN, 1881–1893, wd, bos*
Wood-nymph's Bath. 2. The Wood-nymph. – *UN, 1881–1893, bos*

Announcements and Mottoes

251. Mottoes★ (Artistic Gems) (Picturesque)[161]
No Author, 3/?, G, UN, 1883–89 (F's)

Good Night – Cherubs. – *F 243, BC, 1888–89, ca, wd, ^*
Good Night – Staircase. – *F 243, UN, 1891, ca, d*
Good Night – Wreath of Flowers. – *F 243, UN, 1883–84, ca, bos*

251

252. Announcements[162]
No Author, 14/41? G, BC, m, 1906–07~

252

Adieu. (woman appearing from curtain) – *GEH, 1881–1920, d, wd*
Silence. – *AN, 1906, d, wd*
Happy New Year – Angels. (cherubs?) – *1906, wd*
Merry Christmas – Wreath with Santa. – *MLCM, 1906, wd*
Welcome. (angels with banner and harp) – *AN, 1906, d, wd, bos*
Adieu. (back of train) – *MLCM, 1906, wd, bos*
All Hallow Even. – *E 253, 1881–1920, wd*
Good Luck. (horseshoe) – *E 253, 1881–1920, wd*
Cats on Fence. (Good Night) – *1917–20, wd, bos, ^*
Good Evening. (owl in tree). – *F 245, 1900, ca, wd, bos*
Good Night. (winter sleigh, moonlight) – *1906, wd*
Good Night – Witch on Broom. – *F 245, MOMI, 1900, ca, wd, bos*
Harp and Angel in Wreath of Clovers. – *E 253, 1907, wd, n*
Intermission – Frogs in Pond. – *AN, 1906, s, wd, bos*

Skirt Dancing Effects[163]

253. Skirt Dancing Effects
No Author, 6/20?, G, BC, 1900 i.

253

Owl and Bats in Sky. – *F 245, BC, 1900, ca, wd, bos*
Witch in Sky. – *F 245, BC, 1900, ca, wd, bos, ^*
Good Luck. (horseshoe) – *F 251, BC, 1881–1920, wd*
Harp and Angel in Wreath of Clovers. – *F 252, BC, 1907, wd, n*
All Hallow Even. (Ev'n) – *F 251, BC, 1881–1920, wd*
Mermaid's Home. – *F 245, AN, 1881–93, ca, wd*

Hymns With Limited Distribution[164]

254. Hark the Herald Angels Sing
Wesley, 1/?, S, BAC, ?
Christian Lecture Bureau

1. Hark the Herald Angels Sing. – *F 90, BAC, 1902–03, wd, bos, ^*

255. Jesus Savior, Pilot Me
Hopper, 1/3?, S, BAC, ?
Williams, Brown & Earle

Safe in the Arms of Jesus (Angels kneeling before God). – *F 101, wd, bos*

256. Never Alone
Pickett, 1/4, S, BAC, ?
Williams, Brown & Earle

6. Who like Thyself, my guide and stay can be? – *F 84, 1894, wd*

254

SAVIOUR, like a shepherd lead us,
  Much we need thy tender care,
In thy pleasant pastures feed us;
  For our use thy folds prepare;
    Blessèd Jesus!
  Thou hast bought us, thine we are.

257

257. Savior, Like a Shepherd, Lead Us

Thrupp, 1/3?, S, BAC, ?
Williams Brown & Earle
Also, Albert F. Prieger

Savior Like a Shepherd, Lead Us. (Who like Thyself.) – F84, 1894, wd

258. There is a Fountain Filled With Blood

Unknown, 1/6, S, BAC, ?
McAllister (carried once)

5. Then in a nobler, sweeter song. – F 84, BAC, 1894, wd, ^

3 When at last I near the shore,
  And the fearful breakers roar
'Twixt me and the peaceful rest,
Then, while leaning on Thy breast,
  May I hear Thee say to me,
  " Fear not, I will pilot thee!"

255

256

Then in a nobler, sweeter song,
  I'll sing thy power to save,
When this poor, lisping, star
    tongue
  Lies silent in the grave.

258

Endnotes for Condensed Catalogue Raissoné

These Endnotes use the same abbreviations as the text and text endnotes, found in the Quick Key, p. 91. Lantern slide catalogs are denoted by the name of the distributor and the year of the catalog. For full names, see text notes 34, 100, and 103. Names of Sets are also shortened.

1. Set names and all other related information rely primarily on the *Briggs 1917–20* catalog (text note 24). Care should be taken in referencing these names. This catalog and most others contain non-Beale Sets and Groups with similar names to the Beale Sets, particularly in the categories of Religion and American History.

2. For Secret Societies, the name of the Society itself is used as the author, since Society officials approved the scripts of the rituals. Many of the original Briggs readings or scripts for Beale's work are at GEH or in the BC collections. The two authors most heavily represented in Beale's work are Longfellow and Shakespeare, certainly two of the most popular in the 19th century.

3. In a few cases, the number of "Beale" slides is larger than the number in the Set. This indicates that Beale did several variants of an image for this Set, or that additional slides were made after the initial "Set" was formed.

4. Numbers for both Sets and Groups are taken from the *Briggs 1917–20* catalog (text note 24), except for Secret Societies, which are discussed below. Places where the size of the original Group varies too much to define are marked with a "?" In order to give the most accurate estimate of the "Number of Slides" for a Group, the number of slides for that Group may have been drawn from several applicable sections in the catalogs. For instance, the 19 *Old Testament* Groups are drawn from the "Old Testament" sections plus three sections all entitled "Old Testament, Additional" in the *Briggs 1917–20 catalog.* The eight *New Testament* Groups are drawn from the same catalog's section titles, "Life of Christ, Additional Views, by Beale unless otherwise stated", plus three sections all entitled "New Testament, Additional". (The use of Groups of "Additional" slides was a way to cut down on the expense of reprinting the entire catalog when new slides were added.) Secret Society Groups are drawn from a similar compilation in C. W. Briggs, *List of Slides used in Secret Societies* (Philadelphia, 1917–20?). There is no publisher or date information on the catalog, but it was found in the GEH Sipley Collection and identical pages also appear in a catalog of the same name: Chas. M. Stebbins Picture Supply Co., *List of Slides used in Secret Societies* (Kansas City, MO, 1917–20?). It would appear that the Briggs Co. also distributed un-attributed *Secret Society* catalogs for dealers to brand with their own names, just as it did the *Economic Catalog.* Some Secret Society Groups are based on the 1913 version of the McIntosh catalog, (text note 83). McIntosh had larger slide lists for *White Shrine of Jerusalem, Patriotic Order of America, Grand Army of the Republic,* and *Foresters of America,* and so was used to obtain a more inclusive total Group number for these societies.

5. After the movies became popular, the length of Beale's lantern-slide Sets began to increase, probably in an attempt to compete with the more fluid action of the movies.

6. Briggs, *Catalogue,* text note 24. The many "Lecture Sets" or "Sermons" that are featured in the different catalogs are not counted as Sets or Groups here, even if they contain Beale images, as they often do. These pre-packaged shows for the prospective lanternist are long slide collections (usually 50+ images) on a single topic like *The History of America* or *Life of Christ,* and are usually accompanied by a printed "lecture" or "sermon". They are not listed here because they are so numerous and changeable; because they simply re-format the content covered in the Sets or Groups already discussed; and because they are not intended for a different audience than the standard Sets and Groups, as is, for instance, the re-packaging of (Protestant) Beale Religious slides for the Group, *Catholic Catechism.*

7. Despite its impressionistic nature, the frequency of appearance on eBay today is a useful measure. It is probably the result of three factors: the number of slides originally distributed, the ways in which the slides have been used or stored since, and the forces that are currently bringing them to market. Thus it is likely that the *Knight of Pythias* slides are so common on eBay today – some appear almost every week – because many were originally produced and distributed; because they have been in use until recently; and because many of the Knights chapters are now closing. While the *Knights* slides and some others, are probably over-represented in today's market, slow sellers 100 years ago would not be likely to appear frequently today, and slides that sold well in the Victorian period would be likely to appear more often today.

8. The most commonly seen story Sets are *Ten Nights in a Barroom, Uncle Tom's Cabin,* and (from the Secret Society listings), *The Good Samaritan* and *Damon and Pythias.* The most commonly seen song Sets are *Swanee Ribber, Where is My Wandering Boy Tonight,* and (from the Religion area) the hymns, *Rock of Ages,* and *Nearer My God to Thee.* (Both of these hymns were heavily used by the Secret Societies, as well as churches.) The most popular Parlor Poetry Sets seem to be *Curfew Must Not Ring Tonight,* and *Paul Revere's Ride.*

9. About 525 Beale slides and some over-painted Beale wash drawings of *Hamlet, Romeo and Juliet,* and *The Legend of Sleepy Hollow* are available on line at the web site of the George Eastman House International Museum of Photography and Film. For Sets, the easiest way to access the GEH data base is to use the Google Image function, searching for "George Eastman House + Lantern Slide + Name of Set". If a reference is found, click "Cache". Some of the images from the Set will appear if available. For Groups, the name of the Groups is a less reliable search tool, since the group names are so inconsistent, and some of the names have been created by us. If the Group name does not work, search instead for the name of the key image.

10. Beale did indicate on two sets of Bible designs, presumably created in 1894–95, that they were to be used in a lantern-slide instruction program for International Sunday Schools during the 1895 calendar year. He also signed (in cursive) and dated (1881) all images in *Two Paths of Virtue and Vice,* his earliest clearly dated Set.

11. It would seem logical to simply track Beale's work through the Briggs catalogs, but in fact, as Louis Sipley said, Briggs "seldom put his name on his catalogs or products". Louis Sipley, *Collector's Guide to American Photography* (Philadelphia: American Museum of Photography, 1957), 33. After the 1870s this is quite true. Instead Briggs provided some of his 113 distributors with pre-packaged listings of his slides without his name attached. These lists were then incorporated into different catalogs under different brand names. After 1900 Briggs sometimes offered entire catalogs (the *Economic Catalogs*) that distributors could brand as their own.

12. To create the catalog matrix, we concentrated on combining the catalogs of the T.H. McAllister Company, McIntosh Stereopticon (also called McIntosh Battery and Optical Co.), and Kleine Optical Company. To these three, the largest and most available, we added a few catalogs from the C.T. Milligan, James W. Queen (called N.H. Edgerton for about three years), and C.W. Briggs companies. Beale's work was therefore tracked through a yearly matrix made up of six of Briggs's main distributors. A number of years in the matrix are represented by more than one company, allowing results to be double-checked. The core list was supplemented with catalogs from eight other distributors not cited here, allowing further double-checking. The search for slide dates was facilitated by the fact that the slide listings were frequently in the same format – that provided by Briggs. Distributors' names and catalog titles often changed somewhat over the years; the most common names are given in the citations below. The citations are followed by the matrix years covered by that company's catalogs. These years are indicated by brackets [ ]. T.H. McAllister, *Catalogue of Stereopticon*, text note 34. [1866, '75, '80, '81, '82, '85, '86, '87, '89, '90, '91, '92, '93, '94, '97, '98, '99, 1900, '01, '03, '06, '07, '08, '13]; McIntosh, *Projection Apparatus*, text note 83. [1895, 1900, '07, '09, '12, '13, '16]; O. B. & G. Kleine, Opticians (Kleine Optical Co.), *Catalogue of Stereopticons, Sciopticons, Magic Lanterns and Views* (New York, 1894). [1894, 1903, '04, '05]; C.T. Milligan, *Illustrated Catalogue*, text note 100, 1892, [1875, '77, '79, '82, '87, '92, 1910]; James W. Queen & Co., *Priced and Illustrated Catalogue*, text note 100, 1884, [1876 – produced by N.H. Edgerton for this year only that we use, and then Queen, 1880, '84, '85, '89]; C.W. Briggs. *Untitled Picture Catalog*, text note 121, 1893, *and Catalogue of Economic Series Lantern Slides*, text note 24, 1917–20, [1893, 1917–20]. For Secret Society slides, see Stebbins, *List of Secret Society Slides*, *Catalogue* note 4.

13. The dating data does contain some assumptions, problems, and inconsistencies: We assume that when a slide first appears after 1881 with the same or similar name as a known Beale image, it is in fact by Beale, but we cannot be certain since we usually do not have the ability to actually see the image in the catalog. In general we assume that when the catalogs change the title of a slide from a pre-Beale title to a known Beale title, Beale has revised the image. We assume that when the catalogs attribute an image to Beale, he did it in that year. The catalog matrix mixes the catalogs of different companies, which sometimes treat subjects or Sets differently. Even the catalogs of a single company may be inconsistent, because various sub-catalogs did not necessarily cover the same material. In addition, some of the catalog copies were incomplete; some were so fragile that we were only allowed to copy a few pages (in the pre-digital era); some we were not allowed to copy at all, which made detailed tracking difficult. Some catalogs were issued early in the year, in which case the image we attributed to that year might have actually been created the year before; some were issued late, so the creation could have been the same year. The process of tracking the slides is further complicated because often (especially in the History, Secret Society, and Religion sections) Beale re-drew slides that had been previously listed in the catalog, so a Beale slide may have been created with no indication that it had been re-drawn. Thus the evidence was clearest and most accurate for story Sets; less so for individual slides and Groups. In dating Beale's Sets and Groups, we use the first appearance of several of Beale's slides, but not the appearance of a single image used to "test market" a subject. (About a dozen Sets grow over time from the first few slides to substantially larger numbers; we discuss this in the Set notes.) When we know the exact date of Beale's work from letters, the *Briggs 1890–92 Ledger*, copyrights, etc., we give that specific date. (These works may not appear in the catalog until the next year, and so dates obtained from these sources may be slightly inconsistent with dates derived from catalogs, but the inconsistency is no greater than that within the catalog matrix itself, as explained above.) We also give a specific date when we have two catalogs in a yearly sequence, and so can determine the exact year of a Set's introduction. However, some catalogs contain multiple printed dates – in the case of one Milligan issue, an inside cover date (February 1879), a copyright-page date (1877), and an inside-copyright date for "New Art Slides", 1875 (p. 92). As a result, we use the 1875 date for "New Art Slides", and the 1877 date for everything else, assuming that the cover date of 1879 was a cover change only, designed to give a (misleading) sense of currency. We follow the same procedure in other similar cases.

14. Catalogs are missing for 1883, '88, '96, 1902, '11, '14, '15, '17, '18, '19. Hence the bracketed dates are 1883–84, 1888–89, 1896–97, 1902–03, 1911–12, 1914–16, 1917–20.

There are two exceptions to this pattern, both created by unusual catalog events. The *Briggs 1893* catalog (text note 121) is the first to show pictures of Beale images, so many Beale revisions of previous slides or Sets appear here for the first time. However, it would be unreasonable to assume that Beale created all this work in the single year of 1893. The images could have been produced at any time since he began work in 1881, and we would not have known it because we could not see the revisions pictured. Hence these slides are dated 1881–93. Similarly, the McAllister 1897 catalog provides a new kind of information. In that year, for the first time, McAllister specifically attributed to Beale 92 slides in the "Old Testament", "New Testament" and "Artistic Gem" categories. (Four slides were attributed in 1893.) Because we do not have the 1895 or 1896 McAllister catalogs, we cannot tell if McAllister was making this kind of catalog attribution earlier. Hence the slides that McAllister attributed to Beale in 1897 are dated as 1895–97. (If a slide simply appeared for the first time in 1897, with no catalog attribution, we would use the ordinary catalog matrix, which includes an 1895 McIntosh catalog, and date the images 1896–97.) When a Set with bracketed dates like 1881–93 is placed in a chronological list, as in Fig. 43, or *Appendix 2*, it is placed by the last date in the bracketed pair (1893), since 1893 is the earliest date we are sure of. Conversely, the 1881–93 Set is listed before a 1893 Set, since some slides in the 1881–93 Set may well have been created before 1893. Thus a chronological list would read, 1892, 1881–93, 1893, etc.

15. If a Set (or Group) had two or more clear times of introduction (e.g. beginning with a Set of four, and later expanding in one limited period to 10), both dates are given, separated by a comma. We also provide the dates, if known, of the individual slides, and/or discuss the dating in the notes. There may be a few slides in the Set with other dates.

16. If a Beale individual slide image appears in the catalogs after he began work in 1881, the date of first consistent appearance is used, even if the slide is not specifically attributed to Beale until a later date. If an image exists in the catalogs, is attributed to another artist, and then changes to a Beale attribution, we use the date of the attribution change.

17. It is likely that 60 percent of the <u>total</u> slides – Beale and non-Beale – listed for a Group would have a different date range than the Beale-only slides, which are the only ones counted in dating Beale.

18. This broad range usually occurs because slides, Sets or Groups existed before Beale started work, and he re-drew them at some time that cannot be determined because the names of the slides do not change. Or, there may be so many undated slides in a Group that we cannot apply the 60-percent rule. Or, Beale may not have done many images in the Set or Group. If a few individual slide dates in such a Group are known, they are given. It is possible, in a Group where Beale did only a few slides, that some of the slides by others were created outside of the 1881–1920 date range.

Of the slides attributed by the catalogs to Beale between 1895 and 1897, ten cannot be dated earlier by any other means. These ten are given the dates 1881–1897, since it is impossible to be sure when during that period Beale created them. After 1897, additional slides were attributed to Beale on a regular year-by-year basis, and these year-by-year incremental attributions can be used as dating evidence. In 1899 McAllister began labeling *The Parables of Christ* as, "By Beale unless otherwise stated". Beginning in 1900 McIntosh applied the same practice to the *Parables* as well as to the *Old* and *New Testaments*.

19. Briggs, *Economic Catalogue*, 1917–20, text note 24. Briggs, *Secret Societies*, *Catalogue* note 4. Sometimes these slide names are quotations from the text, sometimes they are descriptions of the image, sometimes they are short titles. And, unfortunately, sometimes the phrasing of the title changes from catalog to catalog, or over time; and sometimes the title of the wash drawing is not the same as the slide. To further complicate things, sometimes different titles were written by Briggs on the verso of the drawing; and sometimes titles were given by Colen or other curators who did not know what slide the drawing went with. Punctuation is also often inconsistent, especially in the treatment of quotations, articles such as "the", capitals, periods, and spelling – e.g. "Persimmons", "Persimmon", "Persimmon's", – all for a single proper name in a single Set. In general, the original formats have been kept, but may have been shortened for space reasons. Slides appear in the same order as in the major catalogs. If there are "additional slides" used in some catalogs, these are interpolated at the appropriate spots. (As more catalogs become available, the dating of slides and Groups will improve.)

20. Because the creative effort for one of these "F" slides occurred earlier, we do not, as indicated in our discussion of Dating, use the "F"-dated slides in calculating the date of a Set or Group. We do, however, count the "F" images as part of the number of Beale slides for the Group.

The name of the slide followed by an "F" may have been changed from the earliest use. If the change is slight, we simply present the new title; if the change is significant, we give the original name or a portion thereof in parentheses afterwards, or cover the change in a note. The date and the rest of the information contained on the line are identical to the earliest use, or almost so. (The "E's" and "F's" and location information may change.) The slides listed with an "F" are sometimes the same date as the earliest use, indicating that they appeared in the same year, and that we are simply showing multiple use. Usually, however, the slides marked with an "F" are in a later Set because "F" means they were **F**irst Used somewhere else. The images with highest multiple use are the "The Samaritan Binds Up His Wounds" from *The Good Samaritan* (Set 145) and "Bethlehem by Night" from *Christmas* (Set 135), both of which are applied in five other contexts.

21. When we are uncertain about any individual attribution entry, we follow that entry with a question mark. If, after considering all factors, we are uncertain about whether or not a slide is by Beale we list it in the *Appendix 3, Slides Possibly by Beale*. There are 31 images in this *Appendix*, together with a summary of the evidence concerning them.

22. We use "wd" for attribution if we know that a drawing exists, or if there is documentation of its previous existence such as a signature on a slide or negative, pre-fire curatorial notes from BAC, photographs, exhibit notices, etc. In the case of BAC, it is likely that some non-Beale drawings were included in the "Beale" collection, as they are in all other large collections. But since both the drawings and the slides were lost, and we are making attributions based only on curatorial notes and non-bos slides, it is possible that a few BAC "wd" attributions are incorrect.

23. Although artistic style is often part of the processes of distinguishing Beale wash drawings from those by other artists, the drawing itself is the focus of attention in most cases. The drawing presents physical paper, paint, and marginalia to examine, and we can usually be quite certain of our facts without relying on style. In these cases, we simply list the attribution source as "wd" for "wash drawing" since the existence of the drawing is the key determiner. Trying to determine "artistic style" attribution by looking only at lantern slides is a difficult matter, because the clues of paper, paint, and marginalia are absent, and because the type and quality of slide coloring can so dramatically affect the "look" of the image. Yet when we cite artistic style as a reference, we must use such slides because the attribution is otherwise impossible – there are no drawings or Beale's Own Slides. Because of this contradiction, we have avoided attributing such images to Beale *solely* on the basis of style, and judge a slide to be "Beale" based on "artistic style" only if there is some sort of supporting evidence such as the fact that the other slides in the Set were by Beale.

24. Many of the *Literature* Sets were reproduced in photographic "bulletin board" spreads in *Grade Teacher* from 1939 to 1944. *Grade Teacher* was the leading elementary teachers' magazine at the time, so this regular monthly feature introduced Beale's work to a whole new generation of millions of children.

25. Some images of *Evangeline* are based on the illustrations of Frank Dicksee. See Henry Wadsworth Longfellow, *Evangeline: A Tale of Acadie* (London: Cassell, Petter, Galpin & Co., 1882). On the verso of drawing # 14, which is matched out from a Dicksee image, Briggs reminded Beale to keep his original slides for the Set "in harmony with it". "Harmony" was the Briggs/Beale term for maintaining "continuity".

26. An early pre-Beale Set of four slides of *Hiawatha*, based on rather crude Currier and Ives lithographs, was dropped in 1882-85. Four similar images reappear after 15 years in 1900, this time by Beale. In 1907 the Set becomes 24. Slides # 10 and # 11 were revised for impact (the "B" version), but the originals were kept in the catalogs as the "A" version, since the images were quite different. Thus the Set is numbered 1–22, but 24 are actually presented. Some of 1907 images rely on an unidentified previous source.

27. The Beale images of *Marley's Ghost* are not copied from the original John Leech drawings that accompanied Dickens's story, but show a familiarity with them. Several unsigned images in Beale's version appear to be based on the English lantern-slide Set by York and Sons. A Set of *Marley's Ghost* by the American slide manufacturer Williams, Brown & Earle combines Beale images and life-model slides.

28. Some images for *Robinson Crusoe* rely on an unidentified previous source.

29. Most images for *Uncle Tom's Cabin* are closely based on the original book illustrations by Hammett Billings. See Harriet Beecher Stowe, *Uncle Tom's Cabin, or Life among the Lowly* (Toronto: Maclear & Company, 1852). Attribution of this very early Set is somewhat uncertain, despite the extant drawings with a Colen provenance, and Beale Owned Slides. The drawings are on brown paper, not Beale's usual grey, though that is typical for early Sets. ("Eva's Dying Farewell" is on grey paper, has Beale notes on the drawing, and is a revision of the earlier image, the drawing for which has been lost.)

30. Most images of *Hamlet* (and the other noted Shakespeare Sets) are closely based on the outline engravings of Moritz Retzsch, *Gallery to Shakespeare's Dramatic Works in Outlines* (New York: Westermann Brothers, 1840).

31. Ibid. A Beale "outline" sketch for slide # 8 of *Macbeth*, including a Briggs "Very Good" notation, is in the BC.

32. See note 30.

33. See note 30. In a letter to Beale of Aug. 20, 1909, Briggs complained of late delivery of the *Othello* designs.

34. Beale used four different matte overlays to create *Pygmalion and Galatea*. They are in the BC.

35. See note 30.

36. The Beale Owned Slides for *Annie and Willie's Prayer* were stolen from Katherine Leddick. We found a label for one of them in one of the Leddick boxes, confirming their previous existence. Four of Beale's initial sketches for the Set are in the BC.

37. Some of the designs for *Curfew* are very loosely based on those in Rose Hartwick Thorpe, *"Curfew Must Not Ring Tonight"* (Boston: Lee and Shepard, Publisher, 1883).

38. For the Set of *Drake's Ode*, the slide "Our Banner in the Sky" (from Set 162) may have been used for slide # 1 after 1899. For slide # 6 Beale created three versions of the American flag, with 42, 45, and 48 stars. Presumably the images were changed to reflect the country's growth, which is how we have dated them, though the *Briggs 1893* catalog still shows the 42 star flag, two years after the country had 45 states.

39. Two images for *Persimmon's* are based on the illustrations of J. Wells Champney. The story is by his wife, Elizabeth. At some unknown date in his career Beale revised an earlier Set which used the Champney drawings, plus two others.

40. It is possible that in some versions of *Independence Bell,* slide # 6 replaced slide # 1, and that slide # 5 v replaced slide # 6.

41. A Set for *John Gilpin*, which we believe to be Beale-Owned Slides, is now held by a Beale relative.

42. In a letter to Briggs, Nov. 22, 1905 (BC), Beale mentions that he will be sending "outlines" (a storyboard) of *John Maynard* to Briggs.

43. Briggs made an entry in his Dec. 1891 *Ledger* for a $16 payment to Beale for the Set of *Nellie's Prayer*. (See text note 66.) The amount is so low for twelve slides that it suggests Beale only matched out the Set. Certainly it is not a typical Beale design.

44. A package of four color prints from *Revere's Ride* was widely distributed to teachers from 1942 to 1958. See Revere Copper and Brass Co., *Paul Revere's Ride: Reproductions from the Famous Beale Paintings* (New York: Revere Copper and Brass Inc. 1942–58).

45. The Beale images of *Pied Piper* were presented as one of a series of large Sunday newspaper supplements featuring Beale's work, syndicated nationally in 1938. For example, "The Pied Piper of Hamlin", *The Syracuse Herald*, Sunday, Jan. 30, 1938.

46. The entire Set of *The Raven* was exhibited at the Whitney Museum of American Art in 1936. See text note 46.

47. The Beale Owned Slides for *Village Blacksmith* were stolen from Katherine Leddick. We know about them only through her notes about her shows, now in the BC.

48. *Saint Nicholas* appears as a Set of five in 1879, before Beale, becomes four by Beale in 1885, and then six by Beale in 1901. There are two versions of slide # 2, probably to improve continuity.

49. We believe that Briggs may have had another artist (Tholey?) begin the *Wreck,* disliked the result, and immediately had Beale re-do all but # 7. All drawings we have examined but # 7 are on Beale's grey paper, and in his artistic style.

50. There are two versions of *America*, one introduced as a three-slide Set in 1893 and then expanded to four in 1901; and a Set of 12 introduced in 1917–20. It is likely that this last Set was "made up" of pre-existing images. We have seen only two slides from it, slide # 7 with a printed label, and slide # 6, which had a handwritten label, so we cannot be sure of the nature of the entire Set. Some of the images from the first version (slides # 2 and # 3) were probably also used in it. *America*, and a number of other Sets, are presented in two full-Set formats: images only; and the same images, reduced in size, accompanied by appropriate verses.

51. The *Comic Songs* slides are usually listed in catalogs under *Comic Subjects*.

52. These images for *Dixie's Land* do not fit the verses in common versions of the song, "Dixie". Numbers 2, 3, 6, 7, and 8 were sold by American National (AN) at auction in 2012.

53. Beale created most of the images for *Home Sweet Home*, but slide # 3 is a non-Beale image of a farmhouse. Beale used a similar house in his images of this Set in order to "harmonize" with this previous image. The variant of slide # 11 appears to have been created to improve continuity.

54. Three Sets, *Killarney* (Set 50), *Holy City* (Set 90) and *Jerusalem the Golden* (Set 91) share a number of images in ways that change over time and with different distributors. Labels on the drawings themselves often reference two different Sets. We have been unable to completely unsnarl this confusion. In particular, there are often different slide numbers for the same image. Thus some images marked "E" (Used Elsewhere) have no clear numbered counterpart in the related Set, and so are indicated as unnumbered "v's" for "variants".

55. The last slide of *Marching* that we present here, a picture of General Sherman's men tearing up the railroad tracks, was never offered as a part of this Set, though it sometimes had the same title. Most catalogs sold it under the *American History* listings as a separate full-image single slide with the title "Sherman's March". Williams Browne and Earle sold it as a song slide (a half-image with words, like the *Illuminated Hymn* format), under the title "Marching Thro' Georgia".

56. This image for *Maryland* was created on a half-sheet of paper, specifically to be used with words in the *Illuminated Hymn* format.

57. In a letter to Briggs, Nov. 22, 1905, now at GEH, Beale discussed the coloring of *Old Black Joe*.

58. A song-slide version of this Set also exists, with the same images, reduced in size, accompanied by appropriate verses.

59. Ibid.

60. A version of *Swanee Ribber* by the Stereopticon and Film Exchange Company mixes Beale images and life-model photographs.

61. This dissolve Set of *Tramp* was created with one large drawing and a flap, or matte overlay, to make the second slide. Compare note 62

62. For the dissolve Set of *Soldier's Dream*, the second image was created using a separate full-sized drawing showing only a small "balloon" to represent the "Vision of Home".

63. There was a 24, a 48, and a 60-slide Set of *Ben Hur*. In a draft letter, Sept. 1909, to Harper Bros. (BC), Beale said he did 34 images for *Ben Hur*. The entire Set changed title to *Jewish Life* in Briggs 1917–20; the slide titles also changed. In *McIntosh 1912*, the Set changed title to *Son of Ben Hur*, and many of the slide titles also changed. See note 114 on *Jewish Life*.

64. There was a 12-slide Set of *Pilgrim's Progress* by Tholey before Beale. Beale added twelve new slides in 1896-97, interspersing them, generally on an every-other-slide basis, within the earlier Set. (This regular integration of Beale slides into pre-existing material is unusual; more often slides were added to achieve a specific effect such as strengthening a climax, or covering additional verses in a poem.)

65. *Quo Vadis* was a Set made up from pre-existing images, with the exception of the Beale slides which were expressly created for it. Different distributors created their own Sets, some containing up to 60 slides.

66. *Other Wise Man* starts as 24 in 1908 then goes to 40 in 1911-12.

67. The catalog attribution for *The Tabernacle* says that Beale's drawing was based on a model. The source of the Set is probably John Dilworth, *Pictorial Description of the Tabernacle in the Wilderness: Its Rites and Ceremonies* (London: Sunday School Union, 1859). This little booklet contains 20 illustrations and presents the story of how Dilworth built a model of the Biblical Tabernacle in order to work out its construction, and explain the significance of its rites to Sunday School students.

68. *Sleepy Hollow* is a close copy of images by F. O. C. Darley. See Washington Irving, *Rip Van Winkle and the Legend of Sleepy Hollow* (Tarrytown, New York: Sleepy Hollow Press, 1974). In a letter to Beale, Nov. 30, 1910 (BC), Briggs complimented him on the way he had handled the adaptation of what were probably the images from *Sleepy Hollow*.

69. Two slides not listed in *Man Without a Country*, # 1 and # 6, are probably by Beale, but are not attributed to him here. Both have only printing on them, so there is no "artistic style" to go by, and there are no wash drawings or Beale's Own Slides or other documentation. They are listed as "Possibly Beale". Slide # 2 is a photograph of Hale.

70. *Rip* is a close copy of Darley. See note 68.

71. See text note 46 re. an exhibit of this Set at the Whitney Museum. The 12 drawings were in the collection of the Whitney until 1950, when they were de-accessioned and transferred to M. Knoedler & Co. for sale.

72. *How Jones Became a Mason* is mentioned in the Jan. 1878 *Magic Lantern* journal, and is first seen as a dissolve Set of four, pre-Beale images in *McAllister 1880*. (See text Fig. 38.) In 1891 it moves from the "Dissolving Views" section to become a Set of four with its own title, and we presume that Beale re-drew the earlier images at that time. The larger Set of 12 was introduced in 1905. Beale's drawings are at the Masonic Texas Grand Lodge, Waco, Texas.

73. *Mr. Spurt* was reproduced in *Ford Times* in June, 1946 in celebration of the 50th anniversary of the Ford Motor Company (BC). See text note 46 re. the Whitney Museum of American Art, where some images from this Set were exhibited.

74. A letter from Beale to Briggs, Nov. 22, 1909 responded to Briggs's criticism of *Mr. Timorous*, slide # 1. Briggs had provided Beale with his own sketches for this Set, and initially did not like Beale's version, but published the image unchanged.

75. Slide # 1 of *Paddy* creates a better image to establish the background of the story than did the variant, which may never have been published.

76. There were 12 images of *Abide* in 1884, ten in 1896–97. The two variant slides were used in different versions of the 10-slide Set, but also, with different titles, in the longer Set.

77. Slide # 9 of *Greenlands* sometimes had a variant dissolve of Christ in a cloud. The *Illuminated Hymn* of *Greenlands* does not use an image from this set, but # 2 from Set 115.

78. *Hold the Fort* was often presented in the catalogs under *Dissolving Views*.

79. See note 58.

80. We have not found *Jerusalem the Golden* in any catalog, except as a single-slide in *Illuminated Hymns* (Set 104), nor have we seen slides of it. Our knowledge of the Set's existence comes from its title, handwritten on the verso of the four wash drawings, along with the slide titles as cited. The order of the slides is unknown. Two of the images ("Angels kneeling before God", "Angels playing trumpets") are in *Rock of Ages* (Set 101), which appeared in 1891, and is pictured in the *Briggs 1893* catalog. Three of the images ("Angels singing", "Angels playing harps", "Angels playing trumpets") are part of *Holy City* (Set 90), which first appeared in 1899. Our hypothesis is that sometime after 1891 (probably after 1899), Briggs considered using the cited images to create a Set of *Jerusalem the Golden*. Whether he actually published it is unknown. See also note 58. A song-slide version also appears, with some images reduced in size, accompanied by appropriate verses.

81. See note 58.

82. There are three Beale versions of *Lead Kindly Light*. The *First Edition* of drawings seems to have been immediately revised, and may not have been made into slides, as we have not seen any. In a letter to Beale, Sept. 20, 1909 (BC), Briggs offered to return the drawings to Beale. The *Variant of the First Edition* (pictured) seems to have been very similar to the first, except for costume changes. It was used for at least a while. The *Second Edition* is called that because Beale wrote that title on the drawings, though it was actually the third if what we call the unused *First Edition* is included in the count. The *Second Edition* showed a plain pilgrim rather than the elaborately costumed protagonist of the *First Variant*, and slides # 1 and # 2 were quite different. It may have been more heavily used at the end of the magic-lantern period. The *Second Edition* exists in a song-slide version.

83. The drawing for image # 4 of *My Mother's Bible* was exhibited at the Whitney Museum of Art in 1936. See text note 46. It is the only image to remain in their collection. Authorship is uncertain.

84. *Near the Cross* was usually listed under *Dissolving Views*. It is not in the *Briggs 1917–20* catalog.

85. *Nearer My God* was widely used by Secret Societies. See also note 58.

86. *Rock of Ages* appeared in an early, pre-Beale Set of four dissolving views based on a single painting by Johannes Oertel. A "new set" of four was introduced in 1887, we assume by Beale. It grew in 1891 to 12 and in 1906 to 18. Beale may also have done the effect slides of "Lightning" and "Rainbow" but they are not counted here, nor among the "Possible Beales" in *Appendix Six* because there is no evidence on which to base attribution, and the Set grew in such a major manner. See also note 58.

87. *Illuminated Hymns* is a separate Set title used in most catalogs. It is unique in that when it was introduced in 1899 it had only one Beale image, but the number of Beale images grew substantially over time. The Set does not appear in *Briggs 1917–20*. These hymns have both the words for a hymn and a single picture on one slide. Some of the images in *Illuminated Hymns* are known through slides in the BC, not from catalog listings. Versions with words and music, but without pictures, also exist for most of these Sets. *America* is listed by the catalogs both as a single slide, and in the multiple-slide words-and-pictures format as shown here. Four other hymns listed under *Illuminated Hymns* also have multiple slides and images, each slide with the words for the associated image: *Red, White and Blue; The Star Spangled Banner; Hold the Fort;* and *Rock of Ages*. Because they, like *America*, make up complete Sets, they are listed as such in this *Catalogue* – Sets 57, 58, 89, 101, and 45 respectively. Several other hymn or song Sets, not included in *Illuminated Hymns*, are presented in similar versions that use all the images, with and without words. All such Sets are mentioned in the *Catalogue* notes. See also *Appendix 6, Illustrated Song Slides*.

88. *St. Paul* starts before Beale as six slides in 1880. In 1896–97, the subject becomes 29 travel views called *Paul's Travels*, probably made directly from existing engravings, each with a short title. In 1899 a new Set of 35 called *Life of St. Paul* is introduced, including three new slides attributed to Beale. Beale also probably redrew some of the *Paul's Travel's* engravings at this time. The Set was expanded to 36 in 1914–16.

89. *Ecclesiastes* is primarily carried in the Secret Society catalogs. All drawings but the first were made half size.

90. The slide, "The Needle's Eye Gate", is designated as a *Golden Bible Text* on the wash drawing, but appears under *New Testament* in the catalogs, hence there are only 12 slides in the *Bible Text* set.

91. Our dating for *Old Testament Sets* 116–124 and 129–134 is slightly different from the rest of Beale's work for the reasons discussed in note 14.

92. *Creation of Earth* (Set 116) has a geological focus and *Creation (of Life)* (Set 117) has a biological focus. *Earth* is sometimes listed as a separate Set, as we have done here, and sometimes included as a group under *Old Testament*. *Life* is always listed as a group under *Old Testament*, and always follows *Earth* in the list, once *Earth* was introduced in 1907.

93. Ibid. In a Briggs letter to Beale, Nov. 26, 1909 (BC) Briggs gave art directions for reworking a pre-existing image of the "Expulsion" slide in *Creation*, and said he was providing tissue overlays. On Nov. 29 he complained that it sounded as if Beale were painting a new figure. Beale responded on that same day, saying that he was overpainting the existing image.

94. A Set called *Life of Joseph* existed in the catalogs in 1877, before Beale, and was dropped after 1894. Beale may have created, or re-drawn some of the images between 1881 and 1894, but we cannot be sure. After 1894, *Joseph* images are listed as part of *Old Testament*, and broken out as a Group by us here.

95. In the Set of *Moses*, the slide "The Burning Bush (Without Moses)" was not listed in the *Old Testament,* but in *Royal Arch, Masonic* (Set 204). It could be used singly, or as a dissolve with "Moses and Angel in Flaming Bush".

96. The *International Sunday School* Set was a series of slides created and promoted for weekly Sunday School use throughout the country during the third and fourth quarters of 1895. It may have been used internationally as well. It was listed as a Set only once that we have seen, in the *1894 McAllister Bulletin No. 27.* Otherwise the slides were integrated into the *Old Testament,* and we have done that with "E's".

97. All but one of the slides for *Samuel* are First Used Elsewhere (F's), making the Group difficult to date.

98. Briggs wrote to Beale on July 20, 1911 regarding the "David Refusing Armor" image in *David,* asking Beale to read the relevant Bible passage and create a drawing, "harmonizing" it with pre-existing drawings. On July 22, Briggs said he had the drawing, but asked for changes. Beale responded on July 29. Apparently the image was misplaced, as Briggs wrote on August 14th asking where it was. (All letters in the BC.)

99. Most slides of *Captives* appear under *Old Testament, Additional* in the catalogs. Related slides are in *The Bible Story in Pictures* (Set 156).

100. Only one slide of *Jonah*, "Jonah and the Whale", is listed in the catalogs. There are two drawings, but we do not know which image the catalogs are referring to. The two images may have been done at different times, as the two whales are not the same, but lacking better data we use the first catalog date for both. Both images were used in Set 159, though the names were radically changed.

101. All but one of the slides for *Christ's Youth* are First Used Elsewhere (F's), making the Group difficult to date.

102. In *Christ's Ministry* we have broken out five slides, all of which begin with "The Calling of …", as Set 138, *Calling of the Disciples.* An underlined note in the list of *Christ's Ministry* indicates where "The Calling" slides were placed in the chronology.

103. Ibid.

104. *Acts*, including Beale slides, is presented as a Group following *New Testament* in McAllister 1897 but does not become a named Set until 1899.

105. See note 96.

106. Those parables dated 1895–97 appear as part of the *New Testament* catalog listings for those three years only, and are then listed separately as *Parables.*

107. *The Good Samaritan* had a number of variants, which generated the catalogs' unique "0" number, used here for the first slide. Wash drawings #s 1 and 2 were made with matte overlays on drawings #s 0 and 1 v.

108. Detailed art directions and Beale's storyboard outline for *The Good Shepherd* are in the BC.

109. *Laborers* appears only in Secret Society catalogs.

110. The dating of The *Prodigal Son* is difficult as most images are based on adaptations of previous engravings. (A Set consisting of the engravings themselves was published by the Williams, Brown and Earle lantern-slide company and is in the BC.) We believe that this same Set of engravings first appears as slides in *Milligan 1877*. It is used by McAllister only in 1880–82, so obviously McAllister did not find it satisfactory. Milligan introduces a new Set in 1892. In 1893 McAllister begins using the *Prodigal Son* again, and in that same year it is also depicted in its revised 8-slide Beale form in the Briggs picture catalog, so we date the Beale Set to that year. In 1902–03, Beale added the last two slides, which are his own composition.

111. In a letter to Briggs, Nov. 22, 1905 (BC), Beale discussed the coloring of *Wicked Husbandmen*.

112. *The Bible Story in Pictures* was available from the Chas. M. Stebbins lantern slide company only, and hence cannot be dated with the catalog matrix. But Stebbins also published a book of the same title, dated 1914, illustrated primarily with Beale slides, so we use that as the Set date.

   See Charles Stebbins (?), *The Bible Story in Pictures* (Kansas City: The Stebbins Publishing Company, 1914).

113. The *Catholic Catechism* was carried only by the Deveraux Slide Company, and so cannot be dated with the catalog matrix.

114. *Jewish Life* is almost identical to *Ben Hur* (Set 64) in images and order. Only the Set title and slide titles have been changed, and two numbered slides added. The Set of *Ben Hur* was dropped from the *Briggs 1917–20* catalog. Since anyone familiar with *Ben Hur* would recognize the *Jewish Life* images as a dramatization of *Ben Hur*, the change in titles may have been a way of avoiding a copyright suit such as that filed by Lew Wallace against the American distribution of the lantern adaptation of *Ben Hur* by the British firm of Riley Bros. See Riley Brothers, *Catalogue of Stereopticons, Magic-Lanterns, and Lantern Accessories,* (New York: Riley Brothers, 1898) 128.

115. *The Photodrama* was not carried by the catalogs. It was produced by the Jehovah's Witnesses, also known as the Watch Tower Bible and Tract Society or the International Bible Students Association. *The Photodrama* was a multi-media program combining lantern slides, movies, and recorded sound, and was shown to between nine and eleven million people using 100 teams of

projectionists. Various versions were produced, beginning in 1912, with the first performances in 1914. The images counted here are from the three-volume book version of the production: International Bible Students Association, *Scenario of The Photodrama of Creation, Vols. 1-3* (London and Brooklyn: International Bible Students Association, 1914). A modern inexpensive reprint, with the slides reproduced in color rather than in the purple and white of the original, is available at www.bibletoday.com. There were more Beale images in some of the projected versions. The pictured slide of "Hell" from this Set was changed from the original wash drawing, possibly in order to emphasize the non-traditional nature of the church's dogma, exemplified in the title printed on the slide itself, "Adam and Eve Now – Traditional Theology".

116. Like *Bible Story in Pictures* (Set 156), *First Christmas* was available only from the Chas. M. Stebbins lantern slide company, and was accompanied by a book with the same title as the Set. Four of the images (dated 1915) were apparently commissioned for the Set, and are copyrighted by Stebbins. See Charlotte Wilder, *The Story of the Very First Christmas* (Kansas City: The Stebbins Publishing Company, 1915).

117. Nineteen of Beale's *American History* images were used by the Homer Laughlin China Company to decorate a complete set of dinnerware, available in red or blue. The dinnerware was sold from 1942 through 1952 (or 1939 to 1958, according to some sources) through F. W. Woolworth, one of the largest department store chains in the world. See Bob Page, Dale Frederiksen, Dean Six, *Homer Laughlin: Decades of Dinnerware* (Greensboro, North Carolina: Page/Frederiksen Publications, 2003) 410–411.

118. Most of the *Americana* slides are listed in a separate section of the catalogs at the end of *American History*. Sometimes the section is unlabeled; sometimes it is called *Army Scenes and Incidents*. The drawing for "Remember the Maine" looks as though it is to create a dissolving image, but we have not seen slides for that effect, so do not count it as a dissolve.

119. Though Beale had only one image in this large Set of *Passing of the Indian*, it was the one that was always used to promote it.

120. The full Set of *Franklin* drawings was exhibited at the Whitney Museum of American Art in 1936. See text note 46.

121. "Lincoln's Debate with Douglas" is unique in that it is an adaptation from an earlier Beale image, "The Farmers' Movement in the West", a Beale etching published in *Frank Leslie's Illustrated Newspaper*, August 30, 1873. Beale's magic-lantern drawing of the "Debate" was made into a 1958 U.S. postage stamp. The "Assassination" drawing is smaller than usual (10" x 10") on grey paper, and appears to be a Beale re-do of an earlier lantern image.

122. The *Washington* Set has both a numbered Set of 12 and another 12 "Additional" which are unnumbered.

123. *Mary Queen of Scots* was adapted from engravings. The artist is unknown. Slides # 1 and 12 may well be by Beale, but there is conflicting evidence so they are listed as Possibly By Beale in *Appendix 7*.

124. A previous owner of the *Seven Wonders* drawings reported that five images were signed (BC files). The seven Beale images were reprinted as one of a series of 16" x 21" Sunday newspaper supplements, syndicated nationally in 1938. Beale's drawings also seem to have formed the basis for some of the illustrations by Mario Larrinaga that were used in Lowell Thomas's 1956 Cinerama production of *Seven Wonders of the World*. See Lowell Thomas, *Seven Wonders of the World* (Garden City, New York: Hanover House, 1956) 94+. Beale's *Seven Wonders* images were also made into a set of Cuban postage stamps in 1997 (BC).

125. The full Set of *Garfield* appears in 1882 with only one Beale slide. The Set disappears from the catalogs by 1888–89.

126. The dissolving view of the *Maine Disaster*, and many of the slides of the *Spanish American War* from Set 189 appeared in many presentations, often mixed with photographs of the War, and sometimes with movies.

127. Ibid. The variant of the "Sinking of the Merrimac" in *Spanish American War* has only an "artistic style" attribution, but it appears in wood-framed slide Sets, which suggests pre-1900, only two years after the Set's creation. That is a further indication that the variant is by Beale. The variant appears to be an effort to further dramatize the scene. The image was used extensively to promote the Set. The last two slides of the Set are a dissolving pair which created a gunboat with a searchlight that could be "turned on" and then moved with a lever. This is one of only three times that Beale created movement on screen through mechanical slides, though there were many cases where he created movement with a rapid dissolve, especially in the Comic Sets (240–244).

128. The first time the *Boer War* appears in the catalog matrix is 1902–03. It was probably introduced in 1900, but in a catalog that we do not have.

129. While discussing *Russo-Japan War* in a letter to Briggs, Aug. 18, 1905 (GEH), Beale writes that he is posting "The Battle of Mukden", and comments on the difficulty of making "two battles in one week". He also discusses the proper coloring of the uniforms. The Set drops out of the catalogs after 1910.

130. Slide five of *The Drunkard's Daughter* is closely copied from an image in *The Drunkard's Children* by George Cruickshank.

131. Image # 2 of *Drunkard's Reform* has been matched out on all four sides. The background of # 3, though the same view, is slightly different. It appears likely that someone other than Beale did the original # 2, which was matched out by Beale (?), who then completed the Set.

132. The song *Father, Dear Father* was often used to accompany the story *Ten Nights in a Bar Room* (Set 199).

133. The last two slides of *Moonshiners* were often listed as a dissolving pair. The Set was created with a matte technique, using cutouts, now at GEH.

134. A pre-Beale slide version of *Ten Nights* is in the BC and appears in an 1875–76 catalog (See Table 2). The existing drawings are reported to be Beale's typical grey paper, and there is a Set of Beale's Own Slides, so he probably reworked the previous images, perhaps copied from a book.

135. *Two Paths* is Beale's earliest clearly dated Set. It is on brownish-grey paper, not Beale's usual grey, as is typical of Beale's early work. All images are signed in cursive, not Beale's usual block signature. The date "1881" follows the signatures. The Set is conceptually related to William Hogarth's *Industry and Idleness*, though the images are entirely different.

136. *William Jackson's Treat* has two titles. *Champagne to the End* is the title used by Milligan from 1882 to 1892. The images may have been from pre-existing art, perhaps from *Puck* magazine. The poem is called *William Jackson's Treat* in all other catalogs once Beale introduces it in 1885, and it is called that in Milligan after 1892.

137. Often *Secret Society* Groups contain a great many slides that were First Used Elsewhere (F's), leaving few slides made specifically for the Group for us to use in dating it. The following Sets did not appear in the catalogs we reviewed: *Brotherhood of the Union* (224), *Moose Lodge* (236), *Tribe of Ben Hur* (237), *American Insurance Union* (238). We know of these Sets only by examining the slides or negatives themselves, and hence cannot date them. There may well be other small Secret Societies that used Beale slides. The flags in Sets 222, 223, 225, 230, 236, and 238 probably came in the three variants of Set 26 in which they were First Used, with the number of stars changing as states were added over a time span, 1888–1920.

138. The first three slides of *Commandery* were probably created with matte overlays, but the overlays are no longer extant, and there is no other evidence, so they are not included here.

139. The *Ascension* is a dissolving Set, sometimes used with *Knights Templar*, sometimes with *Commandery*, and sometimes presented by itself. In *Ascension*, Christ appears to slowly rise, diminish in size, and then fade into the opening in the cloud. There are two versions of Christ. A Beale drawing exists for Christ with one hand raised (1); a negative showing Christ with two hands raised is possibly by Beale (2). We do not know if they were both used in the same version of the Set, or used separately, so we indicate the attribution information for both, using (1) and (2?), for all images involving Christ. Compare note 140 for Set 208. A sixth image for the Set was sometimes offered, presented here as a variant. It could have been a separate slide, or made by simply printing a smaller version of slide number 5.

140. In the *Moveable Ascension*, Christ was made to slowly rise using a lever. The background image of the disciples is slightly different from that in Set 207, and Christ has one hand raised. A variant of the slide, nature unknown, was made for the Colt lantern company. The *Moveable Ascension* is one of only three times that Beale created movement on screen with mechanical means, though he often used both quick and slow dissolves for that purpose. See note 139. There was another form of mechanical *Ascension*, using a vertical crank. We have no evidence that Beale created the image for it.

141. *Blue Lodge* (Set 209) is supplemented with *Blue Lodge Additional*, Set 210. The slides 5a, 5c, 5d are unusual Beale drawing of statues representing the spiritual qualities of Faith, Hope, and Charity. A slide called "5b, Faith", is listed in the catalogs, and may well be by Beale, but we have not seen any direct evidence for attribution.

142. Ibid. *Blue Lodge Additional* is listed as such in most catalogs, but has four subsets: Master Builder (1–12), Creation of Earth (1–8+), Masonic Mark Master, Ecclesiastes (1–10).

143. *The Knights Templar* is an additional order, not a higher degree of freemasonry.

144. The odd numbering of *Oddfellows* follows that in the *Stebbins 1917–20* catalog, which has various degrees and subdivisions: Introductory, Initiatory, First, Second, Special Second, Patriarchal, Subordinate, The Good Samaritan.

145. *Knights of Pythias, First Rank* is primarily a story, that of the faithful friends, Damon and Pythias, traceable to a Greek myth. The story was turned into the play of *Damon and Pythias* by John Banim in 1821. The American actor Edwin Forrest made it famous in America, and it was this play that inspired Justus Rathbone to start the fraternal order of The Knights of Pythias in 1864. There appear to be two versions of the lantern slides, with some Beale images in each, so there are variants of several slides. Numbers 7, 7b, and 8 make up an unusual three-slide dissolve created to capture the movement of the climatic scene. Two of the images appear in 1896–97; 7b does not appear in the catalogs until *McIntosh 1913*.

146. *Third Rank, Pythagoras* contains a unique Beale image, "Hobgoblins". It is Beale's only revolving mechanical slide, and was superimposed over the sorcerer in the first slide, "Ancient Egyptian Arts". It showed a circle of hobgoblins which were masked so that only one was projected at a time. As a crank was turned, the hobgoblins rotated, and appeared to rise – one by one – out of the sorcerer's cauldron.

147. A Set of slides for *Brotherhood* is at the MLCM, but we have not examined them. The drawing for "Seventy Star Flag" is an overlay for a flag, with, in fact, 70 stars in the field. Presumably, it was intended to foreshadow the growth of America. There may be additional Beale slides in this Set, but we have not been able to verify that.

148. We are not sure that both slides of "Burning Bush" were used in *Knights of Malta*. Only one is listed in the catalogs, but there are two images, made with a flap from one drawing. Compare this image of Hell with that pictured for Set 159, where the image may have been changed to fit church dogma. The slogan means "impending doom". The two sizes of "The Hand Rising" were made from the same drawing by simply cropping in to create the larger hand.

149. The first 13 Beale slides listed for *Moose Lodge* are known only from Briggs negatives at GEH. The last, ("Stars and Stripes"), is known from a different 44-slide Set in the BC.

150. *Tribe of Ben Hur* was sold by the lantern slide company George W. Bond & Co. only. A Set of the slides is at the MLCM.

151. *American Insurance Union* is only known from slides in the BC.

152. "Dissolves", meant two or more matched images that transformed from one to the other as the light was shifted from one lantern to another in a paired set of lanerns. Beale's Comic Dissolves created comic motion on screen with a rapid dissolve. He left the background the same, so that it stayed in register when the light shifted from one lantern to the other, but the figures

were in different positions, so that they seemed to suddenly move, creating the comic effect. Compare with the slow dissolve technique discussed in note 155. Most of Beale's comic images are adaptations from pre-existing work, either earlier lantern slides, or trade cards, magazine illustrations, etc. Briggs commented on Beale's comic work in a letter to him of Nov. 22, 1909 (BC). Many of the paired slides listed here appear under "Dissolving Sets" in the catalogs.

153. In the *Comic* Set, the slide "Three Systems of Medicine" is probably based on a cartoon by that name by J. E. Blue, and is the title used in the catalogs. The "Freezing" title is written on Beale's Own Slide. The "Allopathy", etc. title is written on the drawing.

154. *Artistic Gems* was a term often used as a catalog heading, and served as a catchall for a wide variety of images. There is evidence from the negative sleeves that the image from "Good Night, Cherubs" may have also been used, with different lettering, as a Welcome slide. One example of "Good Night, Wreath of Flowers" came with three color tinters, so that the wreath could gradually change colors. There is a different wreath in the "Possible Beale" collection.

155. The term *Dissolves* meant two or more matched images that transformed from one to the other as the light was shifted from one lantern to another in paired lanterns. In most of the following Dissolving Sets, the image was meant to slowly change from one to the other, creating a magical "transformation". In a few, like "Christmas Evening" (Set 246), the "dissolve" consisted simply of contrasting images. Compare to the comic dissolve effect discussed in note 152.

156. The drawing for "Christmas Evening" (pictured) has "Beale Family at Christmas" written on the verso. This was probably written by Arthur Colen as a marketing ploy. It seems unlikely that either Beale or Briggs would use such a phrase, and the scene bears no resemblance to the actual Beale family.

157. Slide # 3 of *Enchanted Grotto* has a lever that moves the arm of the Goddess and the surrounding birds and butterflies. It is one of only three times that Beale created movement on screen through mechanical slides, though there were many cases where he did so with a rapid dissolve, especially in the Comic Sets (240–244).

158. The second Beale slide of *Fire in New York* is matched out from a Currier and Ives print.

159. The "Race" slide of *Steamboat Race* is based on a Currier and Ives image. The "Explosion" is marked "Nisle" on the negative sleeve, but the paper and style fit Beale, and since he created the other two images in the Set, we attribute this one to him as well.

160. In *Dissolving Views*, the 3 "Vesuvius" slides were probably created with flaps, now lost, that went over the extant base painting. There was a fourth optional mechanical effect-slide that would make the fire and smoke seem to erupt into the sky. The following two-slide comic dissolves, which are often found under the catalog rubric *Dissolving Views*, are here located in the following comic Sets or Groups: "Attack of the Monsters" and "Peace and War in the Boarding House" (240); "Schoolboy's First Cigar (241); "Chinese Question", "Fop Past and Present" and "Summit of Happiness" (242); and "Christmas Dissolves" (246).

161. The *Motto* slides are pre-movies, were used for lantern shows, and are broken out here to contrast with the *Announcement* slides (Set 252), which were used for both lantern shows <u>and</u> movies. All *Motto* slides first appeared as *Artistic Gems*, and so the Group is dated here with those "F" dates.

162. Ibid. Not all of the *Announcement* slides appear under the 41 *Announcement* slides in the *Briggs 1917–20* catalog, but all are among the 73 Briggs *Announcement* negatives at GEH. Some of the *Announcement* slides appear in a special Briggs "Safety Slide" format that was designed to withstand the heat of movie projectors.

163. *Skirt Dancing Effect* slides were meant to be projected on the white dress of a dancer, creating a "moving" image. Not all of these appear in the 20 *Skirt Dancing Effects* of the *Briggs 1917–20* catalog, but all appear in the 48 Briggs *Skirt Dancing* negatives at GEH. The image shown is a "Good Night" slide from the BC. For a shirt dance, it would have been used without the words, so we have Photoshopped it to remove the motto.

164. Sets under *Hymns with Limited Distribution* mixed a few Beale images with pictures from other sources, and, unlike *Illuminated Hymns* (Group 104) were carried by only one or two distributors, the names of which are indicated below the usual Set information. More such Beale *Hymns with Limited Distribution* are likely to be found.

Appendix 2

Chronological List of Beale Sets and Groups

The earliest Sets and Groups are listed first. If there are several dates for a Set, it is listed under the earliest. If a Set has a date range (1888–90), we place it by the last date in the pair, e.g. (1890), since that is the only date in the range that we are sure slides were done by. We place a date range like 1888–1890 before the "plain" 1890 dates, since some of the slides in an 1888–90 Set may well have been created prior to 1890. A Set introduced in 1890, i.e. (1890 i) would also precede a "plain" 1890 date, since it probably includes a number of earlier slides. The same logic applies to a range, and a range with a "~," indicating that the 60% rule applies. Thus 1881–90 and 1881–90~ would come before 1888–90 because they would contain earlier slides. Single dates to which the 60% rule is applied (1890~) follow "plain" dates, as there is more "noise" in the dating, with the likelihood of slides both before and after the cited date, e.g. the sequence 1890, 1890~. The combination of these guidelines results in the following sample sequence: 1888, 1889, 1881–1890~, 1888–90, 1888–90~, 1890 i, 1890, 1890~.

See *Chapter 3* and *Introduction to the Condensed Catalogue Raisonné* for a detailed discussion of dating and dating symbols. The Sets below are listed by:
Title, Set Identification Number, and Date.

1881–1889

Life of Garfield, 184.—1882 i
Drunkard's Daughter, The, 194.—1882
Uncle Tom's Cabin, 8.—1882
Two Paths of Virtue and Vice, The, 200.—1882
William Jackson's Treat, 202.— 1885
Tramp, Tramp, Tramp, 61.—1885
Visit of Saint Nicholas. (The Night Before Christmas), 43.—1885~
Leap For Life, A, 31.—1885~
Barbara Feitchie★, 18.—1886
Life of U.S. Grant, 185.—1887 i
Drunkard's Reform, The, 195.—1887
"Father, dear father, come home with me now." 196.—1887
Home, Sweet Home, 49.—1887, 1904
Rock of Ages, 101.—1887, 1891, 1906
Christmas Hymn, A, 86.—1887~
Mottoes★ *(Artistic Gems)*, 251.—1883–89
Patriotic Order Sons of America, 222. —1885–89~
American Mechanics, 229.—1888–89 i

1890–1893

Pygmalion and Galatea, 15.—1890
Life of Washington, 177.—1888–91~
Life of Mary, Queen of Scots, 178.—1891 i
Nellie's Prayer, 34.—1891
Marching Thro' Georgia, 51.—1891
How Jones Became A Mason, 78. —1891, 1905
Commandery (Masonic), 206.—1892~
Rip van Winkle, 76.—1881–93
Drake's Ode to The American Flag, 26. —1881–1893
Ten Nights in A Bar Room, 199. —1881–1893
Christmas Dissolves★, 246.—1881–93

Steamboat Race in Mississippi, 249. —1881–93
Dissolving Views, Misc., 250.—1881–1893~
Artistic Gems, 245.—1881–93~
America, 45.—1893 i
Swanee Ribber (Swanee River), 59.—1893
From Greenland's Icy Mountains (Missionary Hymn), 87.—1893
Prodigal Son, The, 150.—1893~

1894–1895

Knights of Pythias, First Rank, 216. —1891-94, 1896-97~
Knights of Pythias, Third Rank, Pythagoras, 218. —1893–94, 1902–03~
Life of Luther, 105.—1894 i
International Sunday School Lessons for 1895—Third and Fourth Quarters. (Old Testament), 124.—1894
International Sunday School Lessons for 1895—First and Second Quarters. (New Testament), 142.—1894
Seven Ancient Wonders of World, 179. —1894
Courtin', The, 23.—1894
Curfew Shall Not Ring To-Night, 24.—1894
Maud Muller, 33.—1894
Raven, The, 37.—1894
Wreck of the Hesperus, The, 44.—1894
Comic Songs★, 47.—1894
Robinson Crusoe, 7.—1894
Abide With Me, 84.—1894
Blue and The Gray, The★, 19.—1894
Comic, Love★, 243.—1894
Knights of Pythias, Sixth Senator, 219. —1894, 1906~
Comic, Animals★, 240.—1894~
Comic, Children★, 241.—1894~
Comic, Ethnic★, 242.—1894~

Great Supper, The, 147.—1907

Marriage of the King's Son, The, 149. —1907

Talents, The, 152.—1907

Ascension (Knights Templar, Masonic), 207.—1907

Casabianca, 22.—1907

Mrs. Casey and the Billy Goat, 81.—1907

Order of the Eastern Star (Masonic), 212.—1907

1908–1910

Christmas★, 135.—1895–1908~

Life of St. Paul, 106.—1899–1908~

American History, Mexican War, 1846–1848+, 168.—1902–1908~

Knights of the Mystic Chain, 221.—1908 i

Courtship of Miles Standish, The, 1.—1908

Marley's Ghost. (A Christmas Carol), 6. —1908

Unmerciful Servant, The, 153.—1908

Story of the Other Wise Man, The (Fourth Wise Man), 69.—1908, 1911–12

Easter★, 139.—1895–1909~

Joseph★, 122.—1895–1909~

Calling the Disciples★, 138.—1906–09~

Captives in Babylon★, 132.—1907–09~

Othello, 14.—1909

John Gilpin's Ride, 29.—1909

Mr. Timorous and His Bull-Dog, 80.—1909

Healing of the Daughter of Jairus, The, 66.—1910

Bridget's Dream, 77.—1910

Hamlet, 10.—1910

Romeo and Juliet, 16.—1910

Legend of Sleepy Hollow, The, 73.—1910

Carmen, 9.—1910

1911–1917

Calvary, 85.—1911–12

Scottish Rite (Masonic), 205.—1913 i

White Shrine of Jerusalem (Masonic), 211.—1913 i

Foresters of America, 233.—1913 i

Ecclesiastes, 109.—1913

Merry Wives of Windsor, 13.—1913

Blue Lodge Additional (Masonic), 210.—1913~

Bible Story in Pictures, The, 156.—1914 i

Photodrama of Creation, The, 159.—1914 i

Story of the Very First Christmas, The, 160.—1915 i

David★, 131.—1906–16~

Intemperance Subjects, 197.—1914–16 i

Beauty and the Beast, 71.—1914–16

Story of Ruth, 128.—1914–16

Bluebeard, 72.—1914–16

Story of Job, 127.—1914–16 ~

Man Without A Country, The, 75.—1917

1881–20

Moveable Ascensions, 208.—1881–1920

Comic, Miscellaneous Singles★, 244. —1881–1920

How Persimmon's Took Cah ob der Baby, 27.—1881–1920

Tabernacle in the Wilderness, 70. —1881–1920

Transportation★, 170.—1881–1920

U.S. Flags. Miscellaneous★, 172.—1881–1920

Miscellaneous Religious Slides★, 161. —1881–1920

Temperance Miscellaneous★, 203.—1881–1920

Secret Society, Miscellaneous★, 239. —1881–1920

Grand Army of the Republic, 225.—1881–1920

American History, Revolution, 1775–1783+, 166.—*1881–1920*

Jerusalem The Golden★, 91.—1891–1920

Knights of Malta, 226.—1896–1920~

Peter and Philip★, 141.—1906–20~

1917–20

Jewish Life, 158.—1917–20 i

Origin of U. S. Flag, 171.—1917–20 i

Rally Round the Flag, 56.—1917–20 i

Orangemen, 234.—1917–20 i

Order of Maccabees, 235.—1917–20 i

Jr. Order of American Mechanics, 230. —1917–20 i

Laborers in the Vineyard, 148.—1917–20

Maryland, My Maryland, 52.—1917–20

Unknown Dates

Samuel and Saul★, 130.—?

Christ's Youth★, 136.—?

Catholic Catechism, 157.—?

Knights Templar (Masonic), 213.—?

Brotherhood of the Union, 224.—?

Sublime Order of the Cross, 227.—?

Moose Lodge, 236.—?

Tribe of Ben Hur, The, 237.—?

American Insurance Union, 238.—?

Hark the Herald Angels Sing, 254.—?

Jesus Savior, Pilot Me, 255.—?

Never Alone, 256—?

Savior, Like a Shepherd, Lead Us, 257.—?

There is a Fountain Filled With Blood, 258.—?

Appendix 3

Slides Possibly By Beale

These 31 slides may possibly be by Beale, but we cannot be sure because of either conflicting or insufficient evidence. For instance, a catalog may attribute a slide to "Beale," but a Briggs note on the negative sleeve may attribute it to "Tholey," a different Briggs artist. Or the reverse may be true: A wash drawing or negative sleeve may indicate that Beale created or redrew an image, but the listing in the final *Briggs 1917–20* catalog is to the original artist. (This probably happened because the image was so closely associated with the original artist, e.g., Doré's "Tower of Babel.") Or there may be some indication that a slide is by Beale, but not enough for us to attribute it. By its nature, assessment of these slides is tentative, and may well change as more information is obtained.

The slides are organized alphabetically. If a slide is clearly from a Set, that Set name and ID number are given, and individual slides are listed under it. The *Catalogue* abbreviations of "wd" for "wash drawing," and "bos" for "Beale's Own Slide" are used throughout.

"Abide With Me" # 7.

Two angels hovering over cradle. From a Set of 12 that is different from the *Catalogue's* Set # 84. Some of the images are clearly Beale. Slide # 7 looks like Beale, but no wd, or bos or other supporting context.

"Abduction of Helen of Troy"

Large wash drawing in BC. Beale's Own Slide was at BAC. *McAllister 1899* catalog listed Fleury as artist. *Briggs 1917–20* catalog listed Deutsch as artist.

"Ananais Heals Saul's Blindness"

Briggs 1917–20 listed Morelli as artist. Writing on GEH negative sleeve: "Morelli redrawn by Beale." No wd or bos.

"An Angel Destroys Host of Sennacherib"

In a Nov. 30, 1910 Briggs letter to Beale (BC), Briggs wrote that he had asked Beale to redraw an earlier Tholey version of this design, but the negative sleeve is marked "Doré redrawn by Tholey." No wd or bos.

"Angels in Bell Tower"

Wash drawing in BC. *Briggs 1917–20* listed Blashfield as artist for "Christmas Chimes" using this image in *Illuminated Hymns*. No bos.

"Apostles Preaching"

Briggs 1917–20 listed Doré as artist. Wash drawing was at BAC. No bos.

Blue Lodge, Masonic, Set 209—"Scene at Waterfall"

GEH negative looks like Beale. No wd or bos.

Blue Lodge, Masonic, Set 209—"Astronomy"

Wash drawing in BC, with Colen provenance. Grey paper, standard size, but no bos, and drawing does not look like Beale.

"Dream of St. Joseph"

Briggs 1917–20 listed Landelle as artist. Written on GEH negative sleeve: "Misc. Savior. Landelle redrawn by Beale." No wd or bos.

"Elevation of the Cross"

Briggs 1917–20 listed two slides, with Doré and Rubens as artists. Written on GEH negative sleeve: "Doré redrawn by Beale." No wd or bos.

"Elijah in the Wilderness"

Briggs 1917–20 catalog listed Leighton as artist. Written on GEH negative sleeve: "Leighton redrawn by Beale." No wd or bos.

"Fight between the Merrimac and the Monitor, 1862"

Beale's Own Slide in BC. Colen credited AN wash drawing to Beale. Written on GEH negative sleeve: "Tholey." Regular slide in BC has label of "Faulkner & Al[len]. . ." The "Beale" image does not look like Beale.

"Flagellation"

Briggs 1917–20 listed Bouguereau as artist. Written on GEH negative sleeve: "Redrawn by Beale." No wd or bos.

"Give Us Barabbas"

Briggs 1917–20 listed Muller as artist. Written on GEH negative sleeve: "Muller redrawn by Beale." No wd or bos.

Home Sweet Home, Set 49.—Slide # 3, First Chorus.

Image is of a salt box house with well sweep, and does not look like Beale art. It is the only slide not clearly by Beale in the Set. Possibly from the original set of 4. No example of Beale's Own Slide, but the whereabouts of all the Beale's Own Slides for *Home Sweet Home* is unknown. GEH negative shows no Beale printing. No wd.

Man Without a Country, Set 75.

"Title Slide"—Slide # 1.

Beale probably drew this hand-lettered slide, as he did the rest of the Set, but since the image is only printing, it is impossible to make an attribution based on artistic style.. No wd or bos.

"Sentence of the Court"—Slide # 7.

Same explanation as Slide # 1, above.

"Marching Thro' Georgia," Set 51.

Introduced in 1885. Noted as "Beale" on the negative sleeve, and a wash drawing exists in BC, but it is of a different size, color paper, and style than the usual Beale drawings. See note on the Set of *Marching, #* 51.

Mary, Queen of Scots, Life of, Set 178.

"Betrothal of Mary Stuart and Francis II"—Slide # 1.

Beale's Own Slide in BC. Written on GEH negative sleeve: "Tholey." No wd.

"Mary Stuart Led to Execution"—Slide # 12.

Wash drawing at GEH. Beale's Own Slide in BC. Written on GEH negative sleeve: "Tholey."

"Maternal Solicitude"

Bos and wd in BC, but drawn on white paper, and does not look like Beale's style.

"Nailing Christ to the Cross"

Briggs 1917–20 listed Doré as artist. Written on GEH negative sleeve: "Doré, redrawn by Beale. Beale's Misc. Savior." No wd or bos.

"Noah sends out the Dove"—Set # 119

Briggs 1917–20 listed Doré as artist. Written on GEH negative sleeve: "Beale's redrawn." No wd or bos.

"Rally of Troops at Washington"

Wash drawing at BC. Does not look like Beale. Beale's Own Slide in BC. Written on GEH negative sleeve: "Tholey."

"Rateater" (Ratcatcher)

Very detailed, elaborate bed and background in GEH negative looks like Beale's work, but foreground does not. No wd or bos.

"Salome Dancing before Herod"

Briggs 1917–20 listed Rochegrosse as artist. Written on GEH negative sleeve: "Rochegrosse redrawn by Beale." No wd or bos.

"Slaughter of the Innocents"

Briggs 1917–20 listed Doré as artist. Wash drawing was at BAC. No bos.

"Tower of Babel"

Briggs 1917–20 listed 2 slides of this title, by Doré and Brueghel. Some catalogs list as "by Neslie" (Nisle). Written on GEH negative sleeve: "Beale's." Wash drawing was at BAC. Beale's Own Slide in BC.

"Woman Touching hem of Christ's Garment"

Briggs 1917–20 listed Armitage as artist. Written on GEH negative sleeve: "Armitage RA redrawn by Beale." No wd or bos.

Wreath

Untitled washing drawing on grey paper with Colen provenance in BC, but not usual size—10.5" x 10.5." No bos.

Appendix 4

Lantern Slide Companies or Agencies Distributing Beale's Slides

One hundred and twelve different companies are known to have distributed Beale's slides. The list below has been compiled from the *Briggs 1890–92 Ledger* in the Sipley Collection at GEH; from lantern catalogs; and from labels on extant copies of Beale slides, most in the BC.

In the *Briggs Ledger*, a total of 31 lantern-slide accounts are identified, but many of these are so small as to be negligible, and unless there are direct indications from other sources that these companies carried Beale slides, we have not counted them. The 14 companies that Briggs marked as "Dealers entitled to lowest rates," presumably because they were his major customers in 1890, are marked with a "BL+." The largest of these, by far, were McAllister and Milligan. We assume that all these major distributors would have been carrying Beale. Briggs himself provides no direct evidence for that, since in most cases he does not list by title the slides or Sets he sold. However, in all but two cases (Hearn and Harrison, Taylor and Huntington), we have outside confirmation that these major distributors sold Beale slides.

Companies that we ourselves believe to have been major distributors, based on a rough sense of Beale slides extant today, are marked with a "★." Some of the companies that we have marked with a "★"were not considered to be major distributors by Briggs in 1890. In most cases that is probably because they did not became a significant factor until a later period, or because they were distributors of children's slides or other unusual formats.

There are three great centers of the American lantern industry—New York with 21 distributors; Chicago, with 18; and Philadelphia, with 17. Three companies are not American: two of these are Canadian, and one is French.

Additional distributors of Beale images are likely to be found.

A-D

American Slide Co.	Columbus, OH
Amusement Supply Co.—★	Chicago, IL
Armstrong, E. A.	Lincoln, NB
Art Electric Stage Lighting Co.	New York, NY
Bickmore, Prof. A. S.—*BL+*	New York, NY
Bessler Lantern Slide Co. Inc.	New York, NY
Boswell Manufacturing Co.	Chicago, IL
Bosworth Optical Co.	Boston, MA
Bousch and Lomb Optical Co.	Rochester, NY
Briggs, C. W., Co. (BriggsCo)	Philadelphia, PA
Brenkert Light Projection Co.	Detroit, MI
Bubb, U. S.	Milton, PA
Buffalo Stereopticon Entertainers	Buffalo, NY
Buckeye Stereopticon Co.	Cleveland, OH
Button, G. H., Mfg.	Canastota, NY
Chicago Projecting Co.—★	Chicago, IL
Chicago Public Schools Division of Visual Education	Chicago, IL
Chicago Transparency Co.	Chicago, IL
Christian Lantern Slide & Lecture Bureau	Chicago, IL
Cincinnati Regalia Co.	Cincinnati, OH
Cline, Eugene, & Co.—★	Chicago, IL
Colt, J. B., Mfg. Co.—*BL+,* ★	New York, NY
Cornell Photo Supply Co.	Lincoln, NB
Crescent Co.	New London, OH
Devereaux (Deveraux) Slide Co.	New York, NY
DeMoulin Bros. & Co.	Greenville, IL

E-L

E. O. M. Company	Chicago, IL
Edison, Thomas A., Inc.	Orange, NJ
Elite Lantern Slide Co.	New York, NY
Erker Brothers Optical Co.	St. Louis, MO
Excelsior Illustrating Co.	New York, NY
Fellows, Charles T.	Philadelphia, PA
Forester, A. & Co.	Philadelphia, PA
Futterer, A. F.	Los Angeles, CA
Gamel-Barron Co.	Spirit Lake, IO
Gladwish & Mitchell	Montreal, Canada
Hall, James, F.	Philadelphia, PA
Handy, A. D.	Boston, MA
Harbach, Theodore J., Mfg.—*BL+*	Philadelphia, PA
Harsten, Alfred L., and Co.	New York, NY
Hearn and Harrison—*BL+*	Montreal, Canada
Henderson-Ames Co.	Kalamazoo, MI
Herbert, Sidney, Co.	Boston, MA
Holley, J. E.	Cincinnati, OH
(Holley Process, Holley Institute of Visual Instruction)	
Hume, Willis P. (F?)	Oberlin, OH
(Standard Slide Bureau)	
Isaacs, Walter	New York, NY
Jno, W. Robertson (?)	Warren, OH
Kahn, Henry and Co.	San Francisco, CA
Kain, E. W.	Los Angeles, CA
Kansas City Slide Co.	Kansas City, MO
Kanzee Lantern Slides	San Francisco, CA
Keystone Company (Keystone View Co.)	Meadville, PA
Kleine Optical Co.	Chicago, IL
(Kleine, C. B.)	
Kemp, Edward M.	San Francisco, CA
Lauterer, George, Co. (modern)	Chicago, IL
Light, Douglass	Seattle, WA
Lilley, M. C. —*BL+*, ★	Columbus, OH
Lubin, Siegmund	Philadelphia, PA

M–P

Maison de la Bonne	Paris, France
Martin, J. (I?)	Philadelphia, PA
Macoy Publishing and Masonic Supply Co	New York, NY
Manasse, L., Optician—*BL+*	Chicago, IL
Marcy Stereopticon Mfg. Co	Philadelphia, PA
McAllister, T. H., Mfg.—*BL+*, ★	New York, NY
McAllister (T. H.)-Keller Co.	New York, NY
McIntosh Battery & Optical—*BL+*, ★	Chicago, IL
(McIntosh Stereopticon)	
Milligan, C. T. —*BL+*, ★	Philadelphia, PA
Miner, Wendell Co., Inc.	Minneapolis, MN
Montgomery Ward Co.	Chicago, IL
Moore, Bond, & Co.—★	Chicago, IL

(Moore, Hubbel & Co.) Moore, R. M., & Sons	Chicago, IL
Morgan, Paul & Morris	Detroit, MI
National Picture(s) Service, Inc.	Cincinnati, OH
Novelty Slide Co.	New York, NY
Pacific Stereopticon Co.	Los Angeles, CA
Peck and Snyder Co.	Philadelphia, PA
Pettibone Brothers Mfg. Co.—★	Cincinnati, OH
Philadelphia, School District of, Division of Visual Education	Philadelphia, PA
Pierce, H., & Co.	Boston, MA
Prieger, Albert F.	Tampa, FL
Prince, L. M., Mfg. Optician	Cincinnati, OH

Q–S

Quality Slide Co.	Chicago, IL
Queen, James W., & Co.—*BL+*, ★	Philadelphia, PA
Rau, William—*BL+*	Philadelphia, PA
Roe-Goshen	Orange, NJ
Roberts and Fellows—*BL+*	Philadelphia, PA
Scott & Van Altena	New York, NY
Scheidig, J.—*BL+*	New York, NY
Sears Roebuck & Co.—★	Chicago, IL
Solomonson Optical Co.	Cleveland, OH
Spencer Lens Company	Buffalo, NY
Stains, Harry F., Co.	Camden, NJ
Stebbins, Charles M., Optician—★	Kansas City, MO
Stereopticon Film Exchange—★	Chicago, IL
Stieren, Wm. M., Opt. Co.	Pittsburgh, PA
Stilz, Louis E. & Bros. Co.	Philadelphia, PA
Swaab, Lewis M.	Philadelphia, PA

T–Z

Taylor and Huntington—*BL+*	Hartford, CT
(Taylor and Washington?)	
Thompson, A. T.	Boston, MA
Thurston, John H. (Agent for T. H. McAllister.)	Boston, MA
Tolton, H. N., Studio	Lodi, CA
Underwood & Underwood	New York, NY
Union Slide Co.	New York, NY
United Theater Corp.	New York, NY
Univ. of Texas, Visual Instruction Bureau,	Austin, TX
U. S. Slide Co.	Kansas City, MO
Van Allin Co.	New York, NY
Victor Animatograph Co.—★	Davenport, IO
Ward, C. E., Company	New London, OH
Ward-Stilson Co.	Anderson, IN
Weister Lecture Bureau	Portland, OR
Wheeler, Dewitt C.	New York, NY
Williams, Brown & Earle.	Philadelphia, PA
Youth's Companion (Magazine)	New York, NY

Appendix 5

The Beale Method for Dating Catalogs

Once Beale's work is dated, as it is in *The Catalogue Raisonné* and *Appendix 2*, it provides a way to determine the time of publication for the many American magic-lantern catalogs that are undated, or dated only by edition number, or that are dated in a confusing manner—e.g. a catalog of Milligan's that contains three different dates. We call this process the Beale Method for Dating Catalogs. The use of this method is important because correctly dating catalogs creates a chronological framework that allows researchers to then date the creation of lantern slides by artists other than Beale, or by the photographers who created the vast majority of lantern slides. Likewise, it makes it possible to date the development of new kinds of lanterns and related equipment; and to date changes in marketing emphasis designed to accommodate changing tastes and needs, new cultural influences, etc.

Because of the complexities of determining catalog dates, it is best not to simply accept the year attributed to catalogs by museums or libraries, or even the cover dates. Curators and librarians may have made their attributions with limited knowledge of the lantern field, and catalog covers do not necessarily reflect the date of the material inside. Updated covers were often affixed to a catalog that was in fact several years older, and a single "catalog" may in fact be composed of several sections from different time periods. Each catalog should be carefully examined for dates on both the outside and the inside cover, for inside "copyright page" dates, for the dates of any Bulletins or Supplements bound into the catalog, for copyrights on special sections within the catalog, and for internal evidence such as current events. Beale's dates can then be used as an additional check on the information derived from this process. This check can be very valuable because internal sources of dating often yield information only in the form, "The catalog date must be later than xxxx," while the Beale Method can give, in most cases, a precise year date, and at worst a range of two or three years. For some catalogs, Beale's work will be the only means of dating, or the only means of dating the section containing Beale Sets.

There are two caveats to the Beale Method for Dating Catalogs. (1) Beale Groups listed in *The Catalogue Raisonné* should not be used for dating purposes. (Groups do not make good dating evidence because the "60 percent" criterion introduces too much variance to use them as a touchstone.) (2) The Beale Method should not be applied to non-American catalogs, or to the American catalogs of Riley Brothers, a British company operating in the United States for a few years in the 1890s. (These catalogs do not carry Beale slides, but do contain many Sets with titles that are similar to Beale's and could be mistaken for his.)

If an American catalog does contain Beale Sets, and almost all do, it is a simple matter to see which Beale Sets are included and which are not, and then to deduce when the catalog was published. While any dated Beale Set in the chronological listing (*Appendix 2*) can be used for dating, some Sets are better for this purpose than others. The Table below omits all Sets that might mislead someone unfamiliar with lantern catalogs, or the intricacies of Beale's work. For instance, it excludes all Sets that were created by Beale but were also available from foreign sources (e.g. *The Wreck of the Hesperus*). It excludes all Sets that were drawn by some other American artist and then re-drawn by Beale *(e.g. Visit of St. Nicholas),* since the shift from one artist to the other is perceptible only by subtle clues such as changes in the number of slides or the titles of lines. For the Table below we selected from the remaining Sets those that appear in the largest number of catalogs and thus have the greatest dating utility. When using the Table, pay particular attention to the number in parentheses after the title. It indicates the number of slides in the Set to be used for dating. Sets with the same title but a different number of slides were created at a different time.

To use the Beale Method for Dating Catalogs, find one of the Sets below in the catalog. Then work up the timeline until the titles below are no longer found. For example, suppose that *Swanee Ribber* (1893) and all the preceding Sets are included in the catalog, but *Maud Muller* (1894) and the titles that follow are not. It will then be possible to say, "This catalog was created in 1893."

Beale Set Index for Dating Catalogs

Year	Beale set
1882	*Uncle Tom's Cabin* (12)
1885	*A Leap for Life* Set of 4 in 1885, 5 in 1887, 6 in 1891
1886	*Barbara Freitchie* (Single Slide)
1887	*Christmas Hymn* (6)
1890	*Pygmalion and Galatea* (6) First, Dissolving Views. Later a Set.
1891	*Marching Thro' Georgia* (6)
1893	*Swanee Ribber* (8)
1894	*Maud Muller* (6)
1895	*Where is My Wandering Boy?* (6)
1896-97	*Paul Revere's Ride* (8)
1898	*Twenty-Third Psalm* (6)
1899	*Throw Out the Lifeline* (5)
1900	*Evangeline* (24)
1901	*New Born King* (10)
1902-03	*Annie & Willie's Prayer* (6)
1904	*Thanatopsis* (8)
1905	*Little Match Girl* (8)
1906	*Mr. Spurt and His Auto* (8)
1907	*Mrs. Casey and the Goat* (12)
1908	*Marley's Ghost* (24/25) (A Christmas Carol)
1909	*Mr. Timorous & the Dog* (12)
1910	*Carmen* (12)
1911–12	*Calvary* (12)
1913	*Merry Wives of Windsor* (12)
1914-16	*Ruth* (Set of 8 only)
1917	*Man Without a Country* (18)

If the Sets listed above are not in a particular catalog, but other Beale Sets in the *Catalogue* or *Appendix 2* are listed, then it is still possible to use the Beale Method for Dating Catalogs. Check the *Catalogue* title line to be sure the title is a Set and not a Group. Then check any Set notes to be sure that there are no obvious complications. Then proceed as above, but with additional care.

Caution on Edition Numbers, and McIntosh Catalogs

We would like to add a special caution about the use of catalog <u>edition numbers</u>, particularly in the case of the McIntosh Stereopticon Co. Edition numbers were a manufacturer's way to avoid dating catalogs, thus obscuring the fact that the catalogs were not issued yearly. McIntosh in particular used this technique, often adding no new material to his catalogs for many years, but simply creating a new cover with a new edition number. He also used <u>two different edition number sequences</u>, so that it is important not to take one date as a baseline (e.g. the 10th Edition, 1895, which contains both an edition number and a date on the cover) and simply work off the edition numbers to determine the dates of other issues. Each McIntosh catalog should be checked very carefully using internal evidence, followed by the Beale Method for Dating Catalogs.

Illustrated Song Slides Containing Beale Images

A few Beale slides were used in Illustrated Song Sets. Such Sets were sold to movie theaters, and were projected as the songs were sung (or "illustrated") by a live performer who appeared in the breaks between movie reels. The Beale Illustrated Song Slides have not been included as Sets in the *Catalogue Raisonné* because they were marketed to movie theaters rather than to the usual lantern markets, and because their use of Beale images was so limited. See the discussion in Chapter 5.

In general, the listings below follow the conventions presented in the Quick Key at the start of the *Catalogue Raisonné* and detailed in Chapter 3. Two exceptions: (1) No "E" numbers (for Used **E**lsewhere) are given, since we assume that all of these images were **F**irst Used elsewhere (F's). (2) A third line has been added to the headings here. It denotes the slide production company, if known.

Our Thanks to Nancy and Margaret Berg of the Marnan Collection for their help in identifying many of these sets.

1. Betsy Ross March Ballad
Costello, 1/16, S, 1910?
Scott and Van Altena

  2. Betsy Ross showing First Flag. —*F 166, AN, 1899, wd, bos*

2. Boys of the Old Brigade
Weatherly, 3/12, S, 1899
Chicago Transparency Co.

  3. Rally round the flag —*F 162, AN, 1899, s, wd, bos*
10. Stars and Stripes (Am. Flag) —*F26, "When freedom," UN, 1881–93, ca, bos*
11. Hurrah, Hurrah (troops marching) —*F 51, Hurrah, Hurrah, BC, d, wd*

3. Break the News to Mother
Harris, 1/20, S, ?, ?
Chicago Transparency Co.

v 1. Battle of Gettysburg, 1863—*F 169, GEH, 1881–1920, wd, bos*

4. Dawn of Christmas Day
Williams, 3/14+, S, 1909
Scott and Van Altena

  1. (Christmas Evening, Happy Home) —*F 246, MLCM, 1881–93, ca, wd, bos*
  5. (Down the Chimney St. Nicholas Came) —*F 43, RLM, 1900, s, wd, bos*
  7. And Dear Old Santa Claus (?)

14. (A Miniature Sleigh and Eight Tiny Reindeer) —*F 43, RLM, 1883–84, wd, bos,* ^

5. Good Enough for Washington
(If It's Good Enough for Washington,
It's Good Enough for Me)
Shields, 1/?, S, 1908
DeWitt C. Wheeler

The Spirit of 1776—*F 166, MLCM, 1881–1920, wd, bos*

6. Hello Central, Give Me Heaven
Kassel, 1?/? S, 1901
Chicago Transparency Co.

Angel Showing Jerusalem to John.—*F 140, BAC, 1895–97, ca, d, wd, bos*

7. Hymns of the Old Church Choir
Lamb, 2/17, S, ?
Van Allin Co.

  5. Nearer My God (Shall we whose souls) —*F 97, BC, 1895, wd*
15. Rock of Ages (Helping Hand) —*F 101, UN, 1887, bos*

8. Marching Thro' Georgia
Randall, 1/?, S, AN, ?
Scott and Van Altena

  8. "There were Union men," etc. —*F 51, BC, 1891, d, wd*

Appendix 7

List of Books Illustrated by Beale

In September of 1909, Beale was laid off from the C.W. Briggs lantern slide company, which was suffering from the sudden explosion of movie entertainment. Beale began looking for other work. As part of the process, he wrote letters detailing his career, and prepared a list of the books that he had illustrated.

Beale's list is presented here <u>as he wrote it</u>, with minor editorial changes and the addition, in parentheses, of some authors. Beale was employed by the Baker Engraving Co. of Chicago when he worked on many of these books, and often they are illustrated by a group of artists, not by Beale alone. Copies of many of the books are in the BC, and many are now appearing on Google Books, and can be easily accessed online.

Four of the books (or series of books) that Beale illustrated are of special note, so we have a (★) before them. Charles Nordhoff's *Communistic Societies* is a well-known study in early sociology. Allan Pinkerton, who gave his name to his detective agency, published about eighteen books that were the first "true detective" stories. The most famous, illustrated by Beale, was *The Molly Maguires and the Detectives*. Baroness Tautphoeus's *The Initials A – Z* was one of the first great international best-sellers—or, as Beale put it in his cover art, "Best Novel Published." Elizabeth Packard's *Modern Persecution, or Married Women's Liabilities* is considered a classic of the women's liberation movement because of its protest against the unjust confinement of women to mental institutions.

A sentence at the bottom of the list alludes to Beale's work as an illustrator for the Frank Leslie newspapers, but does not provide detail. Nor is detail provided on what must have been thousands of other illustrations that Beale created during his career from 1868 to 1881 as a commercial illustrator for *Leslie's, Harper's, The Daily Graphic,* Baker Engraving, etc. A dozen examples of these are in the BC.

The list of Beale-illustrated books follows:

For Harper & Bros. New York. Illustrated. Charles Nordhoff's
　★ "Communistic Societies of the U.S."

For G. W. Carleton & Co. Publishers, NY.
　★ About a dozen books by Allan Pinkerton.

For Paterson & Bros, Philadelphia. Several books.
　"The Bridal Eve" (by E.D.E.N. Southworth)
　"Bertha's Baby" (by Gustave Droz)
　★ "The Initials A – Z" by Baroness Tautphoeus

For Hubbard Bros., Phila.
　"Life of Garfield" (by Wm. Ralston Balch)

For S. G. Griggs & Co., Chicago.
　"Old Time Pictures and Sheaves of Rhyme" by Benj. F. Taylor
　"Songs of Yesterday" by B. F. Taylor
　"The World on Wheels" by B. F. Taylor
　"Between the Gates" by B. F. Taylor
　"Manual Of Gestures" by Albert M. Bacon, A.M.
　"The Mishaps of Ezekiel Pelter" by Albert M. Bacon

For W. B. Keene, Cook & Co, Chicago
　"A Century of Gossip" by William Nash
　"Against Fate" by Mrs. M. L. Rayne

For Jansen, McClury & Co., Chicago
　"Poems of the Farm and Fireside" by Eugene J. Hall

For the Republican Book and Job Office, Princeton, Ill
　"Reminiscences of Bureau Co.," by N. Matson
　"The Chisholm Massacre," by James M. Wells
　★ "Modern Persecution, or Married Women's Liabilities" by E. P. W. Packard, who published her own book.

From 1868 to 1881, when Frank Leslie died, I was one of his artists, two years in NY and then in Chicago and that direction.

<u>Not on Beale's list</u>:

"Love's Victory" — Sketches for Chapter 10 are in the BC. Author and publisher unknown.

Appendix 8

Selected Bibliography

Note: The magic-lantern catalogs listed in this Bibliography often changed their titles over the years, and sometimes changed the name of the issuing company. The company name and the catalog title given are for the year cited. Other years examined are listed in brackets [ ] after the citation. Company names and catalog titles are usually close enough so that the reader can find the reference. Where it is not, an alternative name or title is given.

Abbreviations in the Bibliography:

GEH = George Eastman House International Museum of Photography and Film

BC = Beale Collection of the Authors

Abel, Richard, ed., *Encyclopedia of Early Cinema*. London and New York: Routledge, 2005.

Abel, Richard. "That Most American of Attractions, the Illustrated Song." In *The Sounds of Early Cinema*, edited by Richard Abel and Rick Altman, 143–155. Bloomington: Indiana University Press, 2001.

Altman, Rick. *Silent Film Sound.* New York: Columbia University Press, 2004.

Barber, Xenophon Theodore. "Evenings of Wonder: A History of the Magic Lantern Show in America." Ph.D. diss., New York University, 1993.

Barter, Judith, ed*., American Drawings and Watercolors—From the Wadsworth Atheneum*. New York: Hudson Hills Press, 1987.

Beale, Joseph Boggs. Letters, Papers, Photographs, Sketches, Drawings, Beale-Owned Slides, Beale-Related Material. Beale Collection of the authors. (Hereafter, BC.)

_____. Letters, Papers, Sketches, Slides, Negatives, Drawings. Sipley Collection, George Eastman House International Museum of Photography and Film. (Hereafter, GEH.)

_____. Diary, Letters, Photographs. Historical Society of Pennsylvania.

_____. For other locations of Beale drawings, see the *Catalogue*.

Beard, Frank. *Lantern Slides of 100 Great Cartoons.* Chicago: Ram's Horn Press, [1900?].

Benerman and Wilson. *Illustrative and Descriptive Catalogue of Magic Lantern Slides, Magic Lanterns, Sciopticons and Lantern Appliances*. Philadelphia, 1875 [1877, 1880 advertisement in *The Magic Lantern*].

Bettmann, Otto L., ed., *The Bettmann Portable Archive: A Graphic History of Almost Everything. . .Presented by Way of 3,669 Illustrations Culled from the Files of the Bettmann Archive. . .Topically Arranged and Cross-Referenced to Serve as an Idea Stimulator and Image Finder.* New York: Picture House Press, Inc., 1966.

Black, Alexander. "Photography in Fiction: 'Miss Jerry,' The First Picture Play." *Scribner's Magazine* 18 (1895): 348–360.

Black, Alexander. *Miss Jerry: With Thirty-Seven Illustrations From Life Photographs by the Author.* New York: Charles Scribner's Sons, 1895.

Black, Alexander. Date Book, Oct. 1895–Dec. 1899. Papers, Rare Books and Manuscripts Division, New York Public Library.

Borton, Terry. *Cinema Before Film: Victorian Magic-Lantern Shows and America's First Great Screen Artist, Joseph Boggs Beale.* Forthcoming.

Borton, Terry, and Debbie Borton, "How Many American Lantern Shows in a Year?" In *Realms of Light: Uses and Perceptions of the Magic Lantern from the 17th to the 21st Century*, edited by Richard Crangle, Mervyn Heard, Ine van Dooren, 105–115. London: The Magic Lantern Society, 2005.

Borton, Terry, "238 Eminent Magic-Lantern Showmen: The Chautauqua Lecturers," *The Magic Lantern Gazette* 5, (Spring 2013): 3–34.

Bordwell, David and Thompson, Kristin. *Film Art: An Introduction.* New York: The McGraw-Hill Companies, Inc., 2004.

Boston Evening Post, Supplement 436 (December 3, 1743). Judson Collection, The Magic Lantern Castle Museum, San Antonio.

Briggs, Casper W. Letters, Agreements of Sale, Ledger. Sipley Collection, GEH, 1893.

_____. *Catalogue of Economic Series Lantern Slides* (Philadelphia: C. W. Briggs Co., 1917–20.

_____. *Untitled Picture Catalog.* Philadelphia, Sipley Collection, GEH, 1893.

Cambridge Reader, A. "My Clerical Lantern Work." *The Optical Magic Lantern Journal and Photographic Enlarger* 6 (October, 1895): 161.

Colen, Arthur W. "Introduction." In *"Paintings by David Blythe: Drawings by Joseph Boggs Beale."* New York: Whitney Museum of American Art, 1936.

———. Modern Galleries, The. Joseph Boggs Beale File. Pennsylvania Academy of the Fine Arts, Philadelphia.

Colt & Co., J. B. *Optical Lanterns and Views.* New York, 1893 [1895].

Crangle, Richard. "What Do Those Old Slides Mean? Or Why the Magic Lantern Is Not an Important Part of Cinema History." In *Visual Delights: Essays on the Popular and Projected Image in the 19th Century,* edited by Simon Popple and Vanessa Toulmin, 17–24. Trowbridge, England: Flicks Books, 2000.

Edgerton, N. H. *Priced and Illustrated Catalogue of Magic Lanterns, Stereopticons, Photographic Transparencies and Colored Views.* Philadelphia, 1876.

Farr, Gail E. "Three Medical Illustrators: The Fabers of Philadelphia." In *Fugitive Leaves from the Historical Collections, Library of the College of Physicians of Philadelphia.* 3 (Spring, 1987): 1–5.

Gaudreault, André. *American Cinema: 1890–1909.* New Brunswick, Rutgers University Press, 2009.

Giannetti, Louis. *Understanding Movies.* Upper Saddle River, NJ: Pearson Prentice Hall, 2008.

Groce, George C. and Wallace, David H. *Dictionary of Artists in America, 1564–1860.* New Haven: Yale University Press, 1957.

Hall, James F. *Illustrated Catalogue of Optical Lanterns, Photographic Transparencies and Colored Views for Luminous Projection.* Philadelphia, 1887 [1867].

Harbach, Theo. J. *Illustrated Catalogue and Price List of Magic Lanterns, Sciopticons, Stereopticons, Photographic Transparencies and Artistically Colored Views,. . .* [etc.] Philadelphia, 1880? [1892].

Herbert, Stephen. ed., *Eadweard Muybridge: The Kingston Museum Bequest.* Hastings, England: The Projection Box, 2004.

Holley, J. E., *The Scared Pageant of the Ages, Vols. 1–8* Cincinnati: Sacred Pageant Society, Inc., 1927.

Holley, J. E and Holley, Carolyn, F., *Bible Lands in Pictures: A Syllabus* (Title uncertain; title page is torn.). Los Angeles: Holley Bible Studies, 1952.

Hollyman, Burnes. "Alexander Black's Picture Plays: 1893–1894." *Cinema Journal* 16 (Spring, 1977): 26–33.

Huhtamo, Erkki, *Illusions in Motion: Media Archeology of the Moving Panorama and Related Spectacles.* Cambridge: The MIT Press, 2013.

Kleine, O. B. & G., Opticians [Kleine Optical Co.]. *Catalogue of Stereopticons, Sciopticons, Magic Lanterns and Views.* New York, 1894 [1903, '04, '05].

Langenheim Brothers [American Stereoscopic Co.]. *Catalogue of Langenheim's New and Superior Style of Colored Photographic Magic Lantern Pictures for the Dissolving View and Stereopticon Apparatus, Carefully Selected From the Best Pictures of the Old and New Masters for Educational, Private and Public Exhibitions. . .[etc.].* Philadelphia, 1861 [1866, '67].

"Professor, The." *Time 26* (August 19, 1935): 44–45.

Pierce, H. *Illustrated Catalogue of Stereopticons and Magic Lanterns of the Best Quality and of Every Variety of the Best Lantern Views and Lantern Novelties.* Philadelphia, 1887.

Magic Lantern, The (Philadelphia, 1874) [1874-1886].

Malan, Dan. "Gustave Doré's Magic Lantern Slides." *The New Magic Lantern Journal 9* (Winter, 2001): 3–6.

Manasse, L. *Illustrated Catalogue of Sciopticons, Stereopticons, Magic Lanterns and Veiws, Mechanical Novelties, etc.* Chicago, 1893 [1887].

Mannoni, Laurent. *The Great Art of Light and Shadow: Archaeology of the Cinema.* Exeter: University of Exeter Press, 2000.

McAllister, T. H. *Catalogue of Stereopticons, Dissolving View Apparatus and Magic Lanterns, with Extensive Lists of Views for the Illustration of All Subjects of Popular Interest.* New York, 1893 [1866, '75, '80, '85, '86, '87, '89, '90, '91, '94, '97, '98, '99, 1900, '01, '03, '06, '07, '08, '13].

McIntosh Stereopticon Company [McIntosh B. & O. Co.]. *Projection Apparatus, Accessories and Slides, Thirty-Seventh Edition.* Chicago, 1913 [1895, 1907, '12, '16].

Milligan, C. T. *Illustrated Catalogue of Stereo-Panopticons, Sciopticons, Exhibitors' Lanterns, and Every Form of First-Class Magic Lantern Apparatus and of Photographic Transparencies and Artistically Colored Views in*

Great Variety, Imported and Manufactured. Philadelphia, 1892 [1875, '77, '79, '82, '87, 1910].

Musser, Charles. *The Emergence of Cinema: The American Screen to 1907, Volume 1.* Berkeley: University of California Press, 1990.

Nelson, Richard Alan. "Propaganda for God: Pastor Charles Taze Russell and the Multi-Media *Photo-Drama of Creation* (1914)." In *Une Invention du Diable? Cinema des Premiers Temps et Religion* edited by Roland Cosandey, André Gaudreault, Tom Gunning. Lausanne: Editions Payot, 1992.

Queen, James W. & Co. *Priced and Illustrated Catalogue of Optical Lanterns, Stereopticons, Photographic Transparencies and Colored Views.* Philadelphia, 1884 [1876, '80,'85, '89].

Ramsey, Terry. *A Million and One Nights: A History of the Motion Pictures Through 1925.* New York: Simon and Schuster, Inc., 1926.

Reed, Walt. *The Illustrator in America.* New York: Society of Illustrators, 2001.

Rhode, Michael. "Drawing on Tragedy." *Hogan's Alley 6* (Winter, 1999): 50–53.

Ripple, Ezra Hoyt. *Dancing Along the Deadline: The Andersonville Memoir of a Prisoner of the Confederacy,* edited by Mark A. Snell. Novato, CA: Presidio Press, 1996.

Robb, Frances Osborn, David M. Robb Jr., and Dale Roylance. *Star Spangled History: Drawings by Joseph Boggs Beale, Magic Lantern Artist, 1841–1926.* Galveston: American National Insurance Company, 1975.

Robinson, David. *From Peep Show to Palace: The Birth of American Film.* New York: Columbia University Press, 1996.

Rossell, Deac. *Living Pictures: The Origins of the Movies.* Albany: State University of New York Press, 1998.

_____. "The Public Exhibition of Moving Pictures Before 1896." *KINtop* 14/15 (2006): 169–205.

Robinson, David, Stephen Herbert, and Richard Crangle, eds., *Encyclopaedia of the Magic Lantern.* London: The Magic Lantern Society, 2001.

Sellin, David. *Thomas Eakins and His Fellow Artists at the Philadelphia Sketch Club.* Philadelphia: The Philadelphia Sketch Club, 2001.

Sipley Collection, GEH. "700 Old Pictures Found in Trunk," undated newspaper article.

Sipley, Louis. "The Pictures of Casper W. Briggs." *Pennsylvania Arts and Sciences* 1 (1936): 228–231.

_____. "Civil War Pictures," "The Magic Lantern," "Photographs on Glass." *Pennsylvania Arts and Sciences,* 4 (July, 1937): 28, 43, 93.

_____. "The First Museum of Photography." *Pennsylvania Arts and Sciences* 5 (1941): 37–66.

_____. "In Celebration of the One Hundredth Year of the C.W. Briggs Company", . . . Invitation to a "Private Exhibition of Works," 29–30 June, 1939. In BC.

_____. *Collector's Guide to American Photography.* Philadelphia: American Museum of Photography, 1957.

Shepard, Elizabeth. "The Magic Lantern Slide in Entertainment and Education, 1869–1920." *History of Photography 2* (April–June 1987): 91–108.

Sobieszek, Robert A. *An American Century of Photography, 1840–1940; Selections from the Sipley/3M Collection.* Rochester: George Eastman House, 1978.

Stieglitz, Alfred. "Some Remarks on Lantern Slides." *Optical Magic Lantern Journal,* 8 (1897): 204–206.

"Speaking of Pictures. . . These Are By A Great Magic-Lantern Artist," *Life* 8 (January 8, 1940): 4–6.

Stebbins Picture Supply Co. *List of Slides used in Secret Societies.* Kansas City, MO, [1917–20?].

Turner, Michael R. ed., *Victorian Parlor Poetry: An Annotated Anthology.* New York: Dover Publications, Inc. 1967.

Vestal, David. "Louis Walton Sipley, A Biography." *Popular Photography,* April, 1968.

Wainwright, Nicholas B. "Education of an Artist: The Diary of Joseph Boggs Beale, 1856–1862." *Pennsylvania Magazine of History and Biography 97* (October 1973): 485–510.

Wilson?, Edward. "Blue's Lantern Comicalities." *The Magic Lantern* 1 (November, 1874): 25–26.

_____. "Blue's Comics." *The Magic Lantern* 1 (January, 1875): 5.

_____. "New Slides." *The Magic Lantern* 1 (July, 1875): 11.

Wilson, Martin. "Lantern Slides." *The American Amateur Photographer* (1900): 440.

Yochelson, Bonnie and Daniel Czitrom, *Rediscovering Jacob Riis: Exposure Journalism and Photography in Turn-of-the-Century New York.* New York: The New Press, 2007.

Index

The index listings for a Beale Set first gives the number of the *Catalogue Raisonné* in parentheses followed by the page number, in the format (22)-108; this Set entry precedes all other page numbers. Illustrations other than those in the *Catalogue* are indicated by an italic page number; the same page may include relevant text. Individual slides are not indexed. Magic-lantern catalogs are indexed by distributors' names (e.g. "McAllister"); full catalog titles may be found in the *Bibliography*. Only those distributors of Beale's slides discussed in the text are indexed; the full list may be found in *Appendix 4.* Commonly used abbreviations are included in parentheses after index entries; see "abbreviations" in index below for full lists.